AYATULLAH IBRAHIM AMINI

al Imam al-Mahdi - The Just Leader of Humanity

First published by Ansariyan Publications 1999

Copyright © 1999 by Ayatullah Ibrahim Amini

All rights reserved. No part of this publication may be reproduced, stored or transmitted in any form or by any means, electronic, mechanical, photocopying, recording, scanning, or otherwise without written permission from the publisher. It is illegal to copy this book, post it to a website, or distribute it by any other means without permission.

First edition

Translation by Abdulaziz Sachedina

Contents

Preface	1
The Mahdi from Among the Descendants of the Prophet	5
The Sunni Traditions on the Subject of the Mahdi	9
The Existence of the Mahdi is Certain	27
The Discussion Among the Companions and the Subsequent...	29
People Awaited the Appearance of the Mahdi	34
The Jurists of Medina and the Mahdi Traditions	38
The Poetry of Di'bil and the Mahdi	41
Manipulation of the Beliefs of the People	45
Fabrication of the Traditions	47
The Family of the Prophet and the Eleven Imams' Predictions...	52
Are these Traditions about the Mahdi Authentic?	59
The Reasons for the Emergence of Belief in the Mahdiism	62
Does it Really Need Explication?	65
The Legend of 'Abd Allah b. Saba	67
The Messianic Leader, Mahdi in Other Religions	69
The Qur'an and Mahdiism	72
The General Prophethood and the Imamate	75
What System Can Make Human Beings Prosperous?	79
The Other-worldly Prosperity	83
The Path of Perfection	85
The Infallibility of the Prophets	87
Rational Proof in Support of the Imamate	89
Textual Proof for the Necessity of the Imamate	93

Will the Imam Be Born at the End of the Time?	100
Descriptions Identifying the Mahdi	102
Mahdi Is Among the Descendants of Husayn b. 'Ali	105
What If the Mahdi Was Well-known?	108
The Traditions from the Ahlul Bayt Are Proofs for All...	113
'Ali b. Abi Talib, the Paragon of the Prophetic Knowledge	117
The Book of 'Ali b. Abi Talib	119
The Heirs to the Prophet's Knowledge:	121
Those Who Saw the Imam of the Age When He Was Small	126
Why Was the Twelfth Imam Not Mentioned in the Will of Imam...	133
Why Did Others Not Know about the Twelfth Imam's Birth?	135
The Mother of the Twelfth Imam	139
The Sunni 'Ulama' and the Birth of the Mahdi	145
The Gifted Children	153
Rising of the People when Naming the Qa'im	155
When Did the Story about the Occultation Begin?	157
The Books on the Subject of the Occultation before the Birth...	161
The Short and Complete Occultation203	164
The Short Occultation and the Contacts with the Shi'a	166
Were these Letters from the Imam in His Own Handwriting?	168
The Number of Deputies	172
'Uthman b. Sa'id, the First Deputy	177
His Miraculous Acts	180
Muhammad b. 'Uthman, the Second Deputy	183
Husayn b. Ruh, the Third Deputy	186
'Ali b. Muhammad Samarri, the Fourth Deputy	189
Is There Any Time Limit to the Complete Occultation?	193

The Philosophy of Occultation	194
What Danger Faced the Imam If He Were Visibly Present?	197
Why Is the Mahdi Afraid of Being Killed?	199
Does Not God Have the Power to Protect the Imam?	200
Is It Not Likely That the Unjust Rulers Would Have Submitted...	201
He Should Remain Silent So That He Would Be Safe	202
He Could Have Negotiated a Treaty of Non-interference with...	203
Why Did He Not Appoint Special Deputies During the Complete...	206
Mr. Hoshyar: Your supposition can be refuted on several...	208
What Is the Benet of Having the Imam in Occultation?	210
The Twelfth Imam Endeavors to Defend Islam during the...	217
The Occultation of the 'Alawid Leaders	225
Violations of Free Expression under the Caliphs	230
The Implications of the Situation	234
Concluding Remarks	237
How Long Will the Hidden Imam Live?	239
The Reasons for Longevity	244
Senility and Its Causes	248
The Long Life of the Twelfth Imam	253
The Article by Justin Glace	257
Research into the Matter of Longevity	260
Further Research on Longevity	264
New Research on Longevity	266
Longevity	268
A Summary of a Russian Study on the Subject of Old Age	270
A Little Known Theory about the Cause of Death	276

Conclusion	279
Those Who Lived a Long Life in History	283
The Story about the Countries that Belong to the Sons of the...	287
Jazira Khadra' (The Evergreen Island)	292
When Will He Appear?	302
The Signs of His Appearance	304
The Story of Sufyani	307
The Story of Dajjal	310
Why Does the Mahdi Not Appear?	330
Another Reason for the Delay in the Appearance of the Mahdi	336
The Preparation for the Emergence Will Take Place Overnight	340
Awaiting Deliverance through the Appearance of the Imam	342
A companion of Imam Baqir by the name of Bashir told the...	347
Investigation into the Traditions against the Rise (qiyam)	352
Governance Within Religion	354
The Obligation to Command the Good and Forbid the Evil	357
Concluding Remarks	358
The Prophet as the Leader of the Muslims	359
Islamic Governance after the Prophet	363
'Ali b. Abi Talib, the Designated Caliph of the Prophet of...	366
Islamic Governance during the Period of Occultation	369
The Obligations of Muslims during the Occultation	371
Two Evidences	375
First Group of Traditions	380

Meaning and Implications of the hadith	383
Second Group of Traditions	389
Investigation into the Meanings and Implications of these...	391
Third Group of Traditions	393
Investigation into the Meanings and Implications of these...	397
Fourth Group of Traditions	399
Investigation into the Meanings and Implications of these...	403
Fifth Group of Traditions	406
Investigation into the Meanings and Implications of these...	408
Conclusions of the Discussion	410
The Destiny of the Unbelievers	418
The Destiny of Jews and Christians	421
Will the Majority of the Peoples on the Earth Be Killed?	426
War Is Inevitable	434
The Mahdi's Defense	436
The World under the Mahdi	439
The Victory of the Prophets	442
The Conduct of the Mahdi	446
The Freshness of the Explanations Offered by the Mahdi	449
The Mahdi and Abrogation of the Ordinances	453
Is It Not Possible that the Mahdi Has Already Appeared?	455
Sayyid 'Ali Muhammad's Acknowledgement of the Hidden Imam's...	460
What Do the Sayyid's Followers Say?	464
The Sayyid Repudiated Any Attribution of Prophethood and...	466
The Bayan and Messianic Claim	468

Preface

In the Name of God, the Merciful, the Compassionate

The month of Sha'ban in the Muslim calendar is a time of celebrations. It is marked with the birth of the third Imam, Husayn b. 'Ali, his half brother, 'Abbas b. 'Ali, his son 'Ali b. Husayn Zayn al-'Abidin, and nally, his renowned descendant, the Qa'im of the *Ahlul Bayt*, the twelfth Imam Mahdi (peace be upon him). I attended a function organized to celebrate the birthday of the twelfth Imam (peace be upon him) on the 15th Night of Sha'ban at one of the high schools in Tehran. It was a well organized affair attended by all classes of people. However, the majority of the participants were educated people, including young, upper class high school students. The function was sponsored by the Islamic Association of that school.

The occasion opened with the recitation of the Qur'an by a young student, who, through his beautiful recitation captured the spiritual dimension of the event. Following him another student recited a poem he had composed about the Hidden Imam (peace be upon him), and a third presented a well-written and very relevant paper about the subject. At the end of the program, Mr. Hoshyar, one of the outstanding teachers of the school, gave a pertinent talk on the topic of the Imam of the Age (peace be upon him), and this brought the evening to a close.

That function left a deep impression upon me. It was not so much its ceremonial side that caught my attention, but rather the experience of being overwhelmed by the spirit of sincerity and piety which owed from the young people. They had brought together religion and knowledge, and were engaged in spreading religious truth and understanding among the people, enlightening their thoughts with faith. The atmosphere at the gathering was dominated by purity of intention and sincerity in the actions of these youths, whose interaction with the audience radiated warmth and consideration.

This enthusiasm among the youth and their religious fervor, guided by clear thinking, made me hopeful about the future of the Muslim community. I almost saw the future leadership of the civilization and the responsibility for the progression of humanity on their shoulders. My eyes were lled with tears of hope and I prayed to God, the Almighty, with all sincerity for the success of the Islamic Association of the students and the schools that had pioneered this sacred mission among the young people.

At that very moment, Engineer Madani, who was seated next to Mr. Hoshyar, raised a question: "Do you really believe in the existence of the Hidden Imam? Is your opinion based on research or do you merely defend such a belief on the basis of your bias?" Mr. Hoshyar replied: "My belief is neither founded upon blind faith nor upon blind imitation. Rather, I have accepted it through careful study and research. In any case, I am still open to do more research and adjust my opinion accordingly."

Mr. Madani continued: "Since the subject of the Imam of the Age is not sufciently clear for me, and so far I have not been able to convince myself of its veracity, I would very much like to discuss the subject and benet from your study and research on the topic."

Dr. Emami: When did the belief in Mahdi become prevalent in the Islamic environment? Was there any conversation about the Mahdi during the time of the Prophet (peace be upon him and his progeny) or was it after his death that the belief became widespread among Muslims? There are some who have written that there was no Mahdiism in the beginning of Islam. It was only in the second half of the rst century (7th century CE) that the idea appeared among the Muslims. There was a group that regarded Muhammad b. Hanayya as the Mahdi and gave the good news to the people about the good fortune Islam would acquire through him. The same group believed that Muhammad b. Hanayya had not died but he was living in Mt. Radwa and one day would return."

Mr. Hoshyar: The belief in Mahdi was widespread during the time of the Prophet. The Prophet (peace be upon him and his progeny) on more than one occasion had announced the future coming of the Mahdi. From time to time he would inform the people about the government of the Mahdi and the signs of his emergence, giving his name and patronymic (kunya). There are numerous hadith-reports that have come down to us from both the Sunni and the Shi'i sources on this subject. Actually some of these reports have been related so frequently, and without interruption in all ages, that nobody can doubt their authenticity. For instance, we read the following hadith reported from 'Abd Allah b. Mas'ud, who heard the Prophet say:

The world will not come to an end until a man from my family (ahl al-bayt), who will be called al-Mahdi, emerges to rule upon my community.[1]

---

[1] The hadith is reported in the majority of the Sunni sources. However, here we cite Majlisi, Bihar al-anwar, Vol. 51, p. 75, who has actually compiled these reports from all the sources in one place, making it convenient to refer to them. Se also, Ithbat al-hudat, Vol. 1, p. 9.

Another tradition reported by Abu al-Hujaf quotes the Prophet saying three times:

Listen to the good news about the Mahdi! He will rise at the time when people will be faced with severe conflict and the earth will be hit by a violent quake. He will fill the earth with justice and equity as it is filled with injustice and tyranny. He will fill the hearts of his followers with devotion and will spread justice everywhere.[2]

The Prophet has declared:

The Day of Resurrection will not take place until the True Qa'im rises. This will happen when God permits him to do so. Anyone who follows him will be saved, and anyone who opposes him will perish. O servants of God, keep God in your mind and go towards him even if it happens to be on the ice, for indeed he is the caliph of God, the Exalted and Gloried, and my successor.[3]

In another hadith the Prophet is reported to have said: "Any one who denies al-Qa'im among my children will have denied me."[4]

In still another hadith the Prophet assured his community by stating:

The world will not come to an end until a man from the descendants of Husayn takes charge of the affairs of the world and fills it with justice and equity as it is filled with injustice and tyranny.[5]

---

[2] Bihar al-anwar, Vol. 51, p. 74

[3] Bihar al-anwar, Vol. 51, p. 65; Ithbat al-hudat, Vol. 6, p. 382

[4] Bihar al-anwar, Vol. 51, p. 73.

[5] Ibid., Vol. 51, p. 66.

The Mahdi from Among the Descendants of the Prophet

Such hadith-reports are abundant. The main idea that runs through all of them suggests that the topic about the future coming of the Mahdi and Qa'im during the time of the Prophet (peace be upon him and his progeny) was well known. In fact, the way these reports speak about the subject indicates that it was not something new which was being presented to the people. On the contrary, they relate the signs and characteristics of the person who would emerge as the Mahdi, as in the statement "the promised Mahdi will be among my descendants."

The following traditions reect such a pattern in their presentation. It is reported from 'Ali b. Abi Talib who said:

I asked the Prophet: "Is Mahdi going to be among our own family or from some other?" He replied: "He will be among us. God will conclude His religion through him, just as He began it with us. It will be through us that people will nd refuge from sedition, just as it was through us that they were saved from polytheism. Moreover, it will be through us that God will bring their hearts together in brotherhood following the animosity sown by the sedition, just as they were brought together in brotherhood in their religion after the animosity sown by polytheism."[6]

Abu Sa'id al-Khudari, a close associate of the Prophet says:

I heard the Prophet declare from the pulpit: "The Mahdi from among my descendants, from my family, will rise at the End of Time, while the heavens will pour rain and the earth will bring forth green grass for him. He will ll the earth with justice and equity as it is lled with tyranny and injustice."[7]

In another tradition from Umm Salma, the wife of the Prophet, there is even more specic information given to the community. The Prophet says: "Mahdi will be among my progeny, among the children of Fatima."[8]

On another occasion the Prophet said:

The Qa'im will be among my descendants. His name will be my name and his patronymic will be my patronymic. His character will be like my own. He will call people to my custom and to the Book of God. Anyone who obeys him would be obeying me, and any one who turns away from him would be turning away from me. Anyone who denies his existence during his concealment would have denied me, and anyone who falsies him would have falsied me. Anyone who conrms his existence would have conrmed my existence. As for those who are engaged in falsifying what I have said about him and thereby mislead my community, I will complain against them to God.

"Those who do wrong shall surely know by what overturn-

---

[6] Ibid., Vol. 51, p. 84; Ithbat al-hudat, Vol. 7, p. 191; Majma' al-zawa'id by 'Ali b. Abi Bakr Haythami (Cairo edition), Vol. 7, p. 317.

[7] Bihar al-anwar, Vol. 51, p. 74; Ithbat al-hudat, Vol. 7, p. 9.

[8] Bihar al-anwar, Vol. 51, p. 75.

ing they will be overturned." *[The Holy Qur'an, 26:227]*[9]

Abu Ayyub Ansari says:

I heard the Prophet (peace be upon him and his progeny) say: "I am the chief of the prophets and 'Ali is the chief of the legatees. My two grandsons are the best among the descendants. The infallible Imams will come forth from among us through Husayn. Moreover, the Mahdi of this community is among us." At that time an Arab stood up and asked: "O Prophet of God, how many Imams are there after you?" He replied: "Equal to the number of the apostles of Jesus and the chiefs of the Children of Israel."[10]

A tradition with similar information has been cited from Hudhayfa, another companion of the Prophet, who heard the Prophet declare:

The Imams after me will be equal to the number of the tribal chiefs among the Children of Israel. Nine among them will be the descendants of Husayn. The Mahdi of this community is among us. Beware! Truth is with them and they are with truth. Thus be careful of the way you treat them after me.[11]

In still another tradition Sa'id b. Musayyib reports from 'Amr b. 'Uthman b. 'Affan, who said:

We heard from the Prophet saying: "The Imams after me will be twelve in number, of whom nine will be from the progeny of Husayn. Moreover, the Mahdi of this community will be among us. Anyone who holds on to them after me holds on to the rope of God; and whoever abandons them has abandoned God."[12]

There are numerous *hadith*-reports of this kind in the sources

---

[9] Bihar al-anwar, Vol. 51, p. 73.

[10] Ithbat al-hudat, Vol. 2, p. 531.

[11] Ibid., p. 533.

[12] Ibid., p. 526.

which one can undertake to examine.

The Sunni Traditions on the Subject of the Mahdi

Dr. Fahimi: Mr. Hoshyar! Our friends know it. But let me tell you that I follow the Sunni school of thought. Hence, the positive evaluation that you have of the Shi'i hadith-reports, I do not share. In all likelihood, extremist Shi'is, for whatever reasons, after having accepted the narratives about the Mahdiism, must have fabricated traditions in support of their views and ascribed them to the Prophet. The evidence for my contention is that the traditions about the Mahdi are recorded only in your Shi'i books. There is no trace of these in our authentic – Sihah – compilations. Yes, I am aware that there are some traditions on the subject in our less reliable compilations.[13]

Mr. Hoshyar: In spite of the most unfavorable conditions under the Umayyads and the 'Abbasids, whose politics and oppressive governments did not allow the discussion or the spread of hadith about wilayat and imamat and the ahl al-bayt or their being recorded

---

[13] Hasan, Sa'd Muhammad, al-Mahdiyya fi al-islam (Cairo, 1373), p. 69; Ibn Khaldun, al-Muqaddima (Cairo edition), p. 311.

in the books of the hadith, your compilations of hadith are not completely void of any traditions on the subject of the Mahdi. If you are not tired I may cite some of them for you.

Engineer Madani: Mr. Hoshyar! Please continue your conversation.

Mr. Hoshyar: Dr. Fahimi! In your compilations, the Sihah, there are chapters devoted to the subject of the Mahdi in which traditions from the Prophet have been recorded. For example, the following:

'Abd Allah reports from the Prophet, who said: "The world will not come to pass until a man from among my family, whose name will be my name, rules over the Arabs."

Tirmidhi has recorded this hadith in his Sahih[14], and comments: "This hadith on the Mahdi is reliable, and has been related by 'Ali b. Abi Talib, Abu Sa'id, Umm Salma and Abu Hurayra":

'Ali b. Abi Talib has narrated from the Prophet, who said: "Even if there remains only a day on earth, God will bring forth a man from my progeny so that he will ll the earth with justice and equity as it is lled with tyranny."[15]

In another hadith Umm Salma narrates that she heard the Prophet say: "The promised Mahdi will be among my progeny, among the descendants of Fatima."[16]

Abu Sa'id al-Khudari says:

The Prophet said: "Our Mahdi will have a broad forehead and

---

[14] Sahih, Vol. 9, p. 74; also, see: Shaykh Sulayman, Yanabi' al-mawadda (1308 AH edition), Vol. 2, p. 180; Muhammad b. Yusuf al-Shafi'i, al-Bayan fi akhbar sahib al-zaman (Najaf edition), p. 57; and other Sunni sources.

[15] Abu Dawud, Sahih, Vol. 5/207; see also all the sources mentioned in note s 2. In addition, see: Shablanji, Nur al-absar, p. 156; Ibn Hajar, al-Sawa'iq al-muharriqah, p. 161; Ibn Sabbagh, Fusul al-muhimma, p. 275; al-Saban, As'af al-raghibin.

[16] Abu Dawud, Sahih, Vol. 2, p. 207; Ibn Majah, Sahih, Vol. 2, p. 519, and the sources mentioned in note s 3.

a pointed nose. He will fill the earth with justice as it is filled with injustice and tyranny. He will rule for seven years."[17]

'Ali b. Abi Talib has related a tradition from the Prophet who informed him:

The promised Mahdi will be among my family. God will make the provisions for his emergence within a single night.[18]

Abu Sa'id al-Khudari has related a tradition from the Prophet who declared:

The earth will be filled with injustice and corruption. At that time, a man from among my progeny will rise and will rule for seven or nine years and will fill the earth with justice and equity.[19]

Greater detail is provided in another hadith reported by Abu Sa'id al-Khudari. In this tradition the Prophet said:

Severe calamity from the direction of their ruler will befall my people during the Last Days. It will be a calamity which, in severity, shall be unprecedented. It will be so violent that the earth with injustice and corruption will shrivel for its inhabitants. The believers will not find refuge from oppression. At that time God will send a man from my family to fill the earth with justice and equity just as it is filled with injustice and tyranny. The dwellers of the heavens and the earth will be pleased with him. The earth will bring forth all that grows for him, and the heavens will pour down rains in abundance. He will live among the people for seven or nine years. From all the good that God will bestow on the inhabitants of the earth, the dead will wish to come to life again.[20]

---

[17] Abu Dawud, Sahih, Vol. 2, p. 208; Fusul al-muhimma, p. 275; and numerous other Sunni sources.

[18] Ibn Majah, Sahih, Vol. 2, p. 519. Also, Ibn Hajar, al-Sawa'iq al-muharriqa, p. 161.

[19] Ahmad b. Hanbal, Musnad, Vol. 3, p. 27.

[20] Ibn Hajar, al-Sawa'iq al-muharriqa, p. 161; Yanabi' al-mawadda, Vol. 2, p. 177.

There are numerous traditions that convey these meanings in your books. I believe we have cited enough reports to make our point.

The Objection Raised by One of the Authors

Dr. Fahimi: The author of the book entitled: Al-Mahdiyya al-islam writes:

Muhammad b. Isma'il Bukhari and Muslim b. Hajjaj Nishaburi, the compilers of the two most authentic books of the Sunni hadith, who recorded these traditions meticulously and with extreme caution in verifying their reliability, have not included traditions about the Mahdi in their Sihah. Rather, these traditions are part of the compilations of Sunan of Abu Dawud, Ibn Majah, Tirmidhi, Nasa'i and Musnad of Ahmad b. Hanbal. These compilers were not careful in selecting traditions and their hadith-reports were regarded by scholars like Ibn Khaldun as weak and unacceptable.[21]

Ibn Khaldun and the Traditions about the Mahdi

Mr. Hoshyar: To elaborate on the topic of the reliability of the hadith on the Mahdi, let us cite Ibn Khaldun's opinion on the matter in full:

It has been well known (and generally accepted) by all Muslims in every epoch, that at the end of time a man from the family (of the Prophet) will without fail make his appearance, strengthen Islam and make justice triumph. Muslims will follow him, and he will gain domination over the Muslim realm. He will be called the Mahdi. Such traditions have been found among the traditions that religious leaders have published. They have been critically discussed by those who disapprove of them and have been often refuted by means of

---

[21] al-Mahdiyya fi al-islam, p. 69.

certain traditions.²²

This was the summary of the opinions held by Ibn Khaldun. He then proceeds to mention the transmitters of these hadith and critically evaluate their reliability or lack thereof, as held by the scholars of transmitted sciences.

Let us respond to some points raised by Ibn Khaldun:

1: Uninterrupted Transmission (tawatur) of the Traditions

Numerous Sunni scholars have recognized the traditions about the Mahdi to have been uninterruptedly transmitted. They have in fact transmitted them uninterruptedly from other sources without raising objections to them. Among these scholars are Ibn Hajar Haythami, in al-Sawa'iq al-muharriqa; Shablanji, in Nur al-absar; Ibn Sabbagh, in al-Fusul al-muhimma; Muhammad al-Saban in As'af al-raghibin; Kanji Sha'i in al-Bayan; and so on. Such an uninterrupted transmission of these traditions compensates for the weakness found in their chain of transmission. According to 'Asqalani, a tradition that is reported in every generation uninterruptedly leads to establish its veracity, and an action taken based upon it is not subject to dispute.²³

A similar opinion is held by Sayyid Ahmad, Shaykh al-Islam and the Sha'ite Mufti, who writes that the traditions about the Mahdi are numerous and mutawatir. Among these some are 'sound' (sahih), others are 'good' (hasan), and still others are 'weak' (da'if). However, he says, the majority are weak traditions and, since they are numerous and their reporters are also in large number, some go towards

---

²² Ibn Khaldun, al-Muqaddimah, p. 311.

²³ Ibn Hajar al-'Asqalani, Nuzhat al-nazar, p. 12.

strengthening the others, and lead to their acceptance as reliable.[24]

Among those who narrate the hadith about the Mahdi are a group of prominent companions of the Prophet. These include: 'Abd al-Rahman b. 'Awf, Abu Sa'id al-Khudari, Qays b. Jabir, Ibn 'Abbas, Jabir, Ibn Mas'ud, 'Ali b. Abi Talib, Abu Hurayra, Thawban, Salman Farisi, Hudhayfa, Anas b. Malik, Umm Salma, and others. Among the Sunni authors who have included these traditions in their books are: Abu Dawud, Ahmad b. Hanbal, Tirmidhi, Ibn Majah, Nasa'i, Tabrani, Abu Nu'aym Isfahani and numerous other compilers of the hadith.

2: Weak Transmission is Not an Issue in All Places

It is important to state that most of the persons who are recognized as being weak in their transmission and are mentioned by Ibn Khaldun have also been accredited by others. In fact, even Ibn Khaldun mentions some of them. Moreover, the weakening of the transmission of a hadith does not have absolute preponderance over its being approved as reliable because special characterization is a subjective matter. Whereas a certain characteristic of a tradition might render it a weak tradition in accord with one researcher, another investigator might nd quite the opposite. Hence, the opinion of the former can be accepted only if the reason for rendering a tradition weak is made clear.

In his Lisan al-mizan 'Asqalani says: The weakening of the tradition assumes preponderance over its accreditation when the reason for doing so is made explicit. Otherwise, the opinion of the person rendering the tradition weak has no value.

Abu Bakr Ahmad b. 'Ali al-Baghdadi writes: It must be pointed out

---

[24] Futuhat al-islamiyya, Mecca edition, Vol. 2, p. 250.

that as for the traditions accepted and used as evidence by Bukhari, Muslim and Abu Dawud, although some of their transmitters have been criticized and have been declared unreliable, the reason for their criticism and unreliability has not been well established and proven by them. Moreover, he says, if weakness and reliability of a tradition are of equal weight, then its weakening is preponderant.

However, if weakness is less obvious than reliability, then there could be varying opinions about that tradition. The best way to resolve this problem of authenticating a tradition is to say that if the reason for weakness is mentioned and if that reason is convincing, then weakness has preponderance over reliability. But if the reason is not mentioned, then reliability has preponderance over weakness.[25]

To be sure, we can not generalize and state with absolute certainty that in all places of dispute over the reliability of a tradition, its being regarded as weak has preponderance over its being considered as reliable. If all points of weakness are made effective, then there would be very few traditions that would be spared from criticism. It is, therefore, important that in such cases careful analysis and rational evaluation are carried out to clarify the truth.

3: Unreliable Simply Because of Being Shi'i

Often a tradition is deemed weak because its transmitter is a Shi'i. For example, Ibn Khaldun, rejected Qutn b. Khalifa, one of the transmitters of the Mahdi traditions, because he was a Shi'i. In this connection he quotes 'Ijli saying that Qutn was good in hadith, but he was somewhat inclined towards Shi'ism.

Again, according to Ahmad b. 'Abd Allah b. Yunus and Abu Bakr b. 'Ayyash, Qutn was unreliable and his traditions were rejected

---

[25] Ibn Hajar al-'Asqalani, Lisan al-mizan, Vol. 1, p. 25.

because of his 'corrupt' beliefs. On the other hand, there were others like Ahmad b. Hanbal, Nasa'i, and so on, who accredited him and regarded his traditions reliable.[26]

Another transmitter by the name of Harun was also regarded as weak because, as Ibn Khaldun tells us, he and his sons were Shi'ites. Some hadith scholars regarded Yazid b. Abu Ziyad a weak transmitter because "he was the leader of the Shi'is" and that he was among the Shi'is of Kufa. Commenting on 'Ammar al-Dhahabi, Ibn Khaldun tells us that although prominent traditionists like Ahmad b. Hanbal, Nasa'i and others had regarded him reliable, Bishr b. Marwan, because of his Shi'ism, considered him weak. Also 'Abd al-Razzaq b. Humam's traditions were regarded as weak because he narrated traditions relating the merits of the family of the Prophet and was famous for his Shi'ism.[27]

4: Difference of Creed

Another excuse used to discredit traditions reported by some pious and truthful individuals was the difference in creed. For example one of the sensitive issues that generated lots of debate and led to an inquisition at that time was that of the createdness of the Qur'an. There were some in the community who believed that the Qur'an was not created in time, and hence, was eternal. Others believed that it had appeared at some point in time and, hence, was created. These two groups were engaged in not only heated arguments, but also mutual condemnation.

A number of the narrators of the hadith believed that the Qur'an was either created in time or that indicated that they had doubts

---

[26] Ibn Khaldun, al-Muqaddimah, p. 313.

[27] Ibid., p. 319.

about the issue. These narrators were discredited and condemned.

The author of Adwa' 'ala al-sunna al-muhammadiya writes:

The scholars had condemned a group of narrators like Ibn Lahi'a as unbelievers. Their sin was their belief that the Qur'an was created. Moreover, it is said that Muhasibi did not accept the inheritance from his father because, he said: "Those who are dualists do not inherit from each other. I do not want my share of inheritance from my father." The reason for his refusal was that his father was a waqi, that is, he was doubtful in expressing his opinion whether the Qur'an was created or not.[28]

Just as extreme religious prejudices and differences became the cause for overlooking the trustworthiness and truthfulness of the narrators (thereby rejecting what they reported), shared belief on a matter and belonging to the same school of thought generated unwarranted trust of the narrators, whose unreliability and corrupt character were overlooked. The situation was so critical that instead of verifying the credibility of the narrator they actually accredited them.

Thus, for example, according to 'Ijli, 'Umar b. Sa'd was among the reliable transmitters of the second generation of the companions of the Prophet, whose traditions people had recorded. This evaluation is contrary to the generally held fact that he was responsible for the murder of Imam Husayn (peace be upon him), whom the Prophet had declared the chief of the youth in Paradise and his beloved grandson.[29]

Such was the case with Bisr b. Artat, who received an ofcial assignment from Mu'awiya. He had massacred thousands of innocent Shi'is and used to publicly curse 'Ali b. Abi Talib, the Prophet's caliph.

---

[28] Abu Rayya, Mahmud, Kitab adwa', p. 316.

[29] Ibid., p. 319.

However, such a person of low character has been excused for these heinous deeds and has been regarded as an independent and learned authority in jurisprudence.[30]

Regarding 'Utba b. Sa'id, Yahya b. Mu'in writes:

He is reliable. Nasa'i, Abu Dawud, and Daraqutni have also regarded him trustworthy. On the other hand, 'Utba b. Sa'id was a companion of the wicked Hajjaj b. Yusuf.

It is not difcult to see the double standards that were applied in accreditation of the traditions reported by individuals whom they favored. Bukhari accepted the traditions reported from Marwan b. Hakam in his Sahih, and relied upon them. And yet Marwan was one of the major causes of the Battle of the Camel, having encouraged and instigated Talha to ght against 'Ali. Then, during the battle, the same Marwan killed Talha.[31]

The author of Kitab adwa' draws our attention to the fact that careful analysis of what these scholars did to authenticate Marwan clearly shows an endeavor to promote a wicked person like Marwan, who favored killing 'Ali, actually killed Talha, and was responsible for the murder of Husayn b. 'Ali. On the other hand, hadith compilers like Bukhari and Muslim discredited prominent scholars and memorizers of the Prophetic traditions like Hammad b. Maslama and the pious and god-fearing Makhul, simply because of their disagreement on some issues related to the creed.[32]

All in all, if any person narrated traditions in praise of the family of the Prophet and 'Ali b. Abi Talib or related traditions agreeing with the Shi'i beliefs, some staunchly Sunni scholars suspected their hadith reports to be unreliable or declared them unconvincing. If this

---

[30] Ibid., p. 321.

[31] Ibid., p. 317.

[32] Ibid., p. 319.

was the treatment of those suspected of Shi'i leanings, then hadith reported by those whose Shi'ism was public knowledge received even more blunt treatment. Their traditions were rejected outright. One need only read Tabari's books to fathom the prejudicial treatment given to the narrators whose beliefs were contrary to the mainstream Sunni faith.

According to Muslim, the compiler of the Sahih Muslim, Tabari says: "I met Jabir Ju'. But I did not record any tradition from him because he believed in raj'a (return of the dead before the emergence of the Mahdi)."[33]

5: Unfounded Prejudice

It is obvious that to pursue an agenda and to follow prejudice is not conducive to objective research. Anyone who intends to do research about a subject and to get to the truth of a matter must discard his unfounded prejudices against and hatred towards it, and then begin his investigation. When, during the process of the investigation, a piece of evidence is found in a tradition, one should investigate its narrator in order to prove his reliability. If the narrator's reliability is conrmed then his tradition should be accepted, regardless of whether he is a Sunni or a Shi'i. It is against the rule of fairness and the method of investigation that the traditions of a reliable narrator be rejected simply because he happens to be a Shi'i or is accused of being one. In fact, fair minded scholars among the Sunnis have been aware of this prejudice.

In this connection 'Asqalani comments:

One of the instances when one should pause in accepting the opinion of the person who is engaged in discrediting a narrator

---

[33] Sahih muslim, Vol. 1, p. 101.

is to investigate whether there exists a difference in the matter of creed between the person who is engaged in discrediting and the narrator who is being discredited.

For example, Abu Ishaq Jawzjani was a Sunni who hated the ahl al-bayt (a nasibi) while the people of Kufa were famous for their Shi'ism. Hence, he discredited the Kufan narrators in the most severe terms. Accordingly, people like A'mash, Abu Nu'aym and 'Abd Allah b. Musa, although the leaders and pillars of narrators of hadith, were declared unreliable by him. Qushayri says: "The motives of the people resemble the pits of re." Consequently, in such instances, a statement about the narrator's reliability has preponderance over a statement about his unreliability.[34]

Similarly, Muhammad b. Ahmad b. 'Uthman Dhahabi, following his account about Aban b. Taghlib's life, writes:

If some one objects to why we declare him trustworthy, in spite of the fact that Aban was among the people of innovation (i.e., Shi'is), I say thus: Innovation is of two kinds. One is a lesser type like the extremism in Shi'ism, or Shi'ism without extremism and sinful deviation. This kind of innovation was common among a number from the second and third generation of the companions of the Prophet, in spite of the fact that their piety and moral probity were beyond reproach.

If it is decided that the traditions reported by such narrators should be rejected, a large number of Prophetic traditions would necessarily have to be rejected. The wrongness of such an opinion is self- evident. The second type of innovation is of a greater type, such as the complete rejection [of the rst three caliphs] and the cursing of Abu Bakr and 'Umar. Indisputably, the traditions reported by this group have no value and should be rejected.

---

[34] Lisan al-mizan, Vol. 1, p. 16.

In short, anyone who undertakes research and wants to discover truth, should not accept such statements of the unreliability of a narrator at face value. Rather, he should try to uncover the reason for discrediting a narrator and whether that person truly deserves such a judgement.

6: Sahih Muslim and Sahih Bukhari and Traditions about the Mahdi

It is important to emphasize that if the traditions about the Mahdi were not recorded by Bukhari and Muslim, this does not mean that the reports were weak in transmission. After all, these two compilers had no intention of shedding light on all the traditions. According to Bayhaqi, Muslim and Bukhari did not intend to search for all the traditions. The evidence is provided by the inclusion of numerous traditions that were recorded by Bukhari and which are not part of Muslim's collection. At the same time, there are traditions in the Sahih of Muslim which were avoided by Bukhari.[35]

Just as Muslim claimed to have recorded only the authentic traditions in his compilation, so did Abu Dawud in his collection. This latter fact has been observed by Abu Bakr b. Dasa who heard Abu Dawud say: "I have recorded 4,800 traditions in my collection of which all are either reliable or close to reliable." In addition, Abu al-Sabah conrms that it was reported to him that Abu Dawud made a similar claim about the traditions in his compilation, Sunan, adding that if he included a weak tradition he made that clear. "Hence any tradition about which I have not made any comment should be regarded as reliable." A similar positive opinion about Abu

---

[35] Sahih muslim, Vol. 1, p. 24.

Dawud's Sunan has been related from Khatabi in the introduction to the present edition by Sa'ati.[36] In short, the traditions in Muslim and Bukhari are not different in reliability from the traditions recorded by other authors of the Sahih. What is important is that their transmitters should be investigated in order to establish their credibility or the lack thereof.

To be sure, the Sahihs of Muslim and Bukhari, whose authority is accepted by all the Sunnis, are not completely devoid of traditions about the Mahdi, although the term mahdi has not been used to express this belief among Muslims. Following is one such hadith:

It is reported from Abu Hurayra that the Prophet said: "What will be your reaction when the son of Mary descends and your Imam is among yourselves?"[37]

There are a number of other traditions on a similar theme in these two compilations. It is also important to bear in mind that Ibn Khaldun has neither totally falsied all the traditions about the Mahdi, nor has he claimed that he does not accept them. The context of Ibn Khaldun's remark about these traditions is provided by his opening statement in this section when he says:

It has been well known (and generally accepted) by all Muslims in every epoch, that at the end of time a man from the family (of the Prophet) will without fail make his appearance, who will strengthen Islam and make justice triumph. Muslims will follow him, and he will gain domination over the Muslim realm. He will be called the Mahdi.

It is evident that he has briey accepted the fact that the belief in the awaited Mahdi is common among Muslims. Moreover, after

---

[36] See the introduction to the Sunan abi Dawud by Sa'ati.

[37] Sahih muslim, bab nuzul 'isa, volume 2; Sahih bukhari, kitab bad' al-khalq wa nuzul 'isa, volume 4.

his critical evaluation of the traditions and their transmitters he concludes the discussion with the following observation:

This is the situation of the traditions about the awaited Mahdi. It has been seen in the books that, with the exception of very few, most of these traditions are regarded as unreliable.[38]

Hence, even at this point he has not rejected all the traditions on the subject. Rather, as he confesses, some of them are authentic.

Furthermore, it is relevant to point out that the traditions on the subject of the Mahdi are not conned only to those mentioned and critically evaluated by Ibn Khaldun. Quite to the contrary, most of the books on hadith, both by the Sunnis and the Shi'ites, narrate traditions in an unbroken chain of transmission which actually comes close to their verication as being credible. Had Ibn Khaldun known about the existence of all these traditions, he would have probably regarded the belief in the Mahdi as deeply rooted in the Islamic revelation.

To conclude this discussion, we can say that it is incorrect to maintain, as some scholars do, that Ibn Khaldun rejected the tradition about the Mahdi. On the contrary, it is these authors who have read into Ibn Khaldun such an opinion.

Other Opinions from Ibn Khaldun:

Ibn Khaldun concludes this section on the traditions concerning the Mahdi thus:

The truth one must know is that no religious or political power's propaganda can be successful, unless power or group feeling exists to support the religious and political aspirations and to defend them against those who reject them, and until God's will concerning

---

[38] Muqaddima, p. 322.

them materializes. We have established this before, with rational arguments which we presented to the reader. The group feeling among the Fatimids and Talibids, indeed, that among all the Quraysh, has everywhere disappeared. The only exception is a remnant of the Talibids – Hasanids, Husaynids, and Ja'farites – in the Hejaz, in Mecca, al-Yanbu', and Medina. They are spread over these regions and dominate them.

They are Bedouin groups. They are settled and rule in different places and hold divergent opinions. They number several thousands. If it is correct that a Mahdi is to appear, there is only one way for his propaganda to make its appearance. He must be one of them, and God must unite them in the intention to follow him, until he gathers enough strength and group feeling to gain success for his cause and to move people to support him. Any other way – such as a Fatimid who would make propaganda for (the cause of the Mahdi) among people anywhere at all, without the support of group feeling and power, by merely relying on his relationship to the family of Muhammad (peace be upon him) – will not be feasible or successful, for the sound reasons that we have mentioned previously.[39]

In response to this assertion by Ibn Khaldun it must be pointed out that there is no doubt that anyone who wishes to revolt and gain power so as to establish a government must have the unquestioning support of his followers in order to reach that goal. Similar conditions must be fullled in the case of the awaited Mahdi and his universal revolution. However, it is not necessary to require that his supporters be among the descendants of 'Ali and the Quraysh.

The reason is that if the government and leadership is based on ethnic and group feeling then the support has to come from that feeling. Moreover, these should be the ones to support him

---

[39] Muqaddima, p. 327.

unquestioningly. This was certainly true in the case of ethnic groups and dynasties that came to power by means of this sense of loyalty and solidarity. In general, a government that comes to power through the specic and limited sense of group feeling is necessarily dependent upon a specic and limited group of supporters. This is true in all such cases of nationalistic, ethnic, and ideological states.

However, if a government is founded upon a specic program, then it has to gain support of those who favor it. And this order can succeed only if a group recognizes the value of the program and desires to implement it by supporting the leadership that is committed to it. The revolutionary program of the Mahdi is of this kind. The Mahdi's program is profoundly universal. It desires that humanity, which is being driven into extreme forms of materialism and opposition to divine commands, respond to the divinely ordained system which rests upon moral and spiritual goals.

It wishes to resolve the problems facing humanity by clarifying the boundaries in such a way as to remove any cause of conict in society. It wants to bring people together under the banner of the Unity of God and universalize submission and service to God. Such a program, if implemented, would end tyranny and injustice and spread peace through justice all over the world.

In order to achieve this universal goal it is not sufcient to rely on the leadership of the descendants of 'Ali, who are spread all over the Hejaz, and to expect that the group feeling would help the Mahdi to reach his universal goal. To be sure, there is a need for the peoples of the entire world to prepare themselves to respond to the call of the Mahdi.

Besides the divine endorsement of this program, the Mahdi's victory is dependant upon a reasonably large and earnest group of people, who, being aware of the merits of the divinely ordained system, would seriously aspire to see such an order implemented.

Moreover, they would be willing to sacrice their lives for that cause. Consequently, if the people see an infallible and incontestable leader who has access to the divine plan for humanity and has divine endorsement of his program, they would not hesitate to assist him in establishing the ideal public order, even if this means that they would have to sacrice their lives.

The Existence of the Mahdi is Certain

There are numerous Prophetic traditions about the Mahdi, reported by both the Sunni and the Shi'i sources. Close examination of the contents of these traditions proves that the subject of the future coming of the Mahdi and the Qa'im was a well established tenet during the Prophet's life time. People anticipated someone who would take upon himself to establish truth and spread the worship of God. Moreover, they expected that person to take charge of purifying the earth and instituting justice. The belief was so wide spread among the people that having veried it in principle they were engaged in discussing its details.

Sometimes they would ask: "From which family would the awaited Mahdi arise?" At other times they wanted to know his name and patronymic. Still at other times they wanted to know the reason why he was called the Mahdi. They wanted to know about his revolution and asked about the signs of his appearance. They also wanted to nd out if the Mahdi and the Qa'im were one and the same person. They were told about the Mahdi's occultation and wanted to understand the reasons and the obligations of his followers while he was in occultation.

The Prophet also, from time to time, used to inform people about the existence of the Mahdi. He would inform them saying: "Mahdi will be among my descendants. He will be among the sons of Fatima, among the descendants of Husayn." At other times he would announce his name and patronymic and give information about the signs of his reappearance and other related matters.

The Discussion Among the Companions and the Subsequent Generations

After the Prophet's death the story of the coming of the Mahdi was often heard among the prominent companions of the Prophet and the following generation. The matter was regarded among the religious truths and was treated as one of the certain future events. The following are some examples of this in the sources:

Abu Hurayra says: "People will pay allegiance to the Mahdi between rukn and maqam."[40] Ibn 'Abbas is reported to have told Mu'awiya that a person among the descendants of the Prophet will rule for forty years at the End of Time. On another occasion a man asked Ibn 'Abbas to inform him about the Mahdi. He said: "I hope that in the near future a young man from our family (the Hashimite) will arise to put an end to civil strife and sedition."[41]

Ibn 'Abbas also specied the descendant of the Prophet as being from

---

[40] Ibn Tawus, Kitab al-malahim wa al-fitan, p. 64. Rukn and maqam are two sacred spots in the grand mosque of Mecca.

[41] Ibid., p. 84.

the children of Fatima. According to another famous companion of the Prophet, 'Ammar Yasir: "At the time when Nafs al-Zakiyya is killed a caller from the heaven will say: 'Your commander is so-and-so.' Following it the Mahdi will emerge and ll the earth with justice and equity."[42]

'Abd Allah b. 'Umar mentioned the name of Mahdi in the presence of an Arab who said: Mahdi is Mu'awiya b. Abu Sufyan. 'Abd Allah said: "It is not as you say. Mahdi is a person behind whom Jesus will offer his prayers."[43]

'Umar b. Qays asked Mujahid if he knew anything about the Mahdi, since he did not believe in what the Shi'a were saying about him. Mujahid said: "Yes, I do. One of the Prophet's companions told me that the Mahdi will not appear until that time when Nafs al-Zakiyya will be killed. At that time he will take the command and will ll the earth with justice and equity."[44]

Nufayl's daughter 'Umayra narrates that she heard Hasan b. 'Ali's daughter saying: "This affair about which you are waiting will not occur until among you some seek to distance themselves from the others and curse each other."[45] The author of Maqatil al-talibiyin Abu al-Faraj Isfahani writes that Fatima, Husayn b. 'Ali's daughter, used to engage in midwifery as a voluntary service to the women of Banu Hashim. Her son used to object to her saying: "We are afraid that you will be recognized as a professional midwife." In reply she would say: "I am awaiting someone. As soon as he is born I will stop assisting in delivery."[46]

---

[42] Ibid., p. 179.

[43] Ibid.

[44] Ibid., p. 171.

[45] Majlisi, Bihar al-anwar, Vol. 52, p. 211.

[46] Maqatil al-talibiyin, p. 160.

Qatada asked Ibn Musayyib: "Is the existence of Mahdi a truth?" He said: "Yes. He is a member of the Quraysh, among the descendants of Fatima." A similar tradition is reported from the famous scholar Zuhri, who also related that the Mahdi will be among the descendants of Fatima. Abu al-Faraj reports an event when Walid b. Muhammad was with Zuhri and a clamor transpired. Zuhri asked Walid to nd out what had caused it. After nding out Walid reported: "Zayd b. 'Ali has been killed and his head has been brought."

Zuhri was upset and said: "Why is this family in haste? Haste has destroyed a number of them." Walid asked: "Will they reach power?" He replied, "Yes, because 'Ali b. Husayn narrated to me on the authority of his father who heard this from Fatima, the Prophet's daughter, who, in turn, heard the Prophet tell her: 'Mahdi will be among your descendants.'" In another place Abu al-Faraj reported a tradition from Muslim b. Qutayba, who said: "One day I went to visit Mansur, the 'Abbasid caliph. He said: 'Muhammad b. 'Abd Allah has revolted and has announced that he is the Mahdi. By God, he is not the Mahdi. Let me tell you something. I have not told nor will I tell this to anyone else besides you. My son Mahdi is not the one mentioned in the traditions. I have just named him Mahdi as a good omen."[47]

Other sources that mention these traditions include the following:

Ibn Sirin used to say that the promised Mahdi will be from this Umma. He will be the one who will lead Jesus in prayers. In another place he reports a tradition from 'Abd Allah b. Harith. He said: "The Mahdi will arise at the age of forty and will resemble the Children of Israel." A variant of this tradition reported by Artat says that the Mahdi will arise at the age of twenty. Another tradition in the same section explains the reason Mahdi was named thus. Ka'b says: "He

---

[47] Maqatil al-talibiyin, p. 167.

was named Mahdi because he will be guided to the hidden matters." 'Abd Allah b. Shurayk used to relate that the Prophet's standard will be with the Mahdi.[48]

Ibn Sirin records several other traditions that speak about the function of the Mahdi. One of these reported from Hakam b. 'Uyayna says that the reporter asked Muhammad b. 'Ali al-Baqir:

We have heard that one among your ahl al-bayt will arise and will establish justice and equity. Is this true? He said: "We are also awaiting his appearance and living in hope."

In another tradition Salma b. Zafar reports:

One day people were talking about the appearance of the Mahdi in the presence of Hudhayfa. Hudhayfa said: "If Mahdi has indeed appeared while you are living close to the Prophet's period and while his companions are living among you, then you are truly fortunate. However, that is not the case. Mahdi will not appear until people are devoured by oppression and tyranny and there is no one absent more beloved and more needed than him."[49]

People were so familiar with the characteristics of the Mahdi that Jarir, the Arab poet, read the following lines of his poem for the Umayyad caliph 'Umar b. 'Abd al-'Aziz in which he compares the caliph with the future Mahdi:

Your presence is a blessing. Your conduct is the conduct of the Mahdi. You are ghting your lower self, and you spend the night in recitation of the Qur'an.[50]

Muhammad b. Ja'far reports that he once told Malik b. Anas his misfortunes. He said: "Wait until the signicance of the verse of the Qur'an:

---

[48] Ibid., p. 147-150.

[49] Ibid., p. 159.

[50] Ibn Qutayba, al-Imama wa al-siyasa, Vol. 2, p. 117.

'Yet We desired to be gracious to those that were abased in land, and to make them leaders, and to make them the inheritors (The Holy Qur'an, 27:5),'

becomes materialized."[51]

---

[51] Maqatil al-talibiyin, p. 359

People Awaited the Appearance of the Mahdi

From all the references to the Mahdi and his appearance in the sources, it is obvious that people were awaiting the coming of the Mahdi from the early days of Islam, and were actually counting the days for that to happen. They regarded the establishment of the legitimate government through his emergence a certainty. This anticipation used to get intense during times of political turmoil and unfavorable social conditions. People expected that the emergence would take place imminently. On many occasions they would adhere to the false pretender or would regard some person to be truly the promised Mahdi. Those whom people thought were the promised Mahdi included the following:

Muhammad b. Hanafiyya

Since he had the name and patronymic of the Prophet, there was a group that believed him to be the Mahdi. According to Tabari, when Mukhtar b. Abu 'Ubayd Thaqa wanted to revolt against the Umayyads and exact revenge from those who had murdered the grandson of the Prophet, Husayn, he ascribed Mahdiism to Muhammad b. Hanayya. And he claimed to be his envoy and his deputy and showed the letters he had brought with him to the people.[52]

Ibn Sa'd tells us that when people wanted to greet Ibn Hanayya they would address him thus: "Peace be to you, O Mahdi!" And he would reply: "Yes, I am the Mahdi, and I shall guide you towards the straight path and prosperity. My name is the same as the name of the Prophet, and my patronymic is also his patronymic. Whenever you want to greet me say: 'Peace be to you O Muhammad; peace be to you O Abu al-Qasim!'"[53]

This and other similar reports indicate that one of the signs of the appearance of the promised Mahdi was the combination of the Prophet's name and patronymic for a person. This is the reason Ibn Hanayya made a reference to this fact for himself. However, careful investigation of historical sources reveals that it was not Ibn Hanayya who made such claims for himself. It was others, like Mukhtar, who introduced him thus.

On his part, sometimes Ibn Hanayya kept silent on the matter, conrming the attribution to him. This policy was probably followed with the hope that the murderers of Karbala would be avenged and the Islamic leadership would revert to its rightful holder. This is supported by another report in which Ibn Hanayya tells the people: "Be aware that the rightful people have a government, which will be established when God desires it. Anyone who witnesses it will be fortunate and anyone who predeceases it will enjoy the blessings of God in the hereafter."[54]

---

[52] Ta'rikh, Vol. 4, pp. 449-494; Ibn Athir, Kamil al-tawarikh, Vol. 1, p. 339, 358..

[53] Tabaqat al-kubra, Vol. 5, p. 66.

[54] Ibid., Vol. 7, p. 71

Muhammad b. Hanayya, in a sermon that he delivered in the presence of some seven thousand people, said: "You have hastened in this matter. Yet, among your descendants are people who, with the help of the family of the Prophet, will wage war against the enemies of God. The government of the family of the Prophet is not concealed from anyone. However, its materialization will take time. I declare solemnly in the name of the One in whose hand is Muhammad's life, the rule will return to the Prophet's family."[55]

Muhammad b. 'Abd Allah b. Hasan

This was another descendant of the Prophet, whom people accepted as the Mahdi. According to Abu al- Faraj, when Muhammad b. 'Abd Allah was born the family of the Prophet rejoiced and quoted the Prophet saying: "The name of the Mahdi is Muhammad." As such, they were hopeful that Muhammad would be the promised Mahdi. They used to adore him. In the gatherings he was mentioned frequently and the Shi'is used to give each other good news about his impending appearance.

In another place Abu al-Faraj reports an account which says that when Muhammad b. 'Abd Allah was born he was named Mahdi with the expectation that he was the Mahdi promised in the earlier sources. However, the leaders of the Talibids used to call him nafs al-zakiyya and, in accord with the divine decree, he would be killed in Ihjar Zayt. One of the slaves of Abu Ja'far Mansūr relates that he was told by Mansur to go and sit near the pulpit and listen to his lectures. Once he heard him say: "Do not entertain any doubt that I am the Mahdi, and the reality is also thus." The slave reported the incident to the Caliph who said: "By God, Muhammad is telling

---

[55] Ibid., Vol. 5, p. 80

falsehood. The truth is that the promised Mahdi is my son."[56]

Salma b. Aslam composed lines about Muhammad b. 'Abd Allah in which he said: "That which is reported in the traditions will materialize when Muhammad b. 'Abd Allah appears among the people and takes charge of the affairs with his hands. Muhammad has a special ring, which God has not given to anyone except him. There will be signs of piety and goodness in him. We hope that Muhammad will be the Imam through whose blessed existence the Qur'an will come to life again. Moreover, through his existence Islam will be revived and reformed, and the poor orphan children and needy families will again live in prosperity. He will ll the earth with justice and equity as it is lled with corruption. And our hopes and aspirations will be fullled."

---

[56] Ibid., pp. 165 and 157

The Jurists of Medina and the Mahdi Traditions

When Muhammad b. 'Abd Allah revolted one of the jurists of Medina by the name of Muhammad b. 'Ajlan also rose with him. After he was killed, Ja'far b. Sulayman, the governor of Medina, summoned Muhammad b. 'Ajlan and asked him: "Why did you rise with that liar?" He then ordered his hands to be cut. Other jurists who were present in the court at that time interceded on his behalf, emphasizing that

Muhammad b. 'Ajlan was a pious jurist of Medina and had erroneously regarded Muhammad b. 'Abd Allah as the Mahdi promised in the traditions.[57]

Another well-known jurist and a prominent scholar of the hadith, 'Abd Allah b. Ja'far also rose with Muhammad b. 'Abd Allah. When the latter was killed he fled from Medina and remained in hiding until he was granted amnesty. One day the governor of Medina passed by him and asked him the reason why he arose with Muhammad b. 'Abd Allah, in spite of his learning in the law and traditions. He replied:

---

[57] Ibid., p. 163.

"The reason I supported and cooperated with him was that I was condent that he was the promised Mahdi, about whom we have been informed in the traditions. I did not doubt Muhammad's Mahdiism until I saw him killed. At that time I knew he was not the Mahdi. I will not fall into anyone else's hoax from now on."[58]

From such accounts it is evident that the subject of the Mahdiism was widespread from those early days of Islam, close to the period of the Prophet. It was accepted as an absolute religious truth and people were awaiting the Mahdi. It was for this reason that the common people, who knew little about the signs for the appearance of the Mahdi and who were downtrodden, believed that Muhammad b. Hanayya and Muhammad b. 'Abd Allah and other pretenders were the promised Mahdi. However, the scholars and those who were well informed about the ahl al-bayt, including Muhammad's own father, knew that he was not the promised Mahdi.

A man came to see 'Abd Allah b. Hasan and asked him when his son Muhammad would rise. He replied: "As long as I have not been killed, he will not rise." The man sighed and said: "From God we originate and to God we shall return. If Muhammad is killed, the umma will collapse." 'Abd Allah said to him: "That is not the case." The man continued and asked when would Ibrahim rise. He said: "As long as I am not destroyed, he will not rise. He too will be killed." Once again the man uttered the same verse and declared that the community had indeed undertaken the path of destruction. 'Abd Allah replied: "That is not so.

Actually their master, the promised Mahdi, is twenty ve years old. And at the time that he rises he will kill all the enemies." When Marwan was told that Muhammad b. 'Abd Allah had revolted, he said: "Neither he nor any other person sharing his father's genealogy

---

[58] Ibid., p. 193.

is the promised Mahdi. Rather, he will be the son of a slave girl." Whenever the Imam Ja'far Sadiq would see Muhammad b. 'Abd Allah he would cry and say: "May my life be a sacrice for him. People are speculating that he is the promised Mahdi.

On the contrary he will be killed. Indeed, his name is not mentioned among the caliphs of this community in the book of 'Ali."[59]

A group of people were sitting around Muhammad b. 'Abd Allah when the Imam Sadiq entered the place. Everyone stood up in respect. He inquired about the affairs and they replied that they had decided to pay allegiance to Muhammad who was the Mahdi. The Imam said: "I advise you to desist from doing so, because the time for the rise of the Mahdi has not approached yet. Moreover, Muhammad is not the Mahdi."[60]

---

[59] Ibid., p. 143.

[60] Ibid., p. 141.

The Poetry of Di'bil and the Mahdi

When Di'bil b. 'Ali al-Khuza'i presented his famous lines in the presence of Imam Rida, he ended his poem with the following lines:

No doubt an Imam will rise – an Imam who will govern according to the name of God and the [divine] blessing.

These lines underscore the certainty with which Di'bil mentioned the rising of the Imam who will rule in the name of God and with God's blessings. On hearing this, Imam Rida wept and said: "The blessed angel has put these words in your mouth. Do you know this Imam?" Di'bil said: "No. But I have heard that an Imam among you will rise and will ll the earth with justice and equity." Imam Rida said: "After me my son Muhammad will be the Imam; following him his son 'Ali will be the Imam; and after 'Ali his son Hasan will be the Imam.

Following Hasan his son will the Proof of God and the Qa'im, who should be awaited while he is in occultation. And when he appears he should be obeyed. He is the one who will ll this earth with justice and equity. But the time of his emergence has not been xed. However, it has been reported by my ancestors that he would appear all of a sudden and in a ash of a moment."⁶¹

There are numerous such reports in the historical sources which, if you wish, you can investigate.

* * *

It was quite late at night and the meeting was adjourned. It was decided that the group would meet the following Friday afternoon.

On the appointed evening friends came together at Dr. Fahimi's house. After the usual formalities and enquiries the session began. Mr. Hoshyar began to speak.

Mr. Hoshyar: There is another matter worth considering as further evidence and related to the topic about the origins of Mahdiism. These are the accounts of individuals claiming to be the Mahdi in the past, whose names have been preserved in the historical sources. These reports suggest that the subject was not only wide spread, but also well authenticated in the early days of Islam. To clarify my point for all those who are gathered here I will mention some of these pseudo-Mahdis.

Muhammad b. Hanayya was regarded as the Mahdi by some Muslims. He was believed to be alive and living an invisible existence in Mount Radwa. He would appear in the future and would ll the earth with justice and equity.⁶² A group called Jarudis among the Zaydis believed that Muhammad b. 'Abd Allah b. Hasan was the Mahdi, and that he was in concealment. They awaited his return.⁶³ The Nawusi's believed that Imam Ja'far Sadiq was the Mahdi, and

---

⁶¹ Yanabi' al-mawadda, Vol. 2, p. 197.

⁶² Shahrastani, Milal wa nihal, Vol. 1, p. 232; Nawbakhti, Firaq al-shi'a, Najaf edition, p. 27

⁶³ Milal, Vol. 1, p. 256; Firaq, p. 62

that he was alive and in occultation. The Waqis believed that Imam Musa b. Ja'far had not died and was in occultation. He would appear in the future and would ll the earth with justice and equity.[64]

A group among the Isma'ilis believed that Isma'il had not died. Rather, he had been declared dead out of fear (taqiyya) of persecution. The Baqiris regarded Imam Muhammad Baqir to be alive and believed that he was the promised Mahdi. The Muhammadis believed that following the death of Imam 'Ali Naqi, the Imam was his son Muhammad. This they believed in spite of the fact that he died during his father's life time. They, furthermore, believed that he was alive and that he was the promised Mahdi.[65] The Jawaziyya believed that the twelfth Imam Hujjat b. al-Hasan had a son and that he was the promised Mahdi. The Hashimis maintained that 'Abd Allah b. Harb Kindi was the Imam. Alive but in occultation, they expected that he would appear in the future. The Mubarakis, among the Isma'ilis, regarded Muhammad b. Isma'il as a living Imam in occultation.[66]

The Yazidi faction maintained that Yazid has ascended to heaven, and will return in the future to ll the earth with justice and equity. The Isma'ilis say that the Mahdi mentioned in the traditions is the same as Muhammad b. 'Abd Allah, known as Mahdi, who became the ruler in Egypt and North Africa. To support their belief they cite the tradition of the Prophet in which he said that in the year 300 the sun would rise from the west.[67]

A group of the Imamis believed that Imam Hasan 'Askari was alive and that he was the Qa'im. He was living an invisible existence and

---

[64] Milal, Vol. 1, pp. 273, 278; Firaq, pp. 67, 80, 83

[65] Muhammad Karim Khurasani, Tanbihat al-jaliyya fi kashf al-asrar al-batiniyya (Najaf, 1351), pp. 40-42

[66] Milal, Vol. 1, pp. 245, 279

[67] Mir Khwand, Tarikh-i Rawdat al-safa, Tehran edition, Vol. 4, p. 181

would appear in the future and would ll the earth with justice and equity. Another group among them held that Imam Hasan 'Askari has died but would come back to life later on and would rise because the meaning of qa'im is 'to rise after death.'[68]

The Qarmatis regarded Muhammad b. Isma'il to be the promised Mahdi. They believed that he was alive and lived in Anatolia. The followers of Abu Muslim believed that Abu Muslim was the living Imam who was in concealment. A group believed that Imam Hasan 'Askari was the Mahdi and that he became alive after death. He continues to live in this state until the time comes when he will ll the earth with justice and equity.[69]

---

[68] Milal, Vol. 1, p. 284; Firaq, pp. 96, 97

[69] Firaq., pp. 47, 97

Manipulation of the Beliefs of the People

These are the names of the people who claimed to be the Mahdi in the early history of Islam. A number of ignorant people accepted their claim and regarded them to be the promised Mahdi. However, the majority of these groups have perished and there remains nothing more than their mention in the books on history. Since that time a number of individuals belonging to Hashimite or non-Hashimite clans from different regions and countries of the world have emerged claiming to be the promised Mahdi.

Historically, such claims have led to insurrections and revolutions, with much bloodshed and destruction of human life.

It is possible to surmise from events related to the appearances of the false messiahs that the subject of Mahdiism and the emergence of the divine savior were among the well established religious truths among Muslims, who anxiously awaited for the appearance of the Mahdi. They also regarded his victory and the defeat of his enemy as imminent. Such expectations of the people became the major source for some ambitious and crafty individuals to manipulate their simple and pure faith – a faith which stemmed from the teachings of the

Islamic revelation – and lay claim to the title of the Mahdi.

It is likely that some of these individuals had no evil design and merely wanted to redress the wrongs committed against the people. Indeed, some of them did not even claim to be the promised deliverer. Rather, it was the common people who, due to ignorance, intolerable living conditions, and an impatience regarding their expectations about the appearance of the Mahdi, took these false messiahs to be the awaited Mahdi.

Fabrication of the Traditions

It was, unfortunately, these conditions that caused circulation of the traditions describing and praising the Mahdi and foretelling the signs of his appearance. These traditions were uncritically accepted and reported in the books. Any impartial scholar can discover these fabricated traditions by undertaking to investigate the historical accounts of the appearance of these pseudo-Mahdis and then to examine the hadith compilations that deal with the characteristics of the Mahdi. Such, for instance, is the case with the tradition in which the Prophet says:

The world will not come to an end until God sends a man from my family, whose name will be the same as mine, and whose father's name will be the same as my father's. He will ll the earth with justice and equity as it is lled with injustice and tyranny.[70]

In this hadith the Mahdi's father is introduced as possessing the name of the Prophet's father, that is, 'Abd Allah. This contradicts many traditions that mention Mahdi's father to be Hasan. Hence, it is

---

[70] Fusul al-muhimma, p. 274

possible to maintain that this hadith was circulated by those who regarded Muhammad b. 'Abd Allah b. Hasan to be the Mahdi. They must have added the sentence 'whose father's name will be the same as my father's' to the original hadith. This is supported by the view held by Muhammad b. Yusuf in his book entitled: al-Bayan. He writes that Tirmidhi relates the same tradition in his compilation without mentioning the additional sentence 'whose father's . . .'. Abu Dawud also reports the same tradition without the additional sentence.

In another tradition recorded by Abu al-Faraj in his Maqatil al-talibiyyin Abu Hurayra is reported to have heard the Prophet saying: "Indeed, the Mahdi's name will be Muhammad b. 'Abd Allah and he will be aficted with a speech defect."[71] This tradition is also a forgery of those who supported Muhammad b. 'Abd Allah b. Hasan's claim to Mahdiism. It is said that he had difculty in speaking and could barely utter certain words. His followers took this defect to be a sign of the Mahdi and forged a tradition to that effect.

The 'Abbasids also fabricated traditions to bolster their claim to this eminent role predicted about the Mahdi. According to one of these traditions, Ibn 'Abbas reported from the Prophet who said to 'Abbas, his uncle: "At the End of Time there will be Mahdi among you through whom right guidance will spread and the res of misguidance will be put out. Indeed, God began this matter with us and will conclude it through your progeny."[72] In another hadith Ibn 'Abbas reports the Prophet saying: "From us, the ahl al- bayt, will arise al-Saffah, al-Mundhir, al-Mansur and al-Mahdi. The Mahdi will be among the descendants of my uncle al-'Abbas."[73] There is little doubt

---

[71] p. 164

[72] Dhakha'ir al-'uqba, p. 206

[73] Ibid., p. 206. See also al-Sawa'iq al-muharriqa, p. 235

that these traditions were forged by the 'Abbasids.

A tradition is related from 'Ali b. Abi Talib regarding the appearance of black banners from the direction of Khurasan. "Among these banners is God's caliph, the Mahdi."[74] This too appears to be fabricated by the 'Abbasids or by the supporters of Abu Muslim Khurasani because the Mahdi will not come from Khurasan, and the black banners were the emblem of the 'Abbasids. There are numerous other traditions that were evidently forged by the 'Abbasid pretenders to promote support for their cause.

In general, to provide legitimacy to the claims of any pseudo-Mahdi, traditions traced back to the Prophet himself were forged and circulated among the followers. Consequently, there is hardly any prominent leader for whom there were no traditions to promote his Mahdiism. The problem was that many of these individuals had died. But their followers refused to accept their death as real. Hence, traditions were fabricated to relate that their revolution would commence after their death and upon their return to life when God commanded them to do so. Al-Fadl b. Musa reports a tradition in which Imam al-Sadiq was asked by Abu Sa'id Khurasani: "Why was he (i.e., the Mahdi) known as al-Qa'im?" The Imam said: "Because he will rise after his death. He will rise for an important task, as commanded by God, the Exalted."[75]

Certainly, this hadith was fabricated by the Waqiyya, who believed that Imam Musa Kazim had not died and would return as the promised Mahdi. Moreover, it is likely that it was fabricated by those who believed that Imam Hasan 'Askari had died, but would rise later on to establish a just society. Actually, in terms of the science of hadith, the chain of transmission is weak, since it includes

---

[74] Yanabi' al-mawadda, Vol. 1, p. 57

[75] Ithbat al-hudat, Vol. 7, p. 27

a person whose reliability is in question. In a similar tradition with a slight variation Abu Sa'id asked Imam al-Sadiq: "Are al-Mahdi and al-Qa'im one and the same?"

The Imam replied: "Yes." Abu Sa'id went on to ask: "Why is he known as the Mahdi?" The Imam replied: "Because he will guide to the hidden matters." "Why is he known as the Qa'im?" The Imam said: "Because he will rise after he dies, that is, dies in the people's remembering that he will rise for the great purpose."[76] It is evident that the two traditions are actually one. In the second tradition death is interpreted as a death of the memory of his name.

The belief that the Mahdi will die and then rise to launch his revolution was accepted by some people who were also responsible for fabricating traditions to support their belief. Thus, Imam Sadiq was asked: "Is there an example of qa'im (rising after death) in the Qur'an?" He said: "Yes. A passage in the Qur'an speaks about the owner of the donkey, whose death was caused by God, and then God brought him back to life."[77]

In a long tradition Mu'awiya b. Abu Sufyan reports from the Prophet the following:

The Prophet said: "After my death an island by the name of Andalusia will be conquered. Afterwards the army of disbelievers will overpower them . . . At that point a man from among the descendants of Fatima, the Prophet's daughter, will rise from the farthest region of the Maghrib. He will be the Mahdi, the Qa'im. He is the rst sign of the Hour."[78]

The tradition was probably fabricated by the Isma'ilis who founded a state in the Maghreb. Many such traditions are single in transmis-

---

[76] Ithbat al-hudat, Vol. 7, p. 34

[77] Ibid., Vol. 7, p. 28

[78] Ibid., Vol. 7, p. 242

sion and, therefore, the information in them cannot be regarded as reliable. More importantly, in comparison to the numerous traditions about the Mahdi reported uninterruptedly, these traditions are not credible at all.

The Family of the Prophet and the Eleven Imams' Predictions about the Mahdi

Dr. Fahimi: What was the belief of the Family of the Prophet and the Imams regarding the Mahdi?

Mr. Hoshyar: Following the Prophet's death the subject of Mahdiism was also under discussion among the Prophet's companions and the Imams. The Family of the Prophet, as the heirs to the Prophet's knowledge and to the intricate matters concerning faith, was the most knowledgeable about the Prophetic traditions. They spoke about the Mahdi and replied to the questions that were posed to them on this subject. Let us cite some examples of these communications by them with some attention to the chronology. Although there are several traditions cited from each one of the Imams and from Fatima Zahra (peace be upon her) we will cite just one from each:

Tradition Narrated by Imam 'Ali about the Future Coming of the Mahdi

The following tradition is related by al-Asbagh who heard 'Ali b. Abi Talib say:

The promised Mahdi will emerge at the End of Time from among us. There is no Mahdi in any nation other than him being awaited.

There are more than fty traditions narrated from 'Ali b. Abi Talib in connection with the future appearance of the Mahdi and his being from among the Family of the Prophet.

Tradition Narrated by Fatima Zahra (peace be upon her)

Fatima Zahra told her son Husayn:

When I gave birth to you, the Prophet came to see me. He took you in his hands and said to me: "O Fatima, take your Husayn, and know that he is the father of nine Imams. From his descendants will appear righteous leaders among whom the ninth will be the Qa'im."[79]

Tradition Narrated by Imam Hasan b. 'Ali

Hasan b. 'Ali said:

There will be twelve Imams following the Prophet. Nine of these Imams will be from the progeny of my brother Husayn. The Mahdi

---

[79] Ithbat al-hudat, Vol. 2, p. 552. There are three more traditions here reported from Fatima Zahra

of this umma will be among them.[80]

Tradition Narrated by Imam Husayn b. 'Ali

Husayn b. 'Ali said:

Twelve Imams will be from among us. The rst among them will be 'Ali b. Abi Talib and the last will be my ninth descendant, the rightful Qa'im. Because of his blessed existence God will bring back the dead earth to life and prosperity. God will give victory to His religion over all other religions, even if this be against the liking of the disbelievers. The Mahdi will disappear from public for a while. During his occultation a number of people will abandon religion, whereas others will remain steadfast and will suffer because of their faith.

This latter group will be asked tauntingly: "If your belief is true, when would your promised Imam rise?" But, remember that whoever perseveres under those unfavorable circumstances when enemies would falsify and harm them, their status will be like those who fought by the side of the Prophet in defending the religion of God.[81]

Tradition Narrated by Imam 'Ali b. Husayn:

'Ali b. Husayn said:

The birth of our Qa'im will be hidden from the people in such a way that they will assert: "He has not been born at all!" The reason for his concealment is that when he begins his revolution he will

---

[80] Ibid., Vol. 2, p. 555. There are four other traditions reported from Imam Hasan

[81] Ibid., Vol. 2, pp. 333, 399; Majlisi, Bihar al-anwar, Vol. 51, p. 133. There are thirteen more traditions reported from Imam Husayn

have no one's allegiance on his neck.[82]

Tradition Narrated by Imam Muhammad Baqir

Muhammad b. 'Ali Baqir told Aban b. Taghlib:

I solemnly declare that the Imamate is the divine covenant that has reached us from the Prophet. The Imams after the Prophet are twelve in number of whom nine are the descendants of Husayn. At the End of Time the Mahdi will also emerge from among us who will protect the religion of God.[83]

Tradition Narrated by Imam Ja'far Sadiq

Ja'far b. Muhammad Sadiq said:

Whoever acknowledges all the Imams, but denies the existence of the Mahdi, is like the one who acknowledges all the prophets but denies the prophethood of Muhammad (peace be upon him).

Someone asked him: "Among whose descendants is the Mahdi?" The Imam responded:

The fth progeny of the seventh Imam [Musa Kazim] will be the Mahdi. However, he will disappear. It is not proper for you to name him.[84]

---

[82] Bihar al-anwar, Vol. 51, p. 135. There are additionally ten traditions reported on the authority of Imam 'Ali b. al-Husayn

[83] Ithbat al-hudat, Vol. 2, p. 559. Additionally, there are sixty-six traditions related on the authority of al-Baqir

[84] Bihar al-anwar, Vol. 51, p. 143; Ithbat al-hudat, Vol. 2, p. 404. There are one hundred and twenty-three additional traditions reported on the authority of al-Sadiq

Tradition Narrated by Imam Musa Kazim:

Yunus b. 'Abd al-Rahman asked Imam Musa b. Ja'far: "Are you the rightful Qa'im?" He replied:

Yes, I am the rightful Qa'im. But the Qa'im who will purify the earth from the enemies of God and will ll it with justice and equity, is my fth descendant. Since he is afraid for his life, he will be in occultation for a long time. During this period of occultation, a group will turn away from religion. But some will remain steadfast in their faith..

He went on to add:

Blessed are those Shi'a who during this period of occultation will continue to be faithful to us and remain steadfast in their loyalty to us and their hostility toward our enemies. Truly, they are from us and we are from them. They are convinced about our Imamate and we acknowledge their fealty to us. By God, blessed are they! They will be with us in Paradise.[85]

Tradition Reported by Imam Ali b. Musa Rida

Rayya b. Salt once asked Imam Rida: "Are you sahib al-'amr (Master of the Undertaking)?" The Imam said:

Yes, I am the Master of the Undertaking. However, I am not that Master of the Undertaking who will ll the earth with justice and equity. How can I be that Master of the Undertaking when you are witness to the prevalent weakness and helplessness? The promised Qa'im will be old in age but young in appearance when he emerges. He will be so powerful and strong that if he extended his hand to the most huge tree it would fall uprooted.

---

[85] Bihar al-anwar, Vol. 51, p. 151; Ithbat al-hudat, Vol. 6, p. 417

And if he screamed among the mountains the rocks would be crushed into pieces. The rod of Moses and the seal of Solomon are with him. That person will be my fourth descendant. God will keep him in occultation for as long as He deems necessary. Then, He will cause him to appear, and through him God will ll the earth with justice and equity as it is lled with tyranny and oppression.[86]

Tradition Reported by Imam Muhammad b. 'Ali Jawad

Imam Muhammad Taqi Jawad told 'Abd al-'Azim Hasani:

Our Qa'im is the same as the promised Mahdi whom you should await and when he appears you should obey. He will be my third descendant. I swear by the God who sent Muhammad as the Prophet and appointed us as the Imams that even if there remains a single day on earth, God will prolong it until the Mahdi emerges and lls the earth with justice and equity as it is lled with injustice and tyranny. God takes care of His affairs overnight just as He managed the affairs of Moses in one night. Moses had gone to fetch re for his family and he returned having been fully designated as God's prophet.

The Imam then added: "Awaiting for the deliverance to come is the best act for our Shi'a."[87]

---

[86] Bihar al-anwar, Vol. 52, p. 322; Ithbat al-hudat, Vol. 6, p. 420. There are additionally eighteen traditions reported on the authority of Imam 'Ali al-Rida

[87] Bihar al-anwar, Vol. 51, p. 156; Ithbat al-hudat, Vol. 6, p. 419. There are five other traditions reported on the authority of Imam Muhammad Taqi

Tradition Narrated by Imam 'Ali Naqi

Imam 'Ali Naqi said: "Following me my son Hasan is the Imam, and following Hasan it will be the Qa'im who will fill the earth with justice and equity."[88]

Tradition Narrated by Imam Hasan 'Askari

Imam Hasan 'Askari told Musa b. Ja'far Baghdadi:

I see you disputing in the matter of the Imam after me. Be aware that anyone who acknowledges the Imams after the Prophet, but rejects the Imamate of my son is like the one who has accepted the prophethood of all the prophets except the prophethood of Muhammad. The one who denies the latter is like the one who has denied all other prophets. The reason is that obedience to the last Imam is like obedience to the first Imam among us. Hence, whoever rejects the last among us is like the one who has rejected the first Imam. Let it be known to you that the occultation of my son will be so much prolonged that people will fall in doubt except for those whose faith God protects.[89]

---

[88] Ithbat al-hudat, Vol. 6, p. 275. There are additionally five traditions related by Imam 'Ali Naqi

[89] Bihar al-anwar, Vol. 51, p. 160; Ithbat al-hudat, Vol. 6, p. 427. In addition, there are twenty one traditions reported on the authority of Imam Hasan 'Askari

Are these Traditions about the Mahdi Authentic?

Engineer Madani: You can follow these traditions only if they are sound and reliable. Do you regard all these traditions about the Mahdi reliable?

Mr. Hoshyar: I do not claim that all the traditions, on the subject of the Mahdi are highly reliable and that all its narrators are trustworthy. However, there are some among these that could be regarded as unquestionably authentic. These traditions, like all other traditions, include authentic, good, reliable, and weak cases. It is not necessary to go through the investigation of each one of them because, as you have noticed, these traditions are so numerous that any fair minded and unprejudiced person can refer to them with condence.

This condence is based on the underlying theme in all of them that the existence of the Mahdi was among the well known subjects of Islam whose seeds were sown by the Prophet himself and whose detailed information was provided by the Imams. It is possible to maintain with certainty that in Islam there are few other subjects which could muster so many related traditions as can be summoned concerning the existence of the Mahdi.

Let me elaborate. From the beginning of his mission until the Farewell Pilgrimage, the Prophet had mentioned the subject of the Mahdi innumerable times. Following the Prophet, Imam 'Ali, Fatima Zahra and other prominent members of the Family, had carried on the tradition of reporting about the future coming of the Mahdi. After all they were the carriers of the Prophetic knowledge. After the death of the Prophet in the year 632 CE, Muslims were counting the days for the Mahdi to appear. This led them to recognize the false pretenders who appeared from time to time in history.

These traditions were reported by all schools of Islamic thought, such as the Sunnis, the Shi'is, the Ash'ari and Mu'tazili theologians, as related by the Arab, Persian, Meccan and Medinese narrators as well as those from Kufa, Basra, Baghdad, and so on. With all these traditions, which actually number more than a thousand, is it possible for any fair minded person to cast doubt in the matter of the future coming of the Mahdi by claiming that these traditions were fabricated by the extremist Shi'is and ascribed to the Prophet?

* * *

It was getting late at night and there was no time to continue the discussion any further. Hence, the decision was made to take up more discussion in the future session to be held at Dr. Fahimi's residence.

People were slowly assembling at Dr. Fahimi's residence. After the usual welcome and hospitality, the session began at eight o'clock. This time it was Engineer Madani who opened the discussion.

Engineer Madani: I remember reading a book some time ago in which the author's thesis was that Mahdiism and the divinely ordained messiah were ideas held by the Jews and pre-Islamic Iranians which spread among the Muslims. Iranians believed that a man named Saoshyant from the descendants of Zoroaster would one day appear and destroy Ahriman, the force of darkness, thereby clearing the earth from corruption. As for the Jews, because they had lost their homeland and had been enslaved by the Chaldeans and Assyrians, one of their prophets had predicted that a messiah would rise, deliver the Jews, and return them to their promised land in the future. Since the origins of the idea of the future savior and deliverer were found amongst the Iranians and the Jews, we may say that this notion came to Muslims through their channels and, hence, cannot be anything more than a legend.

Mr. Hoshyar: I agree that this notion was and is prevalent among other peoples and religious communities. However, its mere prevalence among other communities does not render it a legend! For Islamic notions and rulings to be authentic is it necessary that they ought to be in disagreement with the past religions? Any person wishing to investigate any topic without prejudicial understanding has to begin his research in the primary sources of the particular tradition that deals with the subject in order to assess its validity or lack thereof. It is not proper to begin this investigation in the sources of the traditions that existed before it and then claim that one has discovered the origins of that superstitious belief! Is it possible to say that since the ancient Iranians were believers in Yazdan, the God, and regarded honesty as part of good conduct, that therefore divine worship must be a legend and honesty cannot be part of good morals? Hence, just because other peoples are also awaiting the arrival of a deliverer and a messiah does not disprove the belief among Muslims; nor can it be used as a proof for the belief's veracity.

The Reasons for the Emergence of Belief in the Mahdiism

Dr. Fahimi: One of the authors has adequately narrated the origins of the idea of the future messianic gure. If I may, I would like to relate it in brief for you.

The audience: Please do!

Dr. Fahimi: I am going to restate it in brief. The original legend about the messianic Imam was adopted by the Shi'is from other religious communities, to which they added their own details until it reached its present form. This was done for two reasons:

First, the belief about the birth and emergence of a divine savior was and remains well established among the Jews. They believed that Elijah had ascended to the heavens and would descend at the End of Time to deliver the Children of Israel.

In the early days of Islam, a group of Jews had converted to Islam both for material reasons and in order to destroy Islam from its very foundation. Some among them attained high positions among the Muslims through treachery and dissimulation. Indeed, their sole purpose was to divide the Muslim community and spread dissension among them. The most outstanding example of this subversive character was 'Abd Allah b. Saba.

Second, following the death of the Prophet, his family members, especially 'Ali b. Abi Talib, used to regard themselves as more worthy of the caliphate than other leading Muslims. A small number of the Prophet's companions were also sympathetic to their claims. However, against their expectations, the caliphate was assumed by others rather than by family. This caused bitterness and distress among them until the time when, following the murder of 'Uthman, the caliphate reverted to 'Ali. His supporters were pleased and hoped that the caliphate would not slip out from the hands of the Prophet's family. Engulfed by the civil wars, however, 'Ali could not achieve much and nally was killed by Ibn Muljam. His son Hasan, who followed him in his position, did not succeed in bringing order and nally abdicated the caliphate to the Umayyads.

Hasan and Husayn, the two grandsons of the Prophet, remained in their homes while the government passed into the hands of others. The Prophet's family and its supporters were living a miserable life as the Umayyads and the 'Abbasids squandered the Muslim treasury. These events led to an increase in the number of those who supported the family and raised their opposition to the corrupt rulers throughout in the empire. However, the rulers, instead of redressing the wrongs committed against the innocent populace, increased the intensity of their atrocities by killing or exiling them. In short, after the Prophet's death his *Ahlul Bayt* and their supporters suffered oppression. Fatima was denied her right to inherit from the Prophet. 'Ali's right to the caliphate was denied until later. Hasan was poisoned. Husayn b. 'Ali, his family and companions, were killed at Karbala and the survivors of the tragedy were taken prisoner. Muslim b. 'Aqil and Hani b. 'Urwa were killed mercilessly after being granted amnesty. Abu Dharr Ghiffari was deported to Rabdha. Hujr b. 'Adi, 'Amr b. Humq, Maytham Tammar, Sa'id b. Jubayr, Kumayl b.

Ziyad, and hundreds of other supporters of the Prophet's family were executed. Under orders received from Yazid, the Umayyad, Madina was sacked and hundreds of its residents killed. There are numerous such accounts lling the pages of history. Under these oppressive conditions the lives of the supporters of the *Ahlul Bayt* had become well nigh impossible and they began to look for deliverance. From time to time an 'Alid would take up arms to ght against the oppressors; yet the insurrection would nally be curbed by government forces who would also kill him. These unfavorable circumstances became the major cause for the minority supporters of the *Ahlul Bayt* to despair and look for any ray of hope for deliverance. Evidently, these conditions prepared them thoroughly to accept the belief in the divinely ordained savior, in Mahdiism.

It was at this time that the newly converted and opportunist Jews took advantage of the situation to spread their belief in the divinely ordained messiah. The Shi'is, having been deeply disappointed and having suffered great loss of life and tyranny under the ruling powers, found the belief to be extremely comforting and accepted it wholeheartedly. Nonetheless, they modied it, saying: "This universal deliverer would denitely be from among the wronged ahl al-bayt." Gradually, they embellished it and added to its detail until the idea reached its present complexity.[90]

---

[90] See the thesis presented in the book al-Mahdiyya fi al-islam, pp. 48-68

Does it Really Need Explication?

Mr. Hoshyar: The suffering and persecution of the Prophet's family, the *Ahlul Bayt* and their supporters, as detailed by the book you read, is quite true. However, this detailed analysis of the events that led to such a belief among the Shi'is would have been necessary only if we did not possess knowledge about the origin of the idea in Islam. If you recall, we demonstrated that the Prophet himself spread this belief among Muslims and gave them the information regarding the future restorer. To support this we cited numerous traditions, and not only from the Shi'i sources; we also quoted several traditions from the Sunni collections, the *Sihah*. After having provided all the necessary evidence I do not believe there is any need for further documentation.

In the earlier part of your exposition you mentioned the prevalence of such a belief among the Jews.

This is also true. But your citation of the view that this belief was spread by Jews like 'Abd Allah b. Saba among Muslims is simply untrue. As stated earlier, no less a person than the Prophet himself was the publicizer of the information about this future restorer of Islam. Nevertheless, it is quite possible that Muslims who were formerly Jews afrmed this belief.

The Legend of 'Abd Allah b. Saba

Let me also point out that the existence of a Jew by the name of 'Abd Allah b. Saba is not a proven fact of history. Some scholars believe that the legend was fabricated by those who were hostile to the Shi'is. Moreover, even if it is hypothetically acknowledged that he did exist, attribution of the aforementioned beliefs to him is without evidence or proof. No reasonable person can regard it credible that a newly converted Jew would possess such extraordinary political cunning as to publicly speak about the emergence of the savior of Islam among the *Ahlul Bayt* in the otherwise oppressive conditions which existed under the Umayyads.

Moreover, it is improbable that such a person would undertake to organize an insurrection in secret and call people to pay allegiance to an individual among the Prophet's family to overthrow the caliph, and replace him with the divinely guided Imam, without government ofcials knowing about it. According to those who hold such an opinion, it would seem that a Jewish convert to Islam could undertake to destroy the Muslim religion without any Muslim raising a nger against him! Such an opinion can exist only in the realm of fantasy![91]

---

[91] For further details on the conditions that existed under these caliphal authorities, see: 'Ali al-Wardi, Naqsh-i vu'aaz dar islam, which is the translation of the work from Arabic by Khaliliyan, pp. 111-137. The legend about 'Abd Allah b. Saba has been critically analyzed by Sayyid Murtada 'Askari in his monumental study entitled 'Abd Allah b. Saba; and by Taha Husayn, 'Ali va farzandanash, which is the translation of his book in Arabic by Khalili, pp. 139-143

The Messianic Leader, Mahdi in Other Religions

Engineer Madani: Is belief in the promised Mahdi conned to the followers of Islam, or does it exist in other religions too?

Mr. Hoshyar: In fact, this belief is not limited to the Muslims alone. In almost all religions and heavenly creeds one can nd a similar belief in the future savior. The followers of these religions believe that there will come a time when the world will become corrupt and engulfed in a crisis. Evil and injustice will become the rule of the day. Disbelief will cover the entire world.

At that time, the universal savior of the world will appear. With remarkable divine help he will restore the purity of faith and defeat materialism with the help of divine worship. Not only are the tidings to be found in revealed books like the Zand and Pazand, and Jamaspname of the Zoroastrians, the Torah and other Biblical books of the Jews, and the Gospel of the Christians, such information can also be seen, more or less, among the Brahmins and the Buddhists.

The followers of all religions and traditions maintain such a belief and are awaiting the appearance of such a commanding gure under the divine protection. Each tradition recognizes this gure with a different name and specic title. The Zoroastrians call him Saoshyant (meaning the 'savior of the world'); the Jews know him as the messiah, whereas the Christians regard him as the Savior Messiah. However, each group believes that this divinely ordained savior will be among them.

The Zoroastrians believe he is Persian and among the followers of Zoroaster. The Jews maintain that he will be among the Children of Israel, and the follower of Moses. The Christians think he will be one among them. Muslims believe that he will be among the Hashimites and among the direct descendants of the Prophet. In Islam he has been fully introduced, whereas in other religions this is not so.

It is remarkable that all the characteristics and signs mentioned for this universal savior in other religions are applicable to the promised Mahdi, the son of Imam Hasan 'Askari. It is possible to regard him as Iranian in race because among his ancestors is the mother of the fourth Imam Zayn al-'Abidin who, as the daughter of Yazdgard, the Sassanian king, was a Persian princess. He can also be considered among the Children of Israel, since both the Hashimites and the Israelites are among the descendants of Abraham. The Hashimites are the descendants of Isma'il (Ishmael) and the Israelites are the descendants of Ishaq (Isaac). Hence, the Hashimites and the Israelites are one family. He is also connected to Christians because, according to some traditions, the mother of the present Imam was a Byzantine princess by the name of Narjis (Nargis), who is part of the miraculous story reported in some sources.

It is not appropriate to conne the deliverer of the world, the Mahdi, to one particular nation. He will actually come to ght against all discriminatory claims of racial, creedal and national distinction.

Consequently, he should be regarded as the Mahdi of the whole of humanity. He is the savior and deliverer of the people who worship God. His victory is the victory of all the prophets and all the righteous ones on earth. He will be restoring the religion of Abraham, Moses, Jesus and all of the heavenly revelations, namely, Islam; he will revive the pure religion of Moses and Jesus which had foretold the prophethood of Muhammad.

Let us be clear that we have no intention of proving the existence of the promised Mahdi by referring to the ancient books, nor are we in need of doing so. Our intention is to demonstrate that the belief in the appearance of the unique savior of the world is a common religious belief, stemming from divine revelation, of which all prophets gave glad tidings. All nations are awaiting his emergence, but they have made errors in identifying him.

The Qur'an and Mahdiism

Dr. Fahimi: If the tradition of the Mahdi was authentic, then there would have been some mention of it in the Qur'an. On the contrary, even the word mahdi does not appear in that heavenly book!

Mr. Hoshyar: First, it is not necessary that each and every true subject should be mentioned in all its specic details in the Qur'an. In fact, there are so many particular details that are true and authentic and yet have not been mentioned in the heavenly book. Second, there are a number of verses in that holy book which, however brief, give tidings about the day when the devout worshippers of God and those who support the true religion and those who are worthy of that blessing will rule the earth in its entirety; and the religion of God, Islam, will become the dominant faith over all other religions. Thus, for instance, in the Sura Anbiya' God says:

> "For We have written in the Psalms, after the Remembrance, 'The earth shall be the inheritance of My righteous servants.'" (The Holy Qur'an, Surah al-Anbiya 21:105)

In the Sura Nur God promises:

> *"God has promised those of you who believe and do righteous deeds that He will surely make you successors in the land, even as He made those who were before them successors, and that He will surely establish their religion for them that He has approved for them, and will give them in exchange, after their fear, security: They shall serve Me, not associating with Me anything.'"* (The Holy Qur'an, Surah an-Nur 24:55)

In the Sura Qasas God says:

> *"Yet We desired to be gracious to those that were abased in the land, and to make them leaders, and to make them the inheritors."* (The Holy Qur'an, Surah al-Qasas 28:4)

In the Sura Saff God says:

> *"It is He who has sent His Messenger with the guidance and the religion of truth, that He may uplift it above every religion, though the unbelievers be averse."* (The Holy Qur'an, Surah as-Saff 61:9)

From all these verses it can be briey surmised that the world can look forward to the day when its power and administration will be given into the hands of the believers and those worthy of the divine trust to become leaders and lead humanity and its civilization to its perfection. At that time, Islam will become the dominant religion, and monotheism will replace polytheism. That brilliant period will be marked by the revolution of the divinely designated reformer and savior of humanity, the promised Mahdi. More importantly, that universal revolution will be launched by the deserving Muslims.

The General Prophethood and the Imamate

Dr. Fahimi: I don't know why you Shi'a insist that you should prove the existence of the Imam. You are so unrelenting in your belief that if the Imam does not exist physically, you say he is in concealment. Since the Prophets have already delivered the injunctions from God, why would there be a need for the existence of an Imam?

Mr. Hoshyar: All those proofs that are advanced to prove the necessity of the general prophethood and require God to communicate His injunctions to humankind, also necessitate that an Imam should exist as a proof for the existence of those injunctions and their protection. In order to elaborate on what we have said, it is necessary, however briey, to present rst the proofs that require the existence of the general prophethood and then proceed to prove the existence of the Imam.

If you keep in mind the preliminaries that have been already established and which we will briey touch upon here, the matter concerning the necessity of the general prophethood will become clear to you.

1. A human being has been created in such a way that he cannot run his affairs on his own. He needs the assistance and cooperation of others. In other words, he is created civil and social by nature. Hence, he must act within a society. It is obvious that self-interest and survival are the cause of conict in a social life. Each person in the society is engaged in exerting all his endeavor to benet from limited material resources. In reaching this goal he has to overcome numerous obstacles and compete with other individuals who are equally engaged in attaining the same goal. Under those circumstances individuals become obstacles to each other's goals and, hence, end up stepping upon each other's rights. It is at this point that law is needed to regulate social relations so that people's rights should be protected from being infringed upon, and conicts should be resolved without creating chaos and lawlessness. It is possible to surmise that laws are a precious treasure that have been discovered by human beings. Furthermore, it is probable that from the early days of organizing their society human beings have had access to laws and have always respected them for their own good.
2. A human being has been innately endowed with the capacity to perfect himself and attain prosperity. In his ongoing struggle, a human being has no other purpose than to become truly perfect. All his endeavors are geared towards attaining that lofty goal of perfection.
3. Since a human being is on his way to perfection, attention to the true meaning of perfection has been made part of his natural disposition. Hence, it should be possible for him to attain it, because God does not create anything in futility.
4. The point that a human being is made of body and spirit is well established. He is material through his body; whereas his spirit, although intimately connected with his body is regarded

as belonging to the world of incorporeal beings.

5. Since human being is made of two elements, namely, body and spirit, he is bound to have two kinds of life: this worldly life, related to his body; and the spiritual and contemplative life, related to his soul. Consequently, in relation to each one of them he will have a life of prosperity and damnation.

6. Just as between body and spirit there is connection and relationship, with ensuing unity, so is there a perfect connection and relationship between the material and spiritual life. In other words, the quality of life in this world has a direct impact upon the spiritual life. Likewise, the psychic conditions and other spiritual characteristics have an impact upon the way human acts surface.

7. A human being is on the way to perfection and is attentive to the requirements of innate and natural perfection. Moreover, God has not created life without a purpose. It is incumbent upon God to provide the means to attain the goal and to acquire the perfection intended for humanity so that it is able to distinguish and pursue the path that leads to the attainment of prosperity and avoid that which leads to sinful deviation.

8. By nature a human being is self-centered and pursues his own interests. He is not interested in any other thing than serving his own good and interests. In fact, he endeavors to exploit fellow human beings and take advantage of their endeavors to serve his ends.

9. Although a human being is engrossed in pursuing his own real perfection and is engaged in an intense search of that truth which he believes would lead him to its acquisition, more than often he fails to reach that goal. The reason is that his own egocentric desires and internal emotions overcome his ability to distinguish the straight path. These traits actually

obscure the ability of practical reason to lead humans to that desired perfection, and instead mislead one toward the path of damnation and self- destruction.

What System Can Make Human Beings Prosperous?

Since human beings must live in a society, and since obstacles to preserving one's interest and the exploitation of fellow humans are a necessary part of social life, there is a need for law to control such self-serving interest that could lead to chaos among the people. Such a law can create order in the society only when the following conditions are fullled:

1. Such law has to be comprehensive and effective to cover and administer all spheres of individual as well as collective human activity. It should provide for all the human exigencies without neglecting any aspect of social life. Such a legal system should promulgate laws that would be in conformity with the natural and actual needs of individuals, reecting both the internal reality as well as external conditions of human beings.
2. Such law should lead to the real prosperity of human beings and not merely their imaginary and speculative perfection.
3. Such law should be attentive to the well being of the entirety of humanity, not just a particular group of people or specic

individual.
4. Such law should lay the foundation of a society based on human virtues and the perfection of humanity. It should lead it to the attainment of that lofty goal by putting a high value on earthly life as a means of procuring those virtues and that human perfection, and not as independent of it.
5. Such law should possess the efciency to protect the people from manipulation and chaos, and guarantee the rights of all individuals without discrimination.
6. In its promulgation, this law should be alert to the spiritual needs of the people in such a way that none of its laws should be a cause of harm to the meaningful existence of the people. Nor should it lead to the deviation from the path of perfection.
7. Such law should protect the society from turning away from the right path of humanitarian existence and from choosing the path of destruction.
8. The lawgiver of such a system should be well informed about all the crooked and scrupulous aspects of human encounters and should be knowledgeable about all the judgements given at different times and places.

Undoubtedly, a human being is in need of this kind of law and it is regarded as the necessity of his life. Without such a system in place human life will be in danger. In light of this indispensable need, it is relevant to raise the question of whether human-made law is capable of administering human society justly.

We believe that human-legislated law, inuenced by short-sighted human intelligence, is imperfect and does not possess the ability to administer human society with justice. Some examples would clarify this statement:

1. Human knowledge and information is both limited and decient. The average human being is unaware of all human needs and the laws of nature. He also does not possess sufcient knowledge about good and evil and all aspects of competing interests among various laws and their impact upon the formulation of nal judgements in different places and times.
2. If it is hypothetically admitted that it is possible for human legislators to promulgate such laws, it is undoubtedly impossible to concede that these legislators are aware of the ways in which the worldly and the spiritual life interact with each other to produce actions that suggest their deep roots in human nature. And, even if they are in possession of such an awareness, it is very negligible. Evidently, taking care of that spiritual life is beyond their legislative program. Hence, human prosperity is viewed only from a material perspective. On the contrary, these two aspects of human existence are intimately related, and their division is inconceivable.
3. Since human beings are self-centered, manipulation and exploitation of a fellow human is part of his nature. Every person gives preference to his own interests above the good of others. Hence, conict resolution and the prevention of exploitation are beyond his competence. The reason is that the self- serving goals of the human legislators will never allow them to disregard their own and their supporters' interests and work towards the common good of humanity.
4. Human legislators always promulgate laws shortsightedly. Moreover, they are inuenced by their prejudices, habits and defective thought. Consequently, the laws are enacted to protect the interests of the few, without due attention to the benet and harm that could accrue to others. In these laws the general welfare of humanity has not been the source of legislation.

Indeed, it is only the divinely ordained legal system that is in conformity with the laws of nature and has been promulgated with the purpose of advancing human prosperity in this and the next world. Hence, it is free from every selsh human motive. It is, certainly, enacted to further universal human prosperity. Thus, it is clear that humanity needs the divinely ordained law and God's benevolence makes it necessary that He provide a complete and perfect system through His messengers.

The Other-worldly Prosperity

Even as a human being is constantly occupied with the mundane aspects of life, there is some mysterious life rooted in the depth of his own self to which he hardly pays attention, and he appears to have almost forgotten about it. He is bound to reap prosperity or adversity in relation to this neglected self too. In other words, good thoughts and true beliefs, virtuous conduct and praiseworthy actions that stem from the prosperous self would lead to spiritual perfection and ascendancy as well as to success and excellence, just as erroneous beliefs, immoral behavior and blameworthy conduct, which stem from the perverted self, lead to the impairment, destitution and deviation of the self.

Hence, if a person places himself on the path of perfection, he will permit his essential and real self to be nurtured and rened so as to ascend and revert to its original abode, which is all light and bliss. On the contrary, if he sacrices all the means to attain the perfection of the self by surrendering to the animal appetites, then he will transform himself into a violent, lustful animal, having completely deviated from the straight path.

Consequently, a human being is in need of a carefully structured program for the progression of his inner self without which he cannot expect to travel this hazardous and highly intricate path. By allowing his animal appetites to overcome spiritual and moral perfection, he actually surrenders the ability of his intuitive reasoning to reach sound judgements.

As a result he falls into the darkness of misguidance, destroying his power to carry out the requirements of a virtuous life, judging good to be evil and evil to be good. Indeed, it is only God, the Creator of human beings, who knows the source of human prosperity, the good and the evil, who can provide the right guidance and complete program to attain true perfection and happiness, and to avoid those things that cause destitution and adversity. In sum, a human being needs the Lord Creator also in attaining his prosperity in the Hereafter.

Thus, it is possible to conclude that the Wise God has not exposed humankind, which is potentially capable of realizing prosperity as well as disaster only to the deviating powers of the self. Nor has He abandoned humankind to the forces of ignorance and confusion. Rather, He has endowed humanity with abounding benevolence and kindness by guiding it through the prophets who are selected from among humans. These prophets have been sent with ordinances and laws to direct the lives of the people toward this and other-worldly prosperity and to warn against the tribulations caused by ignoring this guidance. By doing so God has removed all the possible excuses human beings could make for having failed to reach the appointed goal of prosperity.

The Path of Perfection

The path of human perfection leading it to God is embedded in sound belief, righteous action and virtuous conduct. The information about this path was revealed to the Prophets so that they could undertake to call people towards it. It is important to emphasize that this path is not merely a formal path that has no connection in form or essence to the divine goals. Quite to the contrary, it is the path that is real and true, which has its source in the divine lordship. Any one situated in its course can ascend to the highest levels of the limitless universe and paradisaical heavens by going through the inner perfection of the self.

In other words, true religion is such a straight path that whoever situates himself in its course, perfects hisHher essential self and his humanity through the straight, benevolent path and returns to the prosperous abode and the source of all perfection. And anyone who deviates from this straight path has to go through the inhuman path of demonic existence, without any virtues and good conduct to support themselves. Such individuals actually become incapable of treading the precise path of benevolent existence. Indeed, such an individual cannot expect anything better than being damned to perdition and hell re.

The Infallibility of the Prophets

The Divine Benevolence makes it necessary that the prophets be sent as the guides to teach the people religious ordinances and laws so as to lead them to their prosperity in this and the next world. This goal can be accomplished only if the prophets are protected from committing any errors in delivering the divine message to humanity. Otherwise, human beings could make an excuse for not having received authentic directives from God. In other words, a prophet should be immune from any kind of error and forgetfulness in conveying the divine revelation to the people. This is known as *'isma* ('protection' or 'immunity' = 'infallibility'). Moreover, a prophet himself should be an exemplary person, having followed all the divine injunctions in his personal life. It is only then that he can call upon people to follow the divine guidance, demonstrating its validity through his own character and conduct. In this way the people can follow him condently toward their own true perfection. In addition, it is a rationally derived proposition that no person can expect others to carry out moral and religious directives when he himself does not follow the same. A call to the divine path must be exemplied by the prophet.

It is obvious that our own knowledge and perceptions are not free of error, because they are conditioned by the way our sensory perceptions receive them. No one can deny the numerous times when our senses have made errors in perception. However, when that knowledge and those ordinances come in the form of divine guidance from God, delivered through the revelation to the prophets, these are immune from such dangers. In fact, revelation is not the kind of knowledge that is derived from sensory perceptions. Otherwise, it too would have been prone to same dangers as human perceptions are, depriving people of the condence that is necessary in religious ordinances. Religious truth and knowledge about hidden matters is given to the prophets through revelation which descends upon their heart and their inner self. This very truth is experienced by these prophets in their earthly existence, which they convey to the people in accord with their capacity to understand and to follow it. Hence, the religious truth given to the prophets and delivered to the people by them remains immune from any falsehood or error.

It is for this reason that the prophets are protected from disobedience and error of judgement, and are empowered to act upon their knowledge. How can it be otherwise? A person who has attained that level of truth through experience and direct observation cannot be expected to act contrary to that truth.

Moreover, after attaining such a level of perfection he cannot be expected to forfeit that blessing by falling into sinful deviation.

Rational Proof in Support of the Imamate

After having demonstrated the necessity for general prophethood to guide humanity to its this- and next-worldly goals, it is accurate to hold that the same proof can be utilized to establish the fact that, whenever the prophet dies, there must exist in his place someone who can lead the community to those ends. This person should be someone who can continue the work of the prophet in providing the divine ordinances and reach out to the people in their search for the religious and spiritual path. God's purposes cannot be fulfilled without such a person existing among the people to promulgate those laws without errors of omission or commission. Thus, in the absence of the prophet, God's benevolence makes it necessary that there should be someone among the people to make sure that divine revelation is protected from human interference and interpolations, and that divine laws are made accessible to the people at all times.

This outstanding person must also, like the prophet, be immune and protected from committing any error and mistakes in receiving, recording and delivering the divine ordinances to establish the proof that God's guidance for the people is intact. Moreover, he should be fully knowledgeable about the truth of the religious ordinances and should himself act upon those ordinances so that others can bring their own acts and opinions into conformity with his and follow his example in their search for truth, without falling into doubt and confusion and without resorting to excuses for not having found the proof of religious truth. Since the Imam must also be protected from committing any error in carrying out this great responsibility, it must be pointed out that the Imam's knowledge is other than that acquired through sense perception. Hence, his knowledge is different from the knowledge of an ordinary person. Through the Prophet's own guidance the Imam possesses clear insights into religious knowledge. Moreover, he is endowed with direct experience of the truth through his inner eyes. It is because of this that he is protected from any error or forgetfulness, and so acts in accord with this experience and direct observation of religious truth. More importantly, it is this attribute that qualies him to assume the Imamate of the Muslim community.

In other words, there must exist among the people a perfect individual, one possessing absolute faith in God's revelation and exemplifying the best character and personal qualities in order to lead people in the minutest details of God's ordinances. At all these levels he must be protected from error, forgetfulness, and acts of disobedience. He must be *ma'süm*. It is the coming together of faith and action, knowledge and practice, that makes him the personication of all the possible human potentials of perfection. The realization of these potentials indisputably annoints him the leader of humanity. If humanity, at any point, is deprived of this leadership, the situation could lead to the disappearance of the divine ordinances which were proclaimed for the betterment of humankind. Moreover, it could lead to the discontinuation of divine help and could sever the connection between the divine and human realms.

In other words, there should always be a person among the people who is endowed with special guidance from God and is protected through God's benevolence in order for him to provide the necessary guidance and lead the people to their perfection in accord with their divinely endowed potentials. Moreover, through his knowledge and in any way possible, he should aid them in their journey towards their Creator. It is the existence of the sacred presence of the Imam as the Proof of God and as a perfect example of religious life that can make the divine presence known and divine worship possible in a society. Without the Imam's existence God cannot be known or worshipped perfectly. The inner self of the Imam is the receptacle for God's knowledge and divine secrets. It is like a mirror that reects the realities of the material world, and people derive benet from these reections.

Dr. Jalali: Surely, the protection of religious ordinances and laws is not conned to one person who should know it and practice it all. Rather, if all religious ordinances and laws are distributed among the people and if each group learns and puts into practice part of these ordinances, all of them can be protected both from the perspectives of knowledge about and practice of them.

Mr. Hoshyar: Your hypothesis is refutable from two angles:

First, in our previous discussion we have pointed out that there should always be one outstanding person among the people who should be an embodiment of all the possible benevolent qualities and a personication of the religious existence in all its meanings. Moreover, he should be free from any need of acquiring the necessary sciences and education from any other being than God. If such a person is absent among the people, then humanity will be deprived of God's proof and knowledge about God's purposes. To be sure, when any species is left without a purpose its destruction is certain. According to your hypothesis, such a perfect person does not exist because each one of these persons, even when he knows and acts upon a number of those ordinances, is not on that straight path of religion and actually has deviated from it. The reason is that religious ordinances are inevitably too interrelated and profoundly interconnected as a whole for them to be taken in part.

Second, as pointed out earlier, since God's ordinances and laws are sent for the guidance of humanity, they should remain not only constant but should also be safeguarded. All ways to their change, distortion or destruction should remain rmly closed, and they should remain safe from all dangers. This goal can be fullled only when the person in charge of it is protected from error and immune from forgetfulness and disobedience. There is nothing in your hypothesis that guarantees this because the problem of error of judgement and forgetfulness is a possibility for each one of the people. Consequently, the divine ordinances and laws are not immune from any change or alteration and neither so the proof of God's immutable guidance nor the elimination of people's excuse is procurable.

Textual Proof for the Necessity of the Imamate

*M*r. Hoshyar: All that we have said is further attested in the traditions reported on the authority of the ahl al-bayt. If you are interested in an investigation of them you might refer to the books on hadith. Here we will cite some of these for your benet:

One of the companions of Imam Sadiq by the name of Abu Hamza says: I asked the Imam, "Can the earth survive without the presence of the Imam?" He said, "If the earth is devoid of the Imam it will be destroyed."[92]

Al-Washsha', a close associate of Imam Rida says: I asked the Imam, "Can the earth be without an Imam?" He said, "No." I told him that it has been related to us that the earth cannot be without an Imam, except when God is angry with the people. On that he said, "Nevertheless, the earth cannot be void of the Imam, otherwise it will be destroyed."[93]

---

[92] Kulayni, Usul al-kafi, Vol. 1/334

[93] Ibid

Ibn al-Tayyar reports that he heard from Imam Sadiq that if there remained two persons on earth one of them would be the Proof of God. In another tradition Imam Baqir is reported to have declared: "By God, from the time God caused Adam to die until this day, God has not left this earth without an Imam through whom His guidance becomes available to the people. It is this Imam who is the Proof of God for the people. As long as there is a need for God's proof the earth will not be without an Imam."[94]

In another tradition Imam Sadiq is reported to have said: "God has created us in the best form and has appointed us as the caretaker of all the divine knowledge. The tree spoke to us, and through our worship God is being worshipped." The Imam also said: "The vicegerents [of the Prophet] are the gates of divine knowledge. Hence, one should enter religion through them. Without them God cannot be known. It is through the existence of these vicegerents that God will present His argument against His servants."[95]

Abu Khalid, a close associate of Imam Baqir asked the interpretation of the verse that says: "Believe in God, His messenger, and the light which We have revealed." The Imam said:

O Abu Khalid, by 'the light' is meant the Imams. O Abu Khalid, the light of the Imam in the heart of the believer is more brilliant than the sunlight. They are the ones who enlighten the hearts of the believers. God denies and conceals this light from whomever He wishes, as a result of which the heart of that person turns dark and becomes veiled.[96] According to another tradition, Imam Rida said:

When God wills to appoint someone to look after the affairs of humanity, He expands his chest and makes his heart the source

---

[94] Ibid., p. 333, 335

[95] Ibid., p. 368-69

[96] Ibid., p. 372

of realities and wisdom. He continuously endows him with His knowledge so that after receiving it he would not be incapable of answering any question. Moreover, in explaining the realities and providing the right guidance he would not fall into any error or falsehood.

He is free from any corruption and error, he is ma'sūm. He remains all the time the recipient of God's support and assistance, and is protected from sinful deviation. God appoints him to this prominent position so that he becomes the Proof of God's existence on earth. This is God's special favor, which He gives to whomever He pleases. Indeed, God's bounty is extensive.[97]

In yet another tradition the Prophet declared: "Stars are the security for the dwellers of the heavens. If they get destroyed so will the dwellers of the heavens. My family members are the security for the dwellers of the earth. Hence, if they do not exist, the dwellers of the earth will also be destroyed."[98]

In one of his orations Imam 'Ali said:

The earth will not be void of the Qa'im who will stand by the command of God and will provide the proof of God's existence for humanity. Sometimes that proof is manifest and well attested, and at other times it is in fear and hidden. This is to ensure that God's proofs are not terminated. These proofs are few and their whereabouts is not known. I solemnly declare that although they are few their status is extremely elevated. Through them God protects His proof and evidence until that time when they can implant those proofs in those who are like them and cultivate them in their hearts.

The knowledge [given by God] has led them to the true insight and they have attained the spirit of certainty through it. That which bafes

---

[97] Ibid., 1/390

[98] Suyuti, Tadhkirat al-khawass, p. 182

the lovers of wealth and makes it inconceivable for them appears easy and readily accessible to these proofs of God. That which frightens the ignorant, the proofs of God are intimate with it. Their connection to this material world is because of their physical body whose spirits are connected with the highly exalted places. They are God's caliphs and His callers to faith on earth.[99]

In another sermon Imam 'Ali b. Abi Talib has described the excellences of the ahl al-bayt, saying:

The elegances of the Qur'an are about them and they are the treasures of God. When they speak they speak the truth, but when they keep quiet no one can speak unless they speak.

They are the pillars of Islam and the sanctuary of [its] protection. With them truth has returned to its proper position and falsehood has retreated and its tongue is severed from its root. They have understood the religion attentively and carefully, not by mere heresy or from narrators, because narrators of knowledge are many but those who understand it are few.[100]

In short, on the basis of rational and textual evidence one can surmise that as long as human beings live on the earth, there must exist a perfect and divinely protected person among them who could personify all the perfect qualities that the human being can possibly attain. Moreover, such an individual must be responsible, both theoretically and practically, to guide humanity. This person is the Imam, the leader of humankind. Having himself ascended on this sacred path of human perfection he takes it upon himself to call others onto those stages and stations. Hence, he becomes the mediator between the hidden world of the spirit and the human world.

---

[99] Nahj al-balagha, Sermon No. 147, Vol. 3

[100] Ibid., Sermon No. 235

The bounties of the hidden world descend upon him first, and through him reach other human beings. It is obvious that the non-existence of such a person among people would inevitably lead to the absence of any goal for humankind. Such an absence would necessarily lead to the perdition of human society. In the final analysis, regardless of any other proof, this rational and textual evidence confirms that there is no period in history, including our own age, without an Imam. Since there is no manifest Imam at this time, we can say that the Imam is in occultation and lives a concealed life.

* * *

It was quite late in the night. Everyone was tired and it was decided that the discussion would continue at some other time in the near future.

The following session was convened at Dr. Jalali's residence. He was the first person to open the discussion.

Dr. Jalali: A small number of Muslims believe that the Imam of the Age is the son of Imam Hasan 'Askari who was born in the year 256 AH/843 CE. However, they say that he has ascended from this world to the unseen world known as Hurqalya.[101] When humankind reaches maturity and abandons the strife-ridden life of this world, preparing itself to meet and behold the Imam of the Age, it will be able to see him.

One of the leading authorities has written thus in his book:

This [unseen] world had gravitated until it merged with the earth. In the time of Adam he was told: 'Ascend!' And, until now he is

---

[101] The word refers to the mythological universe known to the mystics as very difficult world requiring the strength or courage of Hercules to encounter or accomplish. Tr

ascending. He has not set himself free from the worldly attachments and the lth that sticks with them. He has not reached the clean atmosphere yet. Thus, here it is all darkness. In darkness a human being is searching for a religion and is performing deeds. He has a set of beliefs.

When he frees himself from the dust of the traditions and enters the clean space, he will see the brilliant face of the friend of God [= wali = the twelfth Imam] and benet from his presence without any obstruction, in public. At that time ordinances of religion will become something else, and religion will attain its original form and everything will be different.

Hence, we should ascend to that world where this friend of God is manifest and not wait for him to come to us. If he comes to us and nds us unt we cannot benet from him. Moreover, if he comes to us and we are still in the same state [of ungodly existence], we will not be able to see him. This is also against common sense. On the other hand, if our state changes for better and improves, then we have certainly moved upward in station.

Hence we must realize that we should ascend so that we can reach that world. The name of that world in the language of theosophy is Hurqalya. Thus, as the world ascends to that high level it reaches the station of Hurqalya. In that place the Imam's domain is realized. Truth is spread and falsehood is defeated.[102]

Mr. Hoshyar: The author's intent in this writing is not clear. If he intends to convey that the Imam of the Age (peace be upon him) has relinquished his earthly existence and physical body to ascend to that ideal world, as a result of which he is no more a person existing on this earth needing an earthly form and bound to earthly necessities, this view, besides being in itself irrational, does not conform with the

---

[102] Muhammad Karim Khan, Irshad al-'ulum (Kirman, 1380), Volume 3, p. 401

rational and textual proofs that prove the necessity of the Imamate.

To be sure, these proofs point to the fact that there should exist among people that perfect man in whom all the excellent qualities and virtues should become actualized. Such a person, having attained the straight path of the religion himself, should undertake to show that path and lead the people toward it. It is only then that the Imam could serve as a role model and preserve God's ordinances and serve as a competent authority and proof for God's existence. The twelfth Imam is such a person. To put it differently, the need of the guide and leader is felt where people are moving towards that lofty goal, seeking to be instructed to attain that perfection.

However, if the intent of the author regarding Hurqalya is to x a point in this material world, then we have no disagreement with him in what he believes. But, this more reasonable latter sense does not seem to be congruent with the apparent meaning of his writing. Over all it seems to be an untenable opinion.

Will the Imam Be Born at the End of the Time?

Dr. Fahimi: We can accept this much from what you have said so far, namely, the existence of the Mahdi is among the indisputable religious truths of Islam, about which the Prophet himself had given the information. However, what does it matter if we say that the promised Mahdi is not born yet? Whenever the conditions of the world become favorable God will appoint one of the descendants of the Prophet who will establish the rule of justice and will create conditions for God's sincere worship by destroying the forces of injustice and undertaking to ght against the wrongdoers until victory is gained.

Mr. Hoshyar: To respond to your question, let me begin by pointing out that we have proven by means of all the rational and traditional proofs that no period of human existence is without an Imam, because the absence of the Imam would lead to the decline of humankind. Hence, our age is also not without the Imam.

Moreover, we have established the existence of the Mahdi conclusively by means of the *hadith*-reports from the Prophet and his family. Consequently, we should also obtain a description of his person and character from the same sources. Fortunately, all the characteristics and signs of his existence are covered in numerous reports, leaving no ambiguity or imprecision on that score. However, if we were to read all these reports it would require several sessions, for which I do not believe that you, with your already busy schedule, would have time. Accordingly, I will provide you with a list of these reports and you are free to undertake a further detailed examination to satisfy your interest.

Descriptions Identifying the Mahdi

The contemporary Scholar, Sa Golpaygani, has collected all these traditions in his book: *Muntakhab al- athar*, citing their Sunni and Shi'i sources. Following is the list of the subject and the number of traditions on that subject:

91 *hadith* on: "The Imams are twelve in number, among whom the rst is 'Ali b. Abi Talib and the last is the Mahdi."

94 *hadith* on: "The Imams are twelve, and the last one is the Mahdi."

107 *hadith* on: "The Imams are twelve, nine among whom are the descendants of Husayn, and the ninth is the Qa'im."

389 *hadith* on: "Mahdi is from among the progeny of the Prophet."

214 *hadith* on: "Mahdi is from among the descendants of 'Ali."

192 *hadith* on: "Mahdi is from among the descendants of Fatima."

185 *hadith* on: "Mahdi is from among the descendants of Husayn."

148 *hadith* on: "Mahdi is the nineth descendant of Husayn."

185 *hadith* on: "Mahdi is among the descendants of 'Ali b. al-Husayn."

103 *hadith* on: "Mahdi is among the descendants of Imam Muhammad Baqir."

103 *hadith* on: "Mahdi is among the descendants of Imam Ja'far

Sadiq."

99 *hadith* on: "Mahdi is the sixth descendant of Imam Sadiq."

101 *hadith* on: "Mahdi is among the descendants of Imam Musa al-Kazim."

98 *hadith* on: "Mahdi is the fth descendant of Imam Kazim."

95 *hadith* on: "Mahdi is the fourth descendant of Imam 'Ali Rida."

90 *hadith* on: "Mahdi is the third descendant of Imam Muhammad Taqi."

90 *hadith* on: "Mahdi is among the descendants of Imam 'Ali al-Hadi."

145 *hadith* on: "Mahdi is Imam Hasan 'Askari's son."

148 *hadith* on: "The name of Mahdi's father is Hasan."

47 hadith on: "The name and patronymic of the Mahdi will be that of the Prophet's name and patronymic."[103]

The Prophet (peace be upon him and his progeny) declared:

The Promised Mahdi is among my descendants. His name and patronymic will be the same as mine. In creation and conduct he will be the closest to me. He will live a life of occultation during which people will become confused and lost. At that time, like a brilliant star he will appear and ll the earth with justice and equity, as it is lled with injustice and tyranny.[104]

As you can see from these hadith-reports, the Mahdi has been so clearly identied that there remains no doubt as to his identity. At this juncture, it seems appropriate to remind ourselves that on the basis of some of the prophetic traditions and historical reports one can surmise that the Prophet (peace be upon him and his progeny) had forbidden the combination of his name and patronymic in one

---

[103] See: Lutf Allah al-Safi al-Gulpaygani, *Muntakhab al-athar fi al-imam al-thani 'ashar* (Tehran: Maktabat al-Sadr, nd.)

[104] Majlisi, *Bihar al-anwar*, Volume 51, p. 72.

person. Hence, this has been a rare occurrence in history.

In a hadith reported by Abu Hurayra the Prophet said: "Do not combine my name and my patronymic (kunya) in one person."[105] It was because of this prohibition that when 'Ali b. Abi Talib chose the Prophet's name and patronymic for his son Muhammad b. Hanayya, the Prophet's companions objected to it. 'Ali b. Abi Talib in response to this objection said: "I have a special permission from the Prophet in this matter." A number of the companions conrmed 'Ali's statement.

If the content of this report is connected with the hadith-reports which relate that the Mahdi will have the Prophet's name and patronymic, then it becomes apparent that the Prophet wanted this combining of his name and patronymic to be part of the signs of the future Mahdi from which others were excluded. It was because of this coming together of the Prophet's name and patronymic in the case of Muhammad b. Hanayya that the latter referred to this fact as a sign of his own Mahdiism saying: "Yes, I am the Mahdi. My name is the Prophet's name; and my patronymic is his patronymic."[106]

---

[105] Ibn Sa'd, al-Tabaqat al-kubra, Vol. 1, p. 107

[106] Ibid., Vol. 5, p. 94

Mahdi Is Among the Descendants of Husayn b. 'Ali

Dr. Fahimi: Our scholars accept that the Mahdi will be from among the descendants of Husayn. They refer to the following hadith reported in Sunan of Abi Dawud:

Abu Ishaq relates: "'Ali, while looking at his son Hasan, said, 'This son of mine is the master (sayyid) as declared by the Prophet. Among his progeny will appear a man whose name will be that of the Prophet. He will resemble the Prophet in his demeanor; but he will not resemble him in appearance.'"[107]

Mr. Hoshyar: First, let me point out that in all likelihood, there might have occurred an error in the writing or printing of the hadith. And instead of 'Husayn' it might have recorded 'Hasan'. The reason is that the same hadith has been related in other collections where instead of 'Hasan' it is 'Husayn' to whom the comment is made by 'Ali b. Abi Talib.[108]

Second, there are far too many hadith-reports in the Sunni and Shi'i

---

[107] Sunan, Kitab al-mahdi

[108] Ithbat al-hudat, Vol. 7, p. 208

collections that regard the Mahdi to be from among the descendants of Husayn. As such, this tradition has no validity. Let us examine some examples from the Sunni compilations on this subject:

Hudhayfa relates the following hadith from the Prophet:

The Prophet said: "If there remains no more than a day for the world, God will prolong it until a man from my progeny, whose name will be my name, will emerge." Salman asked: "From which of your progeny will he emerge?" The Prophet replied: "From this son of mine." And, he struck Husayn with his hand.[109]

In another tradition Abu Sa'id Khudari relates that the Prophet (peace be upon him and his progeny) told Fatima:

"The Mahdi of this community behind whom Jesus will pray is among us." Then he struck Husayn's shoulder with his hand and declared: "The Mahdi of my community will be from the descendants of this son of mine."[110]

Once Salman al-Farisi came to see the Prophet when the latter had Husayn in his lap. The Prophet was kissing Husayn's face and mouth and was saying:

You are the master and the son and brother of the master. You are the Imam, son and brother of the Imam. Your are the proof and son and brother of the proof of God's existence. You are the father of nine proofs of God, the nineth among whom will be the Qa'im.[111]

According to these hadith-reports, the Mahdi is among the descendants of Husayn. Hence, one should abandon those reports that say that the Mahdi will be among the descendants of Hasan. Moreover, even if one accepts these latter traditions as being authentic, it can be asserted that both kinds of traditions point to the fact that Mahdi is

---

[109] Dhakha'ir al-'uqba, p. 136

[110] al-Bayan fi akhbar sahib al-zaman, p. 502

[111] Yanabi' al-mawadda, Vol. 1, p. 492

certainly the descendant of both Hasan and Husayn, in the sense that Imam Muhammad Baqir's mother was the daughter of Imam Hasan. The following hadith points to the logical connection between the two kinds of traditions about the Mahdi being from the descendants of Hasan and Husayn:

The Prophet told Fatima: The two grandsons of this community are among us. These are Hasan and Husayn who are the masters of the youths of Paradise. By God, their father is more excellent than they. I solemnly declare in the name of the One who has sent me as a prophet that the Mahdi of this community will emerge from among these two sons of yours at the time when chaos will rule.[112]

---

[112] Ithbat al-hudat, Vol. 7, p. 183

What If the Mahdi Was Well-known?

Dr. Jalali: If the promised Mahdi had been a prominent and well-known personality and if his highly publicized merits and characteristics had reached the ears of the Muslims and the companions of the rightful Imams in the early days of Islam, the road to manipulation and fallacies would have necessarily been closed, and the associates of the Imams and the scholars would not have fallen into an error. On the contrary, one nds that even some of the descendants of the Imams did not have proper information about the subject of the Mahdi.

How, then, did so many individuals claiming to be the Mahdi appear in the early days, introducing themselves as the promised Mahdi of Islam and misleading the people with their false claim? If the Muslims knew the Mahdi by name, and the name of his father and mother, and his patronymic, and that he was the twelfth Imam, and all other details about his age and other characteristics, how did then a group fall into error and regard Muhammad b. Hanayya, Muhammad b. 'Abd Allah b. Hasan, Ja'far Sadiq, Musa Kazim, or other such individuals as the Mahdi?

Mr. Hoshyar: As mentioned earlier, the fundamental belief in the existence of the Mahdi was a well- established tenet of faith among early Muslims. In fact, people did not entertain any doubt in his existence. The Prophet had given detailed information about the existence of the Mahdi, his characteristics, his universal mission of instituting the divine government based on justice and equity and of bringing an end to injustice and tyranny by carrying out necessary reforms. Indeed, the Prophet had given many such glad tidings to the Muslims. Nevertheless, he had not provided them with the cues and the actual characteristics and distinctions of the Mahdi. Rather, one can say that such matters were part of the condential information that was revealed to a few entrusted and loyal followers of Islam. The Prophet had given that condential information about the Mahdi to 'Ali b. Abi Talib, Fatima and other trusted companions, while keeping that secret from the general public, giving them only hints and general information on the subject. The Imams who came after the Prophet followed the Prophet's example and shared only summary information about the Mahdi with the general public. All the detailed particulars on the subject were handed down from one Imam to the succeeding Imams, one after the other. On occasion, the information was divulged to a few trustworthy associates. Over all, the general public and even some of the family members of the Imams, knew very little about the subject.

There were two reasons for the Prophet and the Imams not to indulge in providing detailed information about the future coming of the Mahdi:

First, they wanted to keep the identity of the promised Mahdi secret from the enemies of God and the unjust rulers so that no harm would befall him from that direction. The Prophet and the Imams were fully aware that if the unjust rulers, caliphs and their agents knew the identity of the Mahdi with all the particulars about his parents, their names, and so on, they would not hesitate to prevent his birth even if that meant killing his parents. The Umayyads and the 'Abbasids were determined to hold on to their power by eliminating even the slightest threat to it. They did not pause to commit grievous crimes in order to remain in power. In all likelihood, they would have endeavored to get rid of him, even if it meant killing anyone remotely connected with a challenge to their autocratic rule.

It is important to note that even though the Umayyads and the 'Abbasids were not fully informed about the signs of the Mahdi's appearance, they killed thousands of the descendants of 'Ali b. Abi Talib and Fatima, in order to thwart the potential threat of the Mahdi's revolution. In a hadith related from Imam Sadiq to Mufaddal, Abu Basir and Aban b. Taghlib, the Imam said: "Since the Umayyads and the 'Abbasids had heard that tyrannical rule will be overthrown by our Qa'im, they initiated their hostility against us. They labored to kill the descendants of the Prophet and to destroy subsequent generations with the hope that they could get rid of the Qa'im. But since God was determined to fulll His will, He did not avail the tyrants all the information about the matter."[113]

The case with the Imams was not very different than with the Prophet himself. They lived in fear for their lives. Hence, they practiced 'prudential concealment' (taqiyya) in revealing the details about the Mahdi even to their closest associates and other 'Alawites. Abu Khalid, the close associate of Imams Baqir and Sadiq, once requested Imam Baqir to conrm the name of al-Qa'im for him so that he would perfectly recognize him. The Imam said: "O Abu Khalid, you have asked me something about which if the descendants of Fatima come to know anything, the authorities would cut him into pieces!"[114]

---

[113] Ibn Babüya, Kamal al-din, Vol. 2, 354

[114] Shaykh al-Tusi, Kitab al-ghayba, p. 202

Second, by providing merely general information about the Mahdi, the Prophet and the Imams wanted those weak in their faith not to be overcome by despair at the weakness of God's religion in the face of the unjust powers. In other words, those who had witnessed or heard about the unpolluted and just rule of the Prophet and Imam 'Ali b. Abi Talib in the early days of Islam, had heard about the ultimate victory of true religion and the end of injustice and corruption under Islam. Accordingly, they had accepted the new religion with much hope of seeing an end to all the corruption. However, since they were newcomers to Islam their faith was not that strong. On the one hand, the prevalent turmoil in Muslim society and the unfavorable conditions that ensued had an impact upon these people.

On the other hand, they saw the wicked behavior of the Umayyad and 'Abbasid rulers and the way that that impacted upon society. These unfavorable social and political conditions had made them very perplexed. The concern of the Prophet and the Imams was that people with weak faith would lose hope, with the truth and religion of Islam being overpowered by evil forces, and so these people would abandon Islam. The thing that to a certain extent assured people to remain faithful to Islam and to keep their hearts hopeful was the belief in the deliverance and the revolution of the promised Mahdi.

These Muslims anticipated the revolution of the promised Mahdi to take place any day to redress the injustices in society and to restore universal good order according to the Islamic ideals of justice and equity. It is natural that this hope for a better future in the people would have been effected only when all the true details about the Qa'im's uprising were not clearly known. Otherwise, if the details about the timing, the identity and other related signs of the Mahdi's appearance were public knowledge, such a positive attitude and hope would not have ensued.

Undoubtedly, it was this general, summary information about the future role of the Mahdi that gave the capacity to the downtrodden people in the early days of Islam to bear with patience the unfavorable living conditions under the corrupt and unjust rulers of the Ummayad and 'Abbasid dynasties.

The intended impact of what was foretold about the Mahdi in brief is captured in the report in which Yaqtin, a supporter of the 'Abbasids, asked his son 'Ali b. Yaqtin, one of the prominent associates of the Imam Musa Kazim: "Why is it that things that were predicted about us have been fullled, whereas those about you remain unrealized?" 'Ali b. Yaqtin replied: "The reports that foretold the events came from the same [prophetic] source. However, since the time for your political power has arrived, the prophecies about you are, one by one, being fullled.

But, the time for our rule, that is the rule of the Prophet's family, has not come yet. Hence, they have kept us occupied with the glad tidings and future aspirations. If we had been told that the government of the Prophet's family will not be established for the next two or three centuries, the hearts would have been hard and most of the people would have abandoned Islam. But, the events have been reported in such a way that the hearts are pleased and every day we are looking forward to the establishment of God's government."[115]

---

[115] Ibid., p. 208

The Traditions from the Ahlul Bayt Are Proofs for All Muslims

Dr. Fahimi: One must acknowledge the fact that your traditions identify and describe the Mahdi very well. Unfortunately, such traditions have very little value for a person like me who happens to be a Sunni and who does not attach any signicance to the opinions and actions of your Imams.

Mr. Hoshyar: I am not in the process of proving the Imamate and the wilayat (love of the ahl al-bayt) for you. I want to point out something else for you. It is important to emphasize that the opinions and actions of the Imams among the ahl al-bayt have evidential value and are signicant for all Muslims across the board, regardless of whether they accept them as Imams or not.

The reason is that there are numerous traditions publicized on the authority of the Prophet and regarded as reliable by both the Shi'i and the Sunni in which the Prophet has introduced his ahl al-bayt as the authoritative source of Islamic knowledge and regarded their opinions and actions as sound. For example, the famous tradition about the "two things of high estimation" (al-thaqalayn), the Prophet (peace be upon him and his progeny) said:

I leave among you two things of high estimation. If you hold on to them you will never be led astray. One of these two things is weightier than the other. One of these two is the Book of God which is a link between the earth and the heaven. The second one is my family, my ahl al-bayt. These two trusts will not separate from each other till the Day of Judgement. Hence, exercise care in the way you treat these two.[116]

This hadith has been reported in various forms by both the Shi'i and Sunni sources. Moreover, it has been regarded as an authentic tradition. According to Ibn Hajar, as recorded in his book al-Sawa'iq al-muharriqa, this hadith has been narrated by different sources and through numerous chains of transmission from the Prophet. In fact, more than twenty close companions [of the Prophet] have related it. The Prophet used to attach so much importance to the Qur'an and his ahl al-bayt that on different occasions he had declared their signicance for the well being of the Muslim community in the future, including the Farewell Pilgrimage and the Ghadir, and after his return from his journey to Ta'if.

Another tradition which is widely acknowledged in all Sunni and Shi'i sources is related by Ibn 'Abbas who heard the Prophet declare: "The likeness of my family is the Ark of Noah. Whoever embarks upon it is saved; and whoever stays away from it will perish."[117]

Jabir b. 'Abd Allah Ansari related from the Prophet another widely quoted hadith in which the latter said:

The two sons of 'Ali [Hasan and Husayn] are the leaders of the youths of Paradise. They are my sons. 'Ali, his two sons, and the

---

[116] Dhakha'ir al-'uqba (Cairo, 1356), p. 16; al-Sawa'iq al-muharriqa, p. 147; al-Fusul al-muhimma, p. 22; al-Bidaya wa al-nihaya, Vol. 5, p. 208; (Hydrabad edition), pp. 153, 167; Sibt b. Jawzi, Tadhkirat al-khawass, p. 182

[117] All the sources mentioned in the previous note, in addition to Majma' al-zawa'id, Vol. 9, p. 168

Imams after them, are the Proof of God's existence among the people. They are my gates of knowledge in the community. Any one who follows them will be saved from the Hell Fire; and any one who accepts them as his leader has found the way to guidance. God does not bless any one with their love without making them worthy of the Paradise.[118]

In one of his orations 'Ali b. Abi Talib told the people:

I ask you to verify this, in the name of God: Do you recall what the Prophet said in his last speech: "O people! I leave among you the Book of God and my family? Hold on to them and you will never lose your way, because God, the Wise, has informed and assured me that these two will never part from each other till the Day of Judgement." At that time 'Umar b. al-Khattab got angry and stood up and asked: "Does this statement include all of your family?"

The Prophet replied: "No. This includes my legatees among whom the rst is 'Ali b. Abi Talib, my brother, vizier, heir and caliph. He is the one who has discretionary power over my community. Following 'Ali my son Hasan, following him my son Husayn, and then nine descendants of Husayn are the legatees. They will follow each other until the Day of Judgement. They are the proofs of God's existence for the people, the keepers of divine knowledge, and the repositories of wisdom on earth. Whoever obeys them has obeyed God, and whoever disobeys them has disobeyed God."

When 'Ali's answer reached this point, all those who were present said: 'We bear witness that the Prophet did say all that.'[119]

On the basis of all such traditions that are recorded in the Sunni and Shi'i sources the following conclusions can be drawn:

---

[118] Yanabi' al-mawadda, Vol. 1, p. 54

[119] Jami' ahadith al-shi'a, Vol. 1, Introduction

1. Since the Qur'an will remain with the people until the Day of Judgement, the family of the Prophet, the ahl al-bayt, will also remain with them. Hence, such traditions can be considered as evidence for the existence of the Hidden Imam.
2. The term 'itrat in the hadith actually refers to the twelve legatees of the Prophet.
3. The Prophet (peace be upon him and his progeny) has not abandoned the Muslim community without any guidance. Quite to the contrary, he has actually made his family, the ahl al-bayt, the source of divine knowledge and guidance. He has declared their opinions and actions competent and reliable; and has recommended that one hold on to them until the Day of Judgement.
4. The Imam, then, will never be separated from the Qur'an and its ordinances. Therefore, he has to be perfectly knowledgeable about its injunctions. Just as the Qur'an does not mislead anyone in the matter of guidance, and leads those who adhere to it to salvation, so does the Imam lead the people to their goal without committing any error. If the people follow the Qur'an and the Imams they would certainly be guided to their prosperity. In other words, the Imam is free from any error and deviation.

'Ali b. Abi Talib, the Paragon of the Prophetic Knowledge

In the light of historical and traditional sources it is accurate to assert that the Prophet knew very well that among his companions not all were capable of carrying the burden of the knowledge that was given to him in his position as the Prophet of God. Moreover, the prevalent circumstances in the community were not favorable to spread such information. However, he was also aware that one day the community would need that kind of knowledge. Consequently, he selected 'Ali b. Abi Talib for the purpose of making him the repository of the prophetic knowledge. He personally undertook to teach him and educate him day and night. Hence, what 'Ali reported reects the Prophet's own teachings about Islam. To cite some examples, let us consider the following:

'Ali was brought up under the special care of the Prophet and was all the time in his companionship. In this connection the Prophet informed 'Ali that God had required him to befriend 'Ali and to teach him all he had received from God as a prophet. "You too should take care in learning and recording what I have taught you. God will certainly approve your endeavors," the Prophet guided 'Ali b. Abi

Talib.[120]

Hence, 'Ali used to say: "Whatever I learnt from the Prophet I never forgot."[121] In another report he said: "The Prophet had assigned me a special hour in the night and the day when I used to present myself [to learn from him]."[122]

On one occasion 'Ali was asked: "What is the reason that in comparison to other companions of the Prophet you have the most traditions?" He replied: "Whenever I asked the Prophet something he gave me an answer. And whenever I kept quiet he would begin the conversation."[123]

The Prophet, according to Imam 'Ali, used to ask him to write down what he said. 'Ali asked him if the Prophet thought 'Ali might forget. The Prophet said: "No, because I have prayed to God to make you among those who remembers things and records them. However, I want you to preserve it for your companions and the Imams who will come after you. It is because of the blessed existence of the Imams that the rain falls on earth for the people, their prayers get accepted, the calamities go by them and mercy descends on them." Then the Prophet pointed towards Hasan and said: "This is the second in the line of the Imams," and added, "the Imams will be from the descendants of Husyan."

---

[120] See Manaqib Khwarazmi, p. 199, Kulayni, al-Kafi, Vol. 1, p. 64

[121] A'yan al-shi'a, Vol. 3

[122] Yanabi' al-mawadda, Vol. 1, p. 77

[123] Ibid., Vol. 2, p. 36; Ibn Sa'd, Tabaqat, Vol. 2, Part II, p. 101

The Book of 'Ali b. Abi Talib

To be sure, 'Ali b. Abi Talib was able to comprehend and master the prophetic knowledge through a serious commitment and divine help, attended by divinely endowed talent. This knowledge he put to writing and converted the book to a comprehensive corpus to which he added his own recommendations for the future benet of the community. This matter has been preserved in the hadith-reports related by the ahl al-bayt. For example, we read the following hadith in the collection:

Imam Sadiq said: We have something in our possession which makes us free from any need from the people. However, [because of what we have] people are in need of us. We possess a book which was dictated by the Prophet himself and which is in the hand-writing of 'Ali. It is the comprehensive book that includes all the ordinances about that which is lawful and that which is unlawful.[124]

In another tradition Imam Baqir told Jabir:

O Jabir, if I had expounded for you our belief and tenets we would have destroyed ourselves. In any case, we are relating for

---

[124] Jami' ahadith al-shi'a, Vol. 1, Introduction

you traditions which we collected from the Prophet, just as people collect gold and silver.[125]

'Abd Allah b. Sinan heard Imam Sadiq, who said:

We have in our possession a leather bag, seventy cubits long. It was written by 'Ali under the dictation of the Prophet. It contains all the knowledge that people need to know down to the minutest detail.[126]

---

[125] Ibid

[126] Ibid

The Heirs to the Prophet's Knowledge:

Mr. Hoshyar: Dr. Fahimi, you said earlier that you do not accept the Imamate of the family of the Prophet. However, you must accept the evidential nature of what they say, just as you accept the traditions reported from the companions, and the succeeding generation of Muslims. The reason is that even if you do not accept any one of them as the Imam, you cannot deprive them of their right to relate the reliable traditions on the authority of the Prophet. Undoubtedly, the value of what they relate is many times more than the information transmitted by any ordinary Muslim. A number of Sunni scholars have acknowledged the level of their knowledge, piety and strength of character.[127]

The Imams, time and again, used to say that they do not give opinions based on their own predilections. Rather, their responses were derived from the Prophet's own teachings. In other words, they were the true heirs of the Prophetic knowledge, relating everything

---

[127] There are a number of works authored by the Sunnis that regard the Shi'i Imams as righteous and highly knowledgeable in religious-legal matters. See, for instance, al-Jawzi, Tadhkirat al-khawass, Ibn Sabbagh al-Maliki, Fusul al-muhimma; Shablanji, Nur al-absar; Ibn Hajar, al-Sawa'iq al-muharriqa; and, so on

going back to the Prophet through the Imams. According to Imam Sadiq:

My hadith is my father's hadith. My father's hadith is my grandfather's hadith. My grandfather's hadith is Husayn's hadith. Husayn's hadith is Hasan's hadith. Hasan's hadith is Amir al-Mu'minin's ['Ali b. Abi Talib's] hadith. 'Ali b. Abi Talib's hadith is the Prophet's hadith. And, the Prophet's hadith is what God has told him.[128]

Dr. Fahimi, I ask you to be fair minded. Do you think that the hadith reported on the authority of Hasan and Husayn, the two leaders of the youth of Paradise are not as good as the ones reported by Abu Hurayra, Samra b. Jundab or Ka'b al-Ahbar? How about the hadith related by the pious Imam Zayn al-'Abidin, the righteous Imams Baqir, Sadiq, and so on?

Undoubtedly, the Prophet declared 'Ali and his descendants to be the treasures of prophetic knowledge. He reminded Muslims time and again and in different contexts to look upon them as the sources of reliable knowledge about Islam. More importantly, he encouraged the people to refer to them.

Unfortunately, the direction of Islamic history deviated from its straight course and the community deprived itself of the valuable instruction of the ahl al-bayt, which led to backwardness among Muslims.

Dr. Jalali: I have many more questions in mind. But, since its getting very late, I will leave them for the next session.

Engineer Madani: If you all agree, I would like to hold the next session in my home. We will continue our deliberations there.

On Friday evening the group met at Engineer Madani's house. The session formally began with the question raised by Dr. Jalali.

Dr. Jalali: I have heard that Imam Hasan 'Askari had no son at all!

---

[128] Jami' ahadith shi'a, Vol. 1

Mr. Hoshyar: There are several methods to prove that Imam Hasan 'Askari did have a son:

a) In numerous traditions reported on the authority of the Prophet (peace be upon him and his progeny) and the Imams it is related that Hasan b. 'Ali b. Muhammad 'Askari will have a son who will return to launch a universal reform movement after a long absence and will ll the earth with justice and equity. This matter has been related in various forms in the traditions.

If you recall, we have mentioned a list of hadith-reports in the previous discussion in which it is afrmed that the Mahdi will be the ninth descendant of Imam Husayn; that the Mahdi will be the sixth descendant of Imam Sadiq; that he will be the fth descendant of Imam Kazim; the fourth descendant of Imam Rida; the third decendant of Imam Muhammad Taqi; and so on.

b) In several traditions it is related that the Mahdi will be the son of Imam Hasan 'Askari (peace be upon him). For example, Saqr b. Abi Dalf relates that he heard from Imam 'Ali Naqi who said:

The Imam following me is my son Hasan. After Hasan his son is the Qa'im who will ll the earth with justice and equity just as it is lled with injustice and tyranny.[129]

c) In a number of hadith-reports Imam Hasan 'Askari has informed that the Qa'im and the Mahdi will be his son and that the house of the Imam and the Prophet is protected from falsehood and error. The following is the tradition related by Muhammad b. 'Uthman, the second deputy of the twelfth Imam during the Short Occultation (ghaybat-i sughra), who received it from his father, the rst deputy:

I was in presence of Imam Hasan 'Askari when someone asked him regarding the hadith that was related from his forefathers, namely: "The earth will never be void of the hujjat (God's proof), and any one

---

[129] Ithbat al-hudat, Vol. 6, p. 275

who dies without acknowledging the Imam of the Age dies the death of ignorance." The Imam responded: "Yes, indeed the matter is as clear and real as daylight." The person went on to ask: "Who is the hujjat and the Imam after you?" He said: "After me the hujjat and the Imam will be my son Muhammad. Any one who dies without acknowledging him will die a death of ignorance.

Be aware that my son will go into occultation. The people, because of that, will experience confusion. Those who are unfaithful will perish, whereas those who x the time of his appearance will be uttering falsehood. When the period of his occultation comes to an end he will launch a revolution. I see the white ags waving over his head in Najaf."[130]

d) Imam Hasan 'Askari informed a number of his close companions about the birth of his son. The following are some of those traditions:

1. Fadl b. Shadhan, who died after the birth of the twelfth Imam and before the death of Imam Hasan 'Askari, wrote in his book on Ghayba, relating from Muhammad b. 'Ali b. Hamza, who said: "I heard Imam Hasan 'Askari saying: 'The Proof of God and my successor was born circumcised on the 15th night of Sha'ban, year 255 (870 CE), in the early hour of dawn.'"[131]
2. Another close associate of the Imams, Ahmad b. Ishaq heard Imam Hasan 'Askari say: "Thank God that He did not take me away from this world without showing me my successor. He (my son) is closest to the Prophet in his features and character. God will keep him for a while in occultation and then He will cause him to emerge so that he will ll the earth with justice and

---

[130] Bihar al-anwar, Vol. 51, p. 160

[131] Muntakhab al-athar, p. 320

equity."[132]

3. Ahmad b. Hasan b. Ishaq Qummi related: When the righteous successor [of Imam Hasan 'Askari] was born, a letter came from the Imam 'Askari through Ahmad b. Ishaq. The Imam had written: "A son has been born to me. Keep this matter secret, because I will not divulge it except to my close associates and relatives."[133]

4. Again Ahmad b. Ishaq relates that one day he was with Imam Hasan 'Askari when the latter asked him: "Ahmad, what do you say about the matter in which people have fallen in doubt?" He said: "When your letter announcing the birth of your son arrived, for all of us, that is, men, women, children, old and young, truth became manifest and we believed in what you conveyed to us." The Imam said: "Don't you know that the earth cannot be without God's proof in it?"[134]

5. Abu Ja'far Muhammad b. 'Uthman 'Amri, the second deputy of the twelfth Imam, has related that when the Imam of the Age was born Imam Hasan 'Askari asked for Abu 'Amr, 'Uthman, his father and the rst deputy of the twelfth Imam. When he came the Imam told him: "Buy a thousand pounds of bread and a thousand pounds of meat and distribute it among the Hashimites. Also, arrange for some sheep to be sacriced for my newly born son's head-shaving ceremony ('aqiqa)."[135]

All these traditions provide the necessary evidence that there was a son born to Imam Hasan 'Askari (peace be upon him).

---

[132] Ibid

[133] Ithbat al-hudat, Vol. 6, p. 432

[134] Muntakhab al-athar, p. 345

[135] Ithbat al-hudat, Vol. 6, p. 430

Those Who Saw the Imam of the Age When He Was Small

Dr. Jalali: How can it be possible that a person could have a son and no one in the world would know about him? Moreover, how can it be so that ve years would pass and he would remain unknown? Did not Imam 'Askari live in Samarra? Was not he visited by anyone? Could one believe the only report on the presence of the infant son of the Imam coming from Abu 'Amr 'Uthman b. Sa'id?

Mr. Hoshyar: Although it was clear from the very beginning that, under the circumstances which prevailed in Samarra under the 'Abbasids, the birth of Imam 'Askari's son would be kept secret, there were those trustworthy associates and relatives who had seen the child and had testied to his presence. Let us examine some reports to that effect:

1) Among those who were present at the birth of the twelfth Imam and who reported the event in great detail was Hakima Khatun, the daughter of Imam Muhammad Taqi and the aunt of Imam Hasan 'Askari. The story in brief is recounted by her as follows:

One day I was visiting Imam 'Askari's house. At night, which happened to be the fteenth night of Sha'ban (255 AH/29th July, 870), when I wanted to return to my home, the Imam said: "Aunt, stay with us tonight, because God's friend and my successor will be born this night." I asked: "Which one of your slave-girls is expecting?" He said: "Sawsan."

Hence, I started looking at her to see if there were any signs of pregnancy in her. I could not see any. After breaking the fast and nishing prayers, I slept in the same room as Sawsan. After a while I woke up from my sleep and began to think about what Imam 'Askari had predicted. Then I started performing the midnight prayers. Sawsan also woke up and prepared to perform her prayers. It was getting close to the dawn. But there was no sign of child-birth in her. I was beginning to doubt what the Imam had predicted when he said from his room: "Aunt dear, do not doubt. The time for my son's birth is approaching."

All of a sudden Sawsan's condition started changing. I asked her if everything was alright. She said that she was feeling some discomfort. I began to prepare things that were needed for delivery and took charge of the situation. Within a short while God's friend was born, all clean and pure. Just then Imam 'Askari said: "O Aunt, bring my son to me."

When I took him to the Imam he held him close to himself and stroked his tongue over the infant's eyes. The eyes of the infant opened immediately. Then he stroked his mouth and ears with his tongue, and his head with his hand. At that time the infant began to recite verses from the Qur'an. Then he gave the infant back to me and asked me to take him back to his mother. I brought him to his mother and went home.

On the third day, I came back to Imam 'Askari's house and straight away I went to Sawsan's room to see the child. But I did not see him. I went to the Imam's room. but hesitated to ask about the infant. The

Imam at once informed me: "O aunt, my son is in concealment in God's protection. When I depart from this world and when you see my followers in dispute about my successor, tell those trustworthy among them what you have witnessed in connection with his birth. However, make sure that the event is guarded in secrecy because my son will be in occultation."[136]

2) The two maids at Imam 'Askari's residence have related that when the Imam of the Age was born he sat on his legs and raised his nger toward the sky [bearing witness to the Unity of God]. Then he sneezed and said: "Praise be to God, the Lord of the universe."[137]

3) Abu Ghanim, the servant at Imam 'Askari's house, relates that a son was born to Imam Hasan 'Askari, whom he named Muhammad. "On the third day he showed him to his companions and said: 'This son of mine will be your master and Imam after me. He is the Qa'im who is being awaited by everyone. When the earth is lled with injustice and tyranny, he will rise, and ll it with justice and equity.'"[138]

4) Abu 'Ali Khayzarani relates from the slave girl he had presented to Imam 'Askari that she was present at the time when the twelfth Imam was born. His mother's name was Sayqal.[139]

5) Hasan b. Husayn 'Alawi said: "I personally went to see Imam Hasan 'Askari in Samarra to congratulate him on the occasion of his son's birth." A similar tradition has been related by 'Abd Allah b. 'Abbas 'Alawi.[140]

6) Hasan b. Mundhir reports that one day Hamza b. Abu al-Fath

---

[136] Tusi, Ghayba, pp. 141-42

[137] Ithbat al-hudat, Vol. 7, p. 292; Ithbat al-wasiyya, p. 197

[138] Ithbat al-hudat, Vol. 6, p. 431

[139] Kamal al-din, p. 105

[140] Ithbat al-hudat, Vol. 6, p. 433 and Vol. 7, p. 20

came to see him and informed him: "Last night God granted Imam 'Askari a son. However, he has asked us to keep the matter secret. I asked him his name. He said it is Muhammad."[141]

7) Ahmad b. Ishaq relates that one day he came to see Imam Hasan 'Askari with the intention of asking about his successor. The Imam began the conversation. He said:

O Ahmad b. Ishaq, from the time God created Adam until the Day of Resurrection, God has not and will not leave the earth without His proof. It is because of the existence of this person that calamity is removed from earth and rain falls on it, through which the earth brings forth blessings.

At that juncture Ahmad asked the Imam about his successor. The Imam went in the private quarters of his house and returned carrying a three year old boy whose face was shining like the fourteenth night moon and said:

O Ahmad, if you had not been close to the Imams and highly respected by them I would not have shown my son to you. Know that this boy's name and patronymic are the same as the Prophet's name and patronymic. He is the one who will ll the earth with justice and equity.[142]

8) Mu'awiya b. Hakim, Muhammad b. Ayyub and Muhammad b. 'Uthman 'Amri related the following account:

We were forty people who had come together in Imam Hasan 'Askari's house. The Imam presented his son to us and said: "This is your Imam and my successor. After me you must obey him. Do not get into a dispute on this matter, otherwise you will be destroyed. However, you must remember that after this you will not be able to

---

[141] Ithbat al-hudat, Vol. 6, p. 432

[142] Bihar al-anwar, Vol. 52, p. 23

see him."¹⁴³

9) Ja'far b. Muhammad b. Malik was among the group of the prominent members of the Shi'a that included 'Ali b. Bilal, Ahmad b. Hilal, Muhammad b. Mu'awiya b. Hakim and Hasan b. Ayyub. He relates the following occasion:

We were all gathered at the Imam 'Askari's house to nd out about his successor. We were some forty people there. At that time 'Uthman b. 'Amr stood up and asked: "O son of the Prophet, we have come to ask you about something of which you have better knowledge." The Imam said: "Please be seated." He then left the room asking everyone to remain there. He returned after an hour, having brought with him a small boy whose face was shining like the moon. He then announced: "This is your Imam. Obey him.

And also know that you will no more see him after today."¹⁴⁴

10) Abu Harun reports that he saw the twelfth Imam when his face was shining like the full moon.¹⁴⁵

11) Ya'qub relates that one day he went to visit Imam 'Askari. On the right side of the Imam he saw a room with a curtain hanging on its entrance. He asked the Imam as to who was the Master of the Age. The Imam said: "Raise the curtain!." When he raised the curtain, a boy appeared and came and sat on the Imam's lap. At that time, the Imam told Ya'qub: "This is your Imam."¹⁴⁶

12) 'Amr Ahwazi reported that Imam 'Askari showed him his son and told him that he was the Imam after him.¹⁴⁷

13) A Persian servant related the following:

---

[143] Ibid., Vol. 52, p. 25

[144] Ithbat al-hudat, Vol. 6, p. 311

[145] Ibid., Vol. 7, p. 20

[146] Ibid., Vol. 6, p. 425

[147] Ibid., Vol. 7, p. 16

I was standing at Imam Hasan 'Askari's door when I saw a maid leaving the house with something covered in her hands. The Imam said to her: "Reveal that which you have in your hands." The maid uncovered a beautiful boy. The Imam told me: "This is your Imam." After that one time I never saw that boy again.[148]

14) Abu Nasr, the servant, and Abu 'Ali Mutahhar relate that they saw the son of Imam Hasan 'Askari.[149]

15) Kamil b. Ibrahim relates that he saw the twelfth Imam in the house of Imam Hasan 'Askari. He was four years old and his face was as beautiful as the full moon. The Imam answered his questions before he asked him.[150]

16) Sa'd b. 'Abd Allah recounts: "I saw the Master of the Age as his face was bright like the full moon. He was sitting on his father's lap and responded to the questions I asked."[151]

17) Hamza b. Nusayr, Imam 'Ali Naqi's slave relates from his father: When the twelfth Imam was born the family members in the household of Imam Hasan 'Askari were congratulating each other. When the Imam had grown a little older I was asked to buy daily meat with some bone and it was said that the meat was for "our younger master."[152]

18) Ibrahim b. Muhammad relates:

Once because of fear of the governor I decided to escape from Samarra. I came to Imam Hasan 'Askari's house in order to bid him farewell. I saw a beautiful child next to him. I asked him: "O son of

---

[148] Yanabi' al-mawadda, Bab 82, p. 461

[149] Ithbat al-hudat, Vol. 7, p. 344; Ithbat al-wasiyya, p. 198; Yanabi' al-mawadda, Bab 82, p. 461

[150] Ithbat al-hudat, Vol. 7, p. 323; Yanabi' al-mawadda, p. 461

[151] Bihar al-anwar, Vol. 52, p. 78 and 86

[152] Ithbat al-hudat, Vol. 7, p. 18; Ithbat al-wasiyya, p. 197

the Prophet, who is this child?" The Imam replied: "He is my son and successor."[153]

This was the list of the trustworthy associates, relatives, and servants of Imam Hasan 'Askari who had seen his son in his childhood and who had testied to his existence. When one puts this testimony along side the information given by the Prophet and the Imams, then certainty about the existence of the son of Imam Hasan 'Askari is attained.

---

[153] Ithbat al-hudat, Vol. 7, p. 356. For detailed information on the birth of the twelfth Imam see: Sayyid Hashim Bahrani, Tabsirat al-wali fiman ra'a al-qa'im al-mahdi and Bihar al-anwar, Vol. 51, Bab 1; and Vol. 52, Bab 17 and 19

Why Was the Twelfth Imam Not Mentioned in the Will of Imam Hasan 'Askari?

Engineer Madani: It is said that in his last days when Imam Hasan 'Askari was ill he appointed his mother as the executer of his will so that she could manage his affairs after his death. This matter was ofcially approved by the court. In this will there was no mention of his son. Moreover, his estate was divided between his mother and his brother.[154] Had he had a son then he would have certainly mentioned him in his last will so that he would not be deprived of his share of inheritance.

Mr. Hoshyar: Imam Hasan 'Askari intentionally kept his son's name off his last will so that he would remain immune from all the danger that could come to him from the ruler of the time. In fact, he was so careful in this matter and was so fearful about his son's birth being uncovered that at times, out of necessity, he would employ precautionary dissimulation in the matter of his son with his close

---

[154] Usul al-kafi, Bab mawlid Abi Muhammad al-Hasan b. 'Ali

associates to obscure the situation for them.

One of the companions of Imam Hasan 'Askari by the name of Ibrahim b. Idris relates that the Imam sent him a sheep with a message that he should sacrice it for the latter's having performed the ceremony of shaving off his son's birth hair ('aqiqa), and share the meat with his family. Ibrahim carried out the Imam's order. But when he came to see him the Imam said: "Our child has died." However, once again he sent Ibrahim two sheep with a letter in which the Imam instructed Ibrahim:

In the name of God, the Merciful, the Compassionate. Sacrice these sheep for your master's ceremony of 'aqiqa and eat the meat with your family.

Ibrahim carried out the order. But when he came to see the Imam the latter did not mention anything about it.[155]

Imam Sadiq had also taken similar precautions in his last will. He had appointed ve persons as executors of his will, including the 'Abbasid caliph Mansur, Muhammad b. Sulayman, the governor of Madina, his two sons, 'Abd Allah and Musa, and his wife Hamida, Musa's mother.[156] By doing so he saved the life of his son Musa from imminent danger, because he knew that if his Imamate and legateship became known to the caliph, Mansur would have tried to get rid of his son. As a matter of fact events did happen exactly as Imam Sadiq had thought, because the caliph ordered that if the legatee of the Imam Sadiq was a specic person, then he should be killed.

---

[155] Bihar al-anwar, Vol. 51, p. 22

[156] Usul al-kafi, Bab al-ishara wa al-nass 'ala abi al-Hasan Musa

Why Did Others Not Know about the Twelfth Imam's Birth?

*D*r. Fahimi: The custom is that when a child is born to anyone, then relatives, neighbors, and friends come to know about it. This is true in the case of a person who is well respected. As such no one disputes the existence of a child for that person. How can one believe that the people would have no information about a son born to Imam Hasan 'Askari in spite of the respect that he held among them and that they would have doubts about that and dispute with each other about it?

Mr. Hoshyar: You are correct that normally the situation is exactly the way you have described. However, Imam Hasan 'Askari from the very beginning had decided that he would not divulge any information about the birth of a son to him. Rather, such a decision was made when the Prophet was alive and when other Imams were faced with a situation where secrecy about the birth was among the signs of the last Imam. Thus we have a report which says that Imam Zayn al-'Abidin predicted that: "The birth of our Qa'im will be concealed from the people and that will cause the people to say that he is not born at all, so that when he takes the command no one's allegiance will be on his neck."[157]

In another tradition 'Abd Allah b. 'Ata relates:

I said to Imam Baqir: "Your followers in Iraq are numerous. By God, no one in your family has the status that you have. Why don't you rise?" The Imam said: "O 'Abd Allah, you have allowed nonsensical talk to enter your mind. By God, I am not the promised commander of the affairs." I asked: "Then who is the commander of the affairs?" He said: "Look out for someone whose birth will be concealed from the people. He will be your commander."[158]

Dr. Fahimi: Why did Imam Hasan 'Askari conceal the birth of his son from the people so that they would fall into doubt and perplexity and would be led astray in the matter of Imamate?

Mr. Hoshyar: As I have said earlier, the story of the promised Mahdi was widespread among Muslims from the very early days of Islam. The traditions and the hadith-reports about the subject that were related by the Prophet and the further conrmation of these reports by the Imams had circulated among the people. The rulers of the time were also well aware of these hadith-reports which announced that the promised Mahdi will be among the descendants of Fatima and Husayn.

Moreover, these traditions announced the destruction of unjust governments by the Mahdi, who will establish the rule of justice and equity all over the world.

Consequently, they were in fear of the birth and emergence of the promised Mahdi and were determined to rid themselves of the danger of the revolution of the Mahdi. It was for this reason that the homes of the family members of the Prophet, that is, the Hashimites, and more particularly Imam Hasan 'Askari's home, were

---

[157] Bihar al-anwar, Vol. 51, p. 135

[158] Bihar al-anwar, Vol. 51. p. 34

under constant surveillance and under the watchful eyes of secret agents of the 'Abbasid state.

Mu'tamid, the 'Abbasid caliph, had assigned a number of midwives to conduct espionage missions in the Hashimite families to collect information about pregnancies and child births. When the caliph got the news about Imam Hasan 'Askari's illness, he instructed his agents to keep a constant watch over the house of the Imam. When he heard that the Imam had died, he ordered a search of the Imam's house to nd the whereabouts of his son. In addition, he sent some of these midwives to examine the slave girls of the Imam to determine if they were pregnant. If a woman was found pregnant she was detained and imprisoned.

The midwives suspected one of the women to be pregnant and reported her to the caliph. The caliph ordered her to be conned to one of the rooms and commissioned Tahrir, his servant, to watch over her. He did not set her free until he was sure that she did not carry the Imam's child. He did not stop with the household of Imam Hasan 'Askari. Rather, as soon as the funeral was over he ordered all the houses to be searched and kept under watch.[159]

Now you can appreciate that Imam Hasan 'Askari, living under those dangerous circumstances, could not do anything other than conceal his son's birth from the people so that he would remain immune from their evil designs. The Prophet and his rightful successors, the Imams, used to predict these conditions and inform the people of the twelfth Imam's birth in secret.

However, such stories are not unknown in historical annals. As you know, when Pharaoh came to know that a child would be born among

---

[159] Usul al-kafi, Bab mawlid abi Muhammad al-Hasan b. 'Ali. See also all other sources that mention the adverse conditions under which these women suffered in the hands of the 'Abbasid caliph and his fear of the existence of a son for Imam Hasan 'Askari

the Israelites who would put an end to his kingdom, he attempted to forestall the danger and so sent his spies around to keep a watch over all pregnant women and to kill all the boys and imprison all the girls that were born. With all these criminal acts he did not reach his aim, and God caused the birth of Moses to remain concealed so that the divine aim could be fullled.

As for Imam Hasan 'Askari, in spite of that dangerous situation, he revealed his son to a number of his trusted companions and followers so that they would continue to receive the guidance. Nevertheless, he asked them to keep the matter secret from the enemies and requested that they not even mention his name.

The Mother of the Twelfth Imam

Dr. Jalali: What is the name of the mother of the Master of the Age?

Mr. Hoshyar: His mother was introduced in the sources with various names. Among them are: Narjis, Sayqal, Rayhana, Sawsan, Khumt, Hukayma, and Maryam. If you keep the two following points in mind you will understand the source of this confusion:

a) Imam Hasan 'Askari had several slave girls with different names. On two occasions Hakima Khatun has mentioned these slave girls. At one time she came to visit Imam Hasan 'Askari and saw him seated in the courtyard of his house, surrounded by his slave girls. She asked him: "Which one of these girls is going to be the mother of your successor?" The Imam replied: "It is Sawsan."[160]

In another report Hakima relates the event of the birth of the twelfth Imam, cited earlier, in which Imam Hasan 'Askari requests her to spend the night of 15th Sha'ban (255 AH/870 CE) in his house because a child was going to be born. At that point Hakima asked

---

[160] Bihar al-anwar, Vol. 51, p. 17

him: "Which of your maidens is the mother of the child?" The Imam said: "It is Narjis." Hakima said: "Yes, I too like her the most among your slave girls."[161]

From these two and other similar reports it appears that Imam Hasan 'Askari had several slave girls.

b) As stated earlier Imam Hasan 'Askari's child was born in an extremely dangerous situation because the 'Abbasid caliphs and even some members of the Hashimite clan had been aware of the approaching time for the birth of the Mahdi, who was to end unjust and tyrannical rule and establish justice and equity. Hence, the agents of the 'Abbasids were guarding the homes of the Hashimites in general, and the Imam in particular, day and night. The secret agents of the caliph were involved in searching for the newborn in these homes to deliver him to the caliph.

Having noted these two things, it must be pointed out that it was certainly decreed by God that in such a threatening environment and in such a home of importance a son had to be born to Imam Hasan 'Askari who should remain protected from all sorts of dangers. It was for this reason that all necessary precautions had to be taken. Hence, to begin with, according to the related accounts, there were no signs of pregnancy in his mother. Moreover, Imam Hasan 'Askari did not reveal her real name. In addition, at the time of the delivery only Hakima Khatun, and probably some slave girls were present. This is despite the fact that usually in such circumstances assistance is sought from a midwife and other experienced women. In fact, nobody knew whether Imam Hasan 'Askari was married or not and, if he was married, no one knew the identity of his wife.

On the fteenth night of Sha'ban when it was completely dark, at night, the child was born under fear and veiled circumstances. This

---

[161] Ibid., p. 25

too happened in a home where there were several slave girls of whom none had any visible signs of pregnancy. At the time of delivery, with the exception of Hakima, there was no one present and no one dared to reveal the situation.

For a long while the matter was kept a secret and only later the close, trusted companions of Imam Hasan 'Askari began to inquire and were told about it. Some among the followers believed that God had favored Imam Hasan 'Askari with a son, whereas others denied it. Since all the slave girls lacked visible signs of pregnancy, the story about the dispute over the identity of the child's mother was naturally bound to occur. Some knew the mother to be Sawsan, some Narjis, some Sayqal, and so on. Nobody, except a select few, knew the true state of affairs.

But they were not allowed to divulge that information. Even Hakima, who was the witness and was present during the birth of the twelfth Imam, for the sake of protecting the identity of his mother, sometimes used to mention her name variantly as Narjis, Sayqal or Sawsan, and at other time, as a precautionary measure she would ascribe the child to Imam Hasan 'Askari's mother.

In the year 262 AH/877 CE Ahmad b. Ibrahim came to see Hakima Khatun, the daughter of Imam Jawad. He spoke to her from behind the curtain and asked her about her beliefs. She introduced her Imams and mentioned Muhammad b. Hasan as her last Imam. Ahmad said: "Were you yourself witness to the matter (of his birth) or are you saying this on the basis of what you have heard?" She replied saying that the matter was according to what Imam Hasan 'Askari had written to his mother. So Ahmad went on to inquire as to whom the Shi'a should follow in that matter. Hakima said that they should follow Imam Hasan 'Askari's mother.

Ahmad objected saying: "In this will of testament should we follow one woman?" Hakima responded that actually Imam Hasan

'Askari was following his forefather, Imam 'Ali b. Husayn in this matter. Imam Husayn had made his sister Zaynab his legatee and the knowledge that was possessed by 'Ali b.

Husyan was ascribed to Zaynab. Imam Husyan had done that, added Hakima, so that the matter about the Imamate of 'Ali b. Husayn would remain secret. Then she said: "You are the people who know the traditions. Have not you been informed that the inheritance belonging to the ninth among the descendants of Husayn will be distributed while he is alive?"[162]

As you can see, in this report Hakima has not responded to the inquiry about the last Imam's birth directly. In fact, she has attributed the story to Imam Hasan 'Askari's mother. It is also likely that out of fear for revealing the true state of affairs to the reporter she employed 'prudential concealment' (taqiyya). Or, she simply wanted to present the report in a manner that would generate bewilderment. However, the same Hakima in another place relates the event that led to the marriage of Imam Hasan 'Askari with Narjis Khatun and the birth of the Mahdi, to which she was herself a witness, in great detail. She ends this account with the following statement: "I now see my master (i.e., the twelfth Imam) regularly and talk to him."[163]

In short, the differences of opinion regarding the name of the last Imam's mother is not something unusual. On the contrary they point to the most difcult and even frightful situation at that time.

Moreover, the number of the slave girls that belonged to Imam Hasan 'Askari and the extreme precaution that he took in keeping the matter secret would have necessarily created confusion. It is not unlikely that the story about the serious dispute that erupted between the Imam's mother and brother, Ja'far, the Liar, could have

---

[162] Kamal al-din, Vol. 2, p. 178

[163] Kamal al-din, Vol. 2, pp. 99-103

been part of a state conspiracy masterminded by the caliph in order to extort information about Imam Hasan 'Askari's son.

According to Shaykh Saduq in his Kamal al-din, at the time when Imam Hasan 'Askari's mother got into the dispute with Ja'far, his brother, over the inheritance and when the matter was referred to the caliph, one of the slave girls belonging to Imam Hasan 'Askari by the name of Sayqal claimed to be pregnant. Sayqal was brought to the palace of the caliph, Mu'tamid, and was kept under strict guard and under the watchful eyes of the midwives and other women in the palace to determine the fate of her pregnancy. At that very time, political turmoil as a consequence of the insurrection led by Saffar, the death of 'Abd Allah

b. Yahya, and the revolution of the Zanj engulfed the caliphal state. The 'Abbasids were forced to abandon Samarra. Hence, they became occupied with their own troubles and gave up the surveillance of Sayqal's pregnancy.[164]

There is also another reason for differences in the name of the mother of the twelfth Imam. It is possible to say that all those names were given to one and the same person. That is to say that the twelfth Imam's mother had several names. This explanation is not far fetched because it was customary among Arabs to give several names to a person of importance.

The evidence for this is provided in Shaykh Saduq's Kamal al-din. He himself has related from Ghiyath that Imam Hasan 'Askari's successor was born on Friday, and his mother was Rayhana, who was also known as Narjis, Sayqal, and Sawsan. Since at the time of her pregnancy she had some kind of brilliance over her face, she was known as Sayqal.[165]

---

[164] Kamal al-din, Vol. 2, p. 149

[165] Kamal al-din, Vol. 2, p. 106

To sum this discussion up, it is important to remind ourselves that in spite of some ambiguity in identifying the actual name of the twelfth Imam's mother, there is no doubt that she existed. In other words, such an ambiguity does not detract authenticity from her existence. As you have noticed all the Imams, including Imam Hasan 'Askari, have informed about the existence of a son for the latter. In addition, Hakima, the daughter of Imam Jawad, was a highly trustworthy woman who reported in detail the birth of the Imam. Moreover, a number of trustworthy companions and servants of Imam Hasan 'Askari saw the son and testied to his existence, regardless of his mother's name.

The Sunni 'Ulama' and the Birth of the Mahdi

Dr. Fahimi: If Imam Hasan 'Askari had a son then the Sunni 'ulama' and historians should have recorded that in their books.

Mr. Hoshyar: Yes, indeed there is a group of them who also have related the event of the birth of [Ibn] Imam Hasan 'Askari and have accepted and recorded his and his father's history in their books. Thus, for instance:

1. Muhammad b. Talha Sha'i writes: "Abu al-Qasim Muhammad b. Hasan was born in the year 258 AH/873 CE in Samarra. His father's name was Hasan Khalis. Among the titles [of this last Imam] are: Hujjat, Khalaf Salih (the righteous offspring) and Muntazar (the awaited one)." Following this statement he has related several traditions on the subject of the Mahdi, with the concluding statement: "These hadith-reports conrm the existence of Imam Hasan 'Askari's son, who is in concealment

and will appear later."[166]

2. Muhammad b. Yusuf, following his entry on the death of Imam Hasan 'Askari, writes: "He did not have any child beside Muhammad. It is said that he is the same as the Awaited Imam (imam muntazar)."[167]

3. Ibn Sabbagh Maliki writes: "Section Twelve on the Life of Abu al-Qasim Muhammad, Hujjat, Khalaf Salih, the son of Abu Muhammad Hasan Khalis: He is the twelfth Imam of the Shi'a." Then he has recorded the history of the Imam and has related the traditions about the Mahdi.[168]

4. Yusuf b. Qazughli, after writing his account of the life of Imam Hasan 'Askari, writes: [119] "His son's name is Muhammad, and his patronymic is Abu 'Abd Allah and Abu al-Qasim. He is the Proof of God's existence, the Master of the Age, the Qa'im, and the Muntazar. The Imamate has come to an end with him." Then he reports traditions about the Mahdi.[169]

5. Shablanji in the book entitled Nur al-absar, writes: "Muhammad is the son of Hasan 'Askari. His mother was a slave girl by the name of Narjis or Sayqal or Sawsan. His patronymic is Abu al-Qasim. The Twelver Shi'ites know him as: Hujjat, Mahdi, Khalaf Salih, Qa'im, Muntazar, and Master of the Age."[170]

6. Ibn Hajar, in his al-Sawa'iq al-muharriqa, following the biography of Imam Hasan 'Askari writes: "He has not left a son besides Abu al-Qasim, who is known as Muhammad and Hujjat. That

---

[166] Matalib al-su'al (1287 AH edition), p. 89

[167] Kifayat al-talib, p. 312

[168] Fusul al-muhimma (Second edition), p. 273 and 286

[169] Tadhkirat khawass al-umma, p. 363

[170] Nur al-absar (Cairo edition), p. 342

boy was five years old when his father died."[171]

7. Muhammad Amin Baghdadi in the book entitled: Saba'ik al-dhahab writes: "Muhammad, who is also known as Mahdi, was five years old at the time of his father's death."[172]

8. Ibn Khallikan relates in his biographical dictionary Wafayat al-a'yan: "Abu al-Qasim Muhammad b. al-Hasan al-'Askari is the twelfth Imam of the Imamiyya, that is the Twelver Shi'ites. The Shi'ites believe that he is the one who is the awaited Qa'im and the Mahdi."[173]

9. In Rawdat al-safa Mir Khwand writes: "Muhammad was the son of Hasan. His patronymic is Abu al-Qasim. The Imamiyya acknowledge that he is the Hujjat, the Qa'im, and the Mahdi."[174]

10. Sha'rani writes in his al-Yawaqit wa al-jawahir: "Mahdi is the son of Imam Hasan 'Askari. He was born on the fifteenth night of Sha'ban, 255 AH. He is alive and will remain so until he will emerge with Jesus. Now it is 957 AH. He is, thus, 703 years old."[175]

11. Sha'rani, quoting Ibn 'Arabi's Futuhat makiyya, section 366, writes: "When the earth will be filled with tyranny and injustice the Mahdi will rise and will fill the earth with justice and equity. He will be among the descendants of the Prophet and from the line of Fatima. His grandfather will be Husayn, and his father will be Imam Hasan 'Askari, the son of Imam 'Ali Naqi, the son of Imam Muhammad Taqi, the son of Imam 'Ali Rida, the son of Imam Musa Kazim, the son of Imam Ja'far Sadiq, the son of

---

[171] al-Sawa'iq al-muharriqa, p. 206

[172] Saba'ik al-dhahab, p. 78

[173] Wafayat al-a'yan (1284 AH edition), Vol. 2, p. 24

[174] Rawdat al-safa, Vol. 3, p. 143

[175] al-Yawaqit wa al-jawahir (1351 AH edition), Vol. 2, p. 143

Imam Muhammad Baqir, the son of Imam Zayn al-'Abidin, the son of Imam Husayn b. 'Ali b. Abi Talib."[176]

12. Khwaja Parsa in his book Fasl al-khitab writes: "Muhammad, the son of Hasan 'Askari, was born on fteenth night of Sha'ban, 255 AH/870 CE. His mother's name was Narjis. His father died when he was ve years of age. From that time until now he is in occultation. He is the awaited Imam of the Shi'a. His existence is well established among his companions, trusted associates and family. God will prolong his age as He has done in the case of Elijah and Eliash."[177]

13. Abu al-Falah Hanbali in his Shadharat al-dhahab and Dhahabi in al-'Ibar khabar min ghabar write: "Muhammad is the son of Hasan 'Askari, the son of 'Ali Hadi, the son of Jawad, the son of 'Ali Rida, the son of Musa Kazim, the son of Ja'far Sadiq, 'Alawi, Husayni. His patronymic is Abu al-Qasim and the Shi'a know him as Khalaf Salih, Hujjat, Mahdi, Muntazar, and the Master of the Age (Sahib al- zaman)."[178]

14. Muhammad b. 'Ali Hamawi writes: "Abu al-Qasim Muhammad Muntazar was born in the year 259 AH/874 CE in Samarra."[179]

In short, besides all these above mentioned Sunni scholars there are numerous others who have recorded the birth of Imam Hasan 'Askari's son.[180]

---

[176] Ibid., p. 143

[177] As cited in Yanabi' al-mawadda, Vo. 2, p. 126

[178] Shadharat al-dhahab (Beirut edition), Vol. 2, p. 141; al-'Ibar fi khabar min ghabar (Kuwait edition), Vol. 2, p. 31

[179] Ta'rikh mansuri, microfilm copy of the Moscow manuscript, folio number 114

[180] See the references compiled in the volume Kashf al-astar, by Husayn b. Muhammad Taqi Nuri and Kifayat al- muwahhidin by TTabarsi, especially volume 2

* * *

At this time it was quite late in the night. The meeting was adjourned and it was decided that the following session would be held at Dr. Jalali's residence.

The session began on time. Everyone was anxiously waiting to begin the discussion. Dr. Fahimi formulated his question thus.

Dr. Fahimi: Let us assume that Imam Hasan 'Askari did have a son. But how can one believe that a ve year old lad is appointed to the position of *wilayat* and Imamate? How is it possible that he is given the charge of protecting and effecting the laws of God at that young age and is made the Imam, the leader of the people and God's Proof on earth?

Mr. Hoshyar: It appears that you have imagined the position of the Prophethood and the Imamate to be a trivial thing not requiring any precondition or criterion for anyone who is supposed to protect and effect the divine laws! Moreover, it would seem that you do not require any qualications or personal character and perfection in a person who is to assume such a divinely ordained position –even to the extent that it is possible that Abu Sufyan could take the position of the prophethood occupied by Muhammad b. 'Abd Allah and Talha and Zubayr could assume the Imamate instead of 'Ali b. Abi Talib.

However, a little attention will lead you to the traditions reported on the authority of the *Ahlul Bayt* that the matter of the leadership and guidance of the community is not that simple. Indeed, Prophethood is a divine ofce that requires a qualied individual to be designated to carry out its functions derived from a special spiritual relationship between God and His emissary, a prophet. More importantly, such an individual is endowed with hidden knowledge, and knowledge about God's laws and injunctions which have been revealed to him through God's special favor on him and, hence, both he and the message are free from any error or falsehood.

Similarly, *wilayat* and Imamate are extremely important ofces. The person occupying that position is required to preserve the divine laws and teachings of the Prophet without committing any error or inadvertence in their transmission and their promulgation in the community. Moreover, that person has to be in contact with the hidden source of divine knowledge so that he may receive God's guidance in understanding and illuminating His revelation for humanity. It is because of his knowledge and the actions based on divine guidance that he attains the position of being proclaimed God's Proof (*hujjat*) and His manifestation on earth.

It is obvious that not every person on this earth is capable of fullling these requirements and effecting the laws of God in human society. It is necessary that the person assuming this sensitive position should be endowed with a spiritual and human perfection so as to establish proper contact with the divine source and receive the knowledge and retain it for the community. Moreover, this person must possess both physical and mental qualities most appropriate to the execution of his functions as the leader and guide of the Muslim community. He cannot afford to be fallible and erroneous in conveying the religious truth necessary for the well being of humanity.

Hence, it must be maintained that the Prophet and the Imams are the best in creation. More importantly, it is because of these personal qualities that God, the Almighty, appoints them in the position of a Prophet and an Imam. These qualities are present in them from the time they come into this world. At the appropriate time and as the situation demands, and provided there are no obstacles, they become manifest. It is only then that these individuals become selected and appointed as Prophets and Imams with the mission to carry and effect God's ordinances for humanity. This manifest designation may occur at times after they attain the age of maturity, and at other times even while they are younger in age.

The Qur'an provides the best example of the appointment to the prophethood at a very young age. In the example of Jesus (peace be upon him), the Qur'an speaks about the miracle of Jesus while he was still a baby in the cradle. At that time Jesus introduced himself as a prophet who had brought the revealed message for the Children of Israel. Thus, he says:

> *"Lo, I am God's servant; God has given me the Book, and made me a Prophet. Blessed He has made me, wherever I may be; and He has enjoined me to pray, and to give the alms, so long as I live." (The Holy Qur'an, Surah Maryam 19:29)*

From this and other verses of the Qur'an it is clear that Jesus (peace be upon him) from his very early childhood had been appointed as the Prophet and had been given the Book.

In light of the above, it is correct to say that there is no objection to maintaining that a person could establish relations with the divine sources of knowledge at a very early age and could be appointed to undertake the critical responsibility of promulgating the divine laws with utmost care and accuracy.

Moreover, he could be made completely capable of performing his task and safeguarding the divine trust.

Incidentally, Imam Jawad (peace be upon him), at the time of his father's death was nine or seven years old. It was because of his young age that some among the Shi'is had doubts about his being the Imam. To resolve this problem some of the leading members of the community came to see Imam Jawad and asked him several difcult and complex questions. To all these the Imam was able to give sufcient and satisfactory answers. Moreover, they also witnessed some miracles from him which removed their doubt in his being their Imam at that young age.[181]

Imam Rida had appointed Imam Jawad as his successor and when he found people surprised at his designation he said: "Jesus (peace be upon him) also became a Prophet and a Proof of God at a young age."[182]

Imam 'Ali Naqi also became the Imam at the age of six years and ve months, following his father's death.[183]

So, Dr. Fahimi, the Prophets and the Imams are specially created to carry out the functions assigned to them by God. Hence, it is not proper to compare them with ordinary people and their capacities.

---

[181] Ithbat al-wasiyya, pp. 186-89

[182] Ibid., p. 185

[183] Ibn Shahr Ashub, Manaqib, Vol. 4, p. 397; Ithbat al-wasiyya, p. 194

The Gifted Children

Often among ordinary people one comes across rare individuals endowed with excellent intelligence and immense potential. In fact, they manifest unusual mental powers and faculties of perception superior to an individual of, let us say, forty years of age.

Abu 'Ali Sina, known as Avicenna to Western readers, is regarded among the geniuses of his times. In his autobiography he writes:

Later we all moved to Bukhara, where I was given teachers of Qur'an and Arabic letters (adab). By the time I was ten years old, I had completed the study of the Qur'an and a major part of Arabic letters, so much so that people wondered at my attainments. Then, under the guidance of al-Natili, I began to read the Isagoge [of the Greek neoplatonist philosopher Porphyrius] . . .Almagest [of Ptolemy]. Then

I took up medicine and began to read books written on this subject. Medicine is not one of the difcult sciences, and in a very short time I undoubtedly excelled in it, so that physicians of merit studied under me. At the same time I carried on debates and controversies in jurisprudence. At this point I was sixteen years old.[184]

It is said that Fadil Hindi had mastered all rational and traditional sciences by the age of twelve, and had begun to write a book. The list of the gifted people is long. One only has to open a history of the world to realize that a number of universally recognized individuals were endowed at a young age with uncommon intelligence and a capacity to learn and leave for posterity a wealth of knowledge in different disciplines.

Dr. Fahimi, if other children can be endowed with unique potentials and turn out to be a genius, capable of memorizing hundreds of things and a variety of subjects – provoking wonderment in others – why should it be inconceivable that God in His wisdom appointed the twelfth Imam, God's authentic proof who happens to be a ve year old, to occupy the position of wilayat and to be the exponent and protector of God's ordinances? In fact, the Imams had predicted his attaining that high position at an incredibly young age. Imam Baqir said: "The one who will be entrusted with the command (sahib al-'amr) will be youngest in age and less known than all of us."[185]

---

[184] Ibn al-Qifti, Ta'rikh al-hukama', pp. 413-417

[185] Bihar al-anwar, Vol. 51, p. 38

Rising of the People when Naming the Qa'im

Dr. Jalali: I am sure you know that it is customary among the people to rise when the word qa'im is mentioned. Is there any tradition to support this custom?

Mr. Hoshyar: This custom is common among all the Shi'is around the world. It is related that Imam Rida was present in one of the gatherings in Khurasan when the word qa'im was mentioned. At that he rose, put his right hand on his head and said: "O God, make his deliverance soon and his rising graceful!"[186]

This custom was prevalent even during the time of Imam Sadiq (peace be upon him). Somebody had asked him: "Why is it that one should rise (qiyam) when the Qa'im is mentioned?" The Imam replied:

The one who is entrusted with the command (sahib al-'amr) will have a very long occultation. Because of the utmost love that he has for his followers, whoever remembers him with his title Qa'im, which carries the meaning of awaiting his rule and conveys the impact of

---

[186] Ilzam al-nasib (1351 AH edition), p. 81

the longing for him, he too will show his concern for the faithful. Since the person remembering the Qa'im is also attended by him, it is appropriate to rise out of respect for him and pray to God for his early deliverance.[187]

Hence, the Shi'i custom has a religious root and reects respect and conveys an aspiration, although whether such an act is obligatory or not is unknown.

---

[187] Ibid

When Did the Story about the Occultation Begin?

Dr. Fahimi: I have heard that since Imam Hasan 'Askari died without leaving a son, some opportunistic people like 'Uthman b. Sa'id, fabricated the story about the occultation of the Mahdi in order to preserve their own position in the community.

Mr. Hoshyar: The Prophet and the Imams had long before that informed the people about the impending occultation of the Mahdi. Thus, for instance, the Prophet is reported to have said:

I swear by the One Who prompted me to give you the good news that the Qa'im among my descendants, in accordance with the covenant that reaches him from me, will disappear. [The situation will be such] that most of the people will say: "God does not need the progeny of Muhammad." Others will doubt his very birth. Whoever lives during [this period of occultation] should cling to his faith and not let the Satan approach him through the channel of doubt and cause him to abandon my religion, just as he had caused your parents [Adam and Eve], to be thrown out of Paradise. Undoubtedly, God has made Satan friend of those who do not believe.[188]

Asbagh b. Nubata relates the occasion when Amir al-Mu'minin 'Ali b. Abi Talib remembered the Qa'im and said: "Be aware that he will disappear in such a way that an ignorant person will say: 'God does not need the progeny of Muhammad.'"[189]

Imam Sadiq advised his followers saying: "If you hear the story about your Imam's occultation, do not deny it."[190] There are some 88 hadith-reports on this subject.

It was because of these traditions that Muslims regarded the occultation necessary for the Qa'im. It was considered to be one of his characteristics. In fact, anyone who claimed to be the promised Mahdi or was fancied to be so was necessarily believed by his supporters to be in occultation. Abu al-Faraj Isfahani, in his description of one of such claimants, writes: "'Isa b. 'Abd Allah reports that Muhammad b. 'Abd Allah b. Hasan [b. 'Ali b. Abi Talib] lived in concealment from the very early childhood and was named Mahdi."[191]

Sayyid Muhammad Himyari, the well known poet during the Umayyad period, relates that he used to hold exaggerated beliefs about Muhammad b. Hanayya, including the belief that he was in occultation. For a long time he held such erroneous beliefs until that time, as he says, God favored him and he was saved from them by Imam Sadiq's right guidance. The event is described thus by him:

When I was fully convinced about the Imamate of Ja'far b. Muhammad [Sadiq] through well demonstrated proof, I went to see him one day and asked him: "O son of the Prophet, there are traditions

---

[188] Ithbat al-hudat, Vol. 6, p. 386

[189] Ibid., p. 393

[190] Ibid., p. 350

[191] Maqatil al-talibiyyin, p. 165

about the occurrence of occultation that have reached us from your forefathers which regard occultation among the denite things. Would you kindly inform me as to whom these traditions speak?" The Imam replied: "This occultation will occur for the sixth of my descendants. He is the twelfth Imam after the Prophet, of whom the rst is 'Ali b. Abi Talib and the last is the Qa'im, Baqiyyat Allah (the Remnant of God), and the Master of the Age. I solemnly declare that even if his occultation lasts for as long as the age of Noah, he will not leave this world until he rises and lls it with justice and equity."

Sayyid Himyari adds:

When I heard this from my master Ja'far b. Muhammad the truth became evident for me. I apologized to him for the erroneous belief that I held before that and composed a poem on the subject.[192]

Hence, the story of occultation of the Mahdi was not invented by 'Uthman b. Sa'id. It was God who foreordained it for him, and the Prophet and the Imams had informed the people about it before his father Imam Hasan 'Askari was born. Tabarsi, in his book on the history of the Prophet and the Imams entitled, I'lam al-wara, writes:

The traditions about the ghaybat of the twelfth Imam were in circulation before his, his father's, and his grandfather's birth. They were recorded and cited by the Shi'i traditionists who lived during the time of Imams Baqir and Sadiq. Among these highly trusted traditionists is Hasan b. Mahbub. He wrote a book entitled Mashikha a century before the occultation of the twelfth Imam in which he recorded traditions about the occultation. One of the traditions published in this book included the following hadith reported from Abu Basir, who relates:

I asked Imam Sadiq: "Abu Ja'far [Imam Baqir] said, 'The Qa'im among the descendants of Muhammad will have two occultations,

---

[192] Kamal al-din, Vol. 1, pp. 112-115

one long and the other short.'" Hearing this Imam Sadiq said, "Yes, that is so. One of the two occultations will be longer."

Tabarsi then draws his conclusion and writes:

Do you see how with the materialization of the two occultations for Imam Hasan 'Askari's son the prediction in the hadith came to be true?[193]

Muhammad b. Ibrahim b. Ja'far Nu'mani was born during the Short Occultation (ghaybat-i sughra), and when he wrote his book on Ghayba the twelfth Imam was eighty and some years old. He writes the following on page 6:

The Imams had foretold the occurrence of the occultation. If the occultation had not occurred, this very point would have become the source of falsication of the belief of the Shi'a Imamiyya (i.e., the Twelvers). But God manifested the truthfulness of the Imams' predictions by means of causing the Imam to go into occultation.

---

[193] I'lam al-wara (Tehran edition, 1378 AH), p. 416

The Books on the Subject of the Occultation before the Birth of the Twelfth Imam

The story of the Mahdi and the twelfth Imam's occultation was told by the Prophet, 'Ali b. Abi Talib, and the rest of the Imams from the very early days of Islam. It was well known among the early companions to the extent that some scholars and narrators of hadith-reports, including the close associates of the Imams, had written books on the subject long before the twelfth Imam or his father and grandfather were born. In these books the hadith about the promised Mahdi and his occultation were recorded. The names of these authors and the titles of their works are preserved in the biographical dictionaries (kutub al-rijal). Thus, for instance:

1. 'Ali b. Hasan b. Muhammad Ta'i, a companion of Imam Kazim, wrote a book on ghaybat. He was a jurist and was regarded as reliable in his transmission of hadith.[194]

---

[194] Rijal Najashi, Vol. 2, p. 77; Rijal Tusi, p. 357; Fihrist Tusi, p. 92

2. 'Ali b. 'Umar A'raj Ku, a companion of Imam Kazim, wrote a book on ghaybat.[195]
3. Ibrahim b. Salih Anmati, a companion of Imam Kazim, wrote a book on ghaybat.[196]
4. Hasan b. 'Ali b. Abi Hamza, who lived during the time of Imam Rida, was also an author of a book on ghaybat.[197]
5. 'Abbas b. Hisham Nashiri Asadi was a prominent gure and a reputable person. He was among the companions of Imam Rida. He died in the year 220 AH/835 CE. He also wrote a book on ghaybat.[198]
6. 'Ali b. Hasan b. Faddal was a learned man and reliable in his transmission of religious information. He was among the companions of Imams Hadi and Hasan 'Askari. He wrote a book on ghaybat.[199]
7. Fadl b. Shadhan Nishaburi was among the jurists and theologians. He was among the companions of Imams Hadi and Hasan 'Askari. He died in the year 260 AH/873 CE. He wrote a book on the subject of the Qa'im of the Family of Muhammad and his ghaybat.[200]

It is important to keep in mind that the story about ghaybat is not something new in Islam. It has deep religious roots and was always discussed and debated from the time of the Prophet (peace be upon him and his progeny). Consequently, the possibility that

---

[195] Rijal Najashi, Vol. 2, p. 79

[196] Rijal Najashi, Vol. 2, p. 86; Fihrist Tusi, p. 3

[197] Rijal Najashi, Vol. 2, p. 132; Fihrist Tusi, p. 50

[198] Rijal Najashi, Vol. 2, p. 119; Rijal Tusi, p. 384; Fihrist Tusi, p. 147

[199] Rijal Najashi, Vol. 2, p. 119; Rijal Tusi, p. 384; Fihrist Tusi, p. 147

[200] Rijal Najashi, Vol. 2, p. 167; Rijal Tusi, p. 420 and 434; Fihrist Tusi, p. 150

a person like 'Uthman b. Sa'id invented and disseminated it is absolutely unfounded. Such an accusation cannot come about from any one other than a prejudiced individual. Moreover, if we append the following three propositions together, then the matter of the occultation of the Imam of the Age becomes certain:

1. On the basis of rational demonstration as well as numerous hadith-reports related from the Prophet and the Imams, it is certain that the existence of the Imam and the Proof of God on earth is necessary for the survival of humanity. Therefore, there is no time when the earth could be without the Imam.
2. On the basis of numerous hadith-reports, there can be no more than twelve Imams.
3. On the basis of many reports, both in the books on hadith and history, it is a fact that eleven of these twelve Imams have lived and died.

These three propositions make it necessary to conclude that the existence of the Imam Mahdi is beyond any doubt, and that since he does not live a visible existence, he must be in occultation.

The Short and Complete Occultation203

Dr. Jalali: What is the meaning of 'short' and 'complete' occultation?

Mr. Hoshyar: It means that the twelfth Imam (peace be upon him) remained concealed from the public at two different times. The first period extends from the time of his birth in 255 or 256 AH/868 or 869 CE or from the time of his father, Imam Hasan 'Askari's death in 260 AH/873 CE, to the year 329 AH/940 CE. During this time, although he lived an invisible existence as far as the public was concerned, he was not completely cut off from them. Rather, he maintained regular contact with his followers through his deputies, who were able to reach him and present to him their needs and inquiries. The existence of the Imam during this period that lasted some 74 or 69 years is known as ghaybat-i sughra.

The second period extends from the year 329/940, with the termination of the deputyship of his prominent and trustworthy associates, to the time when he will emerge from the state of the occultation to lead humanity to establish the rule of justice and equity on earth. This period of occultation is known as ghaybat-i kubra.

Both the Prophet and the Imams (peace be upon them) had informed people about the two forms of occultation for the Mahdi. Thus, for instance, Ishaq b. 'Ammar relates a hadith he heard from Imam Sadiq:

The Qa'im will have two forms of occultation: one long and the other short. During the rst occultation his special followers will know his whereabouts; during the second occultation, except for a few very special followers of his in his religion, no one will have any information about his whereabouts.[201]

In another tradition Imam Sadiq said:

The one who is entrusted with the command (sahib al-'amr) will have two forms of occultation. One of them will be so long that a group of the people will say that he has died; others will say he has been killed; still others will say he has disappeared. Very few will remain who will still have faith in his existence, and will continue to be steadfast. At this time no one will have any information about his whereabouts except his very few followers.[202]

---

[201] Ithbat al-hudat, Vol. 7, p. 69; Bihar al-anwar, Vol. 52, p. 155

[202] Bihar al-anwar, Vol. 52, p. 153. There are eight more traditions on this subject

The Short Occultation and the Contacts with the Shi'a

Dr. Fahimi: I have heard that after the short occultation began, there were some charlatans who, taking advantage of the ignorance of the ignorant masses, claimed to be the deputies and 'gates' (bab = 'mediator' between the Imam and his followers) of the Hidden Imam. They cheated the people and pocketed a lot of their wealth. Could you take some time to explain who exactly these deputies were and what kind of contact and relationship there was between the Imam and his followers, and in what form?

Mr. Hoshyar: During the short occultation people in general were deprived of a more normal contact with the Imam. However, the relationship was not completely severed. It was maintained through some special individuals known as bab ('mediator'), na'ib ('deputy'), and wakil ('representative'). It was through these individuals that the people established contact with their Imam, asking questions of him and seeking his assistance in their affairs. The share of the Imam from the khums (the 'fth') was delivered to the Imam through his deputy. Sometimes, they used to ask for material help from the Imam; at other times they used to seek permission to go for hajj or other kinds of travel; still at other times they would ask the Imam to pray for their sick or to pray for a child for them.

The Imam used to respond to these requests through different individuals who represented him among them in different parts of the Muslim world. In the performance of all these tasks there were specic individuals who executed the will of the Imam. There were times when the requests were made in letters to the Imam and, accordingly, he would respond in writing. These 'signed notes' from him were known as tawqi'.

Were these Letters from the Imam in His Own Handwriting?

Dr. Jalali: Who wrote these letters? Was it the Imam himself or someone else?

Mr. Hoshyar: It is said that the Imam himself wrote these letters or notes. In fact, his handwriting was well known among his associates and the contemporary scholars. They used to recognize it well. There is some evidence to that effect in the sources. For instance, Muhammad b. 'Uthman 'Amri says: "A signed note was issued from the Imam and the handwriting was well known to me."[203]

Ishaq b. Ya'qub relates that he had sent a letter asking questions to the twelfth Imam through Muhammad b. 'Uthman. He received the reply in the Imam's own handwriting.[204]

Shaykh Abu 'Amr 'Amiri relates: Ibn Abi Ghanim Qazwini had a dispute on a matter with a group of the Shi'is. For resolving it they wrote a letter to the Imam explaining the matter. The response came

---

[203] Bihar al-anwar, Vol. 51, p. 33

[204] Bihar al-anwar, Vol. 51, p. 349

from the Imam in his own handwriting.²⁰⁵ According to Shaykh Saduq, the letter that his father had received from the Imam was in his possession.²⁰⁶

These aforementioned individuals have borne the testimony that the letters they received or were in their possession were from the Imam himself, in his own handwriting. However, we do not know the way they determined that it was the Imam's handwriting. The reason is that with the occultation it was not possible to see the Imam. In addition, there were some who reported contrary to what these aforementioned individuals were claiming. For example, Abu Nasr Hibat Allah relates that the signed notes were issued by 'Uthman b. Sa'id and Muhammad b. 'Uthman, in the same handwriting that was used during the time of Imam Hasan 'Askari.²⁰⁷

In another report the same person relates that Abu Ja'far 'Amri died in the year 304 AH/916 CE. He had been the deputy of the Imam for over fty years. People used to bring their donations to him and signed notes were issued to them in the same hand writing as during the time of Imam Hasan 'Askari.²⁰⁸ In yet another report he says that the signed notes of the Imam were issued by Muhammad b. 'Uthman, in the same handwriting as they were issued during the time of his father, 'Uthman b. Sa'id.²⁰⁹

'Abd Allah b. Ja'far Himyari relates: "When 'Uthman b. Sa'id died, the signed notes of the Imam of the Age were issued in the same handwriting in which we used to receive earlier letters."²¹⁰

---

[205] Bihar al-anwar, Vol. 53, p. 178

[206] Anwar al-nu'maniyya (Tabriz edition), Vol. 2, p. 24

[207] Anwar al-nu'maniyya (Tabriz edition), Vol. 2, p. 24

[208] Bihar al-anwar, Vol. 51, p. 352

[209] Bihar al-anwar, Vol. 51, p. 306

[210] Ibid., Vol. 51, p. 350

On the basis of all these reports it can be surmised that the notes that were received by the people during 'Uthman b. Sa'id and Muhammad b. 'Uthman's time were in the same handwriting as those that were received during the time of Imam Hasan 'Askari. Thus, these could not be in the handwriting of the twelfth Imam. Rather, it can be maintained that Imam Hasan 'Askari had a special scribe who was in charge of writing the letters and who continued to do so also under these two deputies, namely, 'Uthman and his son Muhammad. It is also plausible to maintain that some of these letters were dictated directly by the Imam, whereas others were dictated by someone other than him. However, it is important to state that from the evidence provided in the biographies of the Shi'i scholars living during the short occultation, the contents of these letters were trusted by the Shi'is, were regarded as coming from the Imam himself, and were accepted as authentic. They used to write to the Imam about their points of dispute. And, when the response came for them, they used to submit to his judgement.

'Ali b. Husayn b. Babawayh corresponded with the Imam in occultation and requested him to pray for a son for him. To be sure, he received a response from the Imam.

One of the prominent scholars who was born during the short occultation and had been in touch with the deputies of the Imam was Muhammad b. Ibrahim b. Ja'far Nu'mani. In his book entitled Ghayba he conrmed the deputyship of some prominent associates of the eleventh and twelfth Imams. After relating some hadith on the subject of the ghaybat, he writes:

During the rst occultation there were the mediators between the Imam and the people, carrying out [the duties of the Imam], having been designated [by him], living among the people. These were the eminent persons and leaders from whose hands emanated cures derived from the knowledge and the intricate wisdom which they possessed, and the answers to all the questions which were put to them about the problems and difculties [of religion]. This was the short occultation, the days of which have come to an end and whose time has gone by. Now it is the time of the complete occultation.[211]

It appears that the signed notes received from the Imam served as special signs and documentation which the Shi'is and their scholars accepted. Shaykh Hurr 'Amili writes:

Ibn Abi Ghanim Qazwini used to argue with the Shi'is on the matter of the successor to the Imamate. He used to say: "Imam Hasan 'Askari had no son." The people wrote to the Imam. Their custom was to write on a white sheet with a pen without ink so that it would serve as a sign of miracle. To this they received the answer from the Imam (peace be upon him).[212]

---

[211] Kitab al-ghayba, p. 91

[212] Ithbat al-hudat, Vol. 7, p. 360

The Number of Deputies

There is difference of opinion regarding the number of deputies of the twelfth Imam. Sayyid Ibn Tawus in his book entitled Rab'i al-shi'a has mentioned their names as follows:

1. Abu Hashim Dawud b. al-Qasim
2. Muhammad b. 'Ali b. Bilal
3. 'Uthman b. Sa'id
4. Muhammad b. 'Uthman
5. 'Umar al-Ahwazi
6. Ahmad b. Ishaq
7. Abu Muhammad al-Wajna'
8. Ibrahim b. Mahziyar
9. Muhammad b. Ibrahim[213]

Shaykh Tusi introduces the names of the deputies of the Imam as follows:

From Baghdad 'Uthman b. Sa'id and his son Muhammad b.

---

[213] Ithbat al-hudat, Vol. 7, p. 360

'Uthman, Hajiz, Bilali, and 'Attar; from Kufa 'Asimi; from Ahwaz Muhammad b. Ibrahim b. Mahziyar; from Qumm Ahmad b. Ishaq; from Hamadan Muhammad b. Salih; from Rayy Shami and Asadi; from Azerbaijan Qasim b. 'Ala'; and from Nishabur Muhammad b. Shadhan.[214]

However, the deputyship of the four prominent members of the community is famous among the Shi'is. These are:

1. 'Uthman b. Sa'id 'Amri (260 AH/874 CE)
2. Muhammad b. 'Uthman 'Amri (d. 304 AH/916 CE)
3. Husayn b. Ruh Nawbakhti (d. 326 AH/937 CE)
4. 'Ali b. Muhammad al-Samarri (d. 329/940 CE) 'Uthman b. Sa'id, the First Deputy

He was among the most trustworthy and eminent companions of Imam Hasan 'Askari and was his representative among the Shi'a. According to Bu 'Ali and Mamqani, "'Uthman b. Sa'id was thoroughly reliable and highly respected because of his impeccable character. He served as the agent of the Imam Hadi, Imam Hasan 'Askari, and Imam Qa'im (peace be upon them)35." Such an opinion of him was universally held by all other authors of biographical dictionaries. Thus, 'Allama Bihbahani, in addition to praising 'Uthman, says that he was actually accredited by the Imams Hadi and Hasan 'Askari[215].

Ahmad b. Ishaq relates the incident in which he asked the tenth Imam Hadi regarding the person with whom the Shi'a should deal and whose guidance they should accept as coming from the Imams. The Imam said: "'Uthman b. Sa'id is my trusted agent. If he relates

---

[214] Rijal Mamqani (Najaf edition, 1352 AH), Vol. 1, p. 200; Ithbat al-hudat, Vol. 7, p. 294

[215] Minhaj al-maqal (Tehran edition, 1307 AH), p. 219

something for you then he is telling the truth. Listen to him and obey him because I trust him." When Imam Hasan 'Askari was asked a similar question he mentioned both 'Uthman and his son Muhammad as his trusted agents. Moreover, he also required his followers to listen to and obey Uthman. These reports were so widespread among the companions of the last Imams that they became the source of the respect and trust with which 'Uthman b. Sa'id was held.[216]

On one occasion Muhammad b. Isma'il and 'Ali b. 'Abd Allah came to Samarra to visit Imam Hasan 'Askari. There was a group of Shi'a visiting the Imam at that time. Suddenly, the servant came and announced that a group of villagers, shabbily dressed, were seeking permission to enter the presence of the Imam. The Imam said: "They are Shi'a from the Yemen." Then he told the servant to ask 'Uthman to be prepared for the visitors. Within a short while 'Uthman was ready. The Imam said to him: "'Uthman, you are our trusted agent. Receive the goods this group has brought." This elevation of 'Uthman, according to the narrators of the report, was done in order to let the Shi'a know the status of 'Uthman. In fact, towards the end of that visit Imam Hasan 'Askari declared to the group saying: "Let it be known to you that 'Uthman b. Sa'id is my agent and his son will be the agent of my son Mahdi."[217]

Imam Hasan 'Askari revealed his son to the group of forty people among his followers, including 'Ali b. Bilal, Ahmad b. Hilal, Muhammad b. Mu'awiya, and Hasan b. Ayyub and said: "This is your Imam and my successor. Obey him! Know that after this time for a while you will not see him. Listen to what 'Uthman b. Sa'id says and follow his instructions because he [Uthman] is the successor of

---

[216] Bihar al-anwar, Vol. 51, p. 348

[217] Bihar al-anwar, Vol. 51, p. 346

your Imam. The management of the affairs of our people will be in his hands."[218]

His Miraculous Acts

In addition to these favorable statements from the Imams accrediting 'Uthman b. Sa'id, there are miraculous acts (karamat) ascribed to him. These acts actually provide further evidence to bolster the truthfulness of his statements. For instance, Shaykh Tusi in his Kitab al-Ghayba, relates the following story from a number of persons belonging to Nawbakht family, including Abu al-Hasan Kathiri:

A person brought some goods [belonging to the twelfth Imam] from Qumm and the vicinity to 'Uthman b. Sa'id. When the person wanted to leave 'Uthman b. Sa'id said: "You have been entrusted with something else too. Why have you not delivered it?" The person said: "There is nothing else left." 'Uthman b. Sa'id told him to go back and search for it. After a few days of searching the person returned to report that he had not found anything on him. At that 'Uthman b. Sa'id asked him: "What happened to the two pieces of cloth that were handed to you by so and so?" The person said: "By God, you are right. But I have forgotten about them, and now I do not know where they are."

Once more he returned to his place and searched for the material, but could not nd it. He came and told 'Uthman b. Sa'id about that. 'Uthman said: "Go to so and so, the cotton seller, to whom you delivered two bundles of cotton. Open the bundle on which such and such is written. You will nd that entrusted material in it." The man went and did what 'Uthman b. Sa'id had asked him to do. He

---

[218] Bihar al-anwar, Vol. 51, p. 346

found the material and brought it to him.[219]

Muhammad b. 'Ali Aswad, another agent of the Imam, was given a piece of cloth by a woman for 'Uthman b. Sa'id. He took it with some other clothes to 'Uthman. 'Uthman asked him to hand it to Muhmmad b. 'Abbas Qummi. He did so. After that 'Uthman b. Sa'id sent him a message which said: "Why have you not delivered the cloth given by the woman?" Muhammad b. 'Ali Aswad remembered the cloth and searched for it until he delivered it to him.[220]

Shaykh Saduq has narrated another incident in his Kamal al-din. He writes:

A man from Iraq brought the Imam's share (sahm imam) to 'Uthman b. Sa'id. 'Uthman returned the money and said: "Deduct from it that which you owe to your cousins." The man was surprised to hear that. When he investigated his goods he found that he owed part of the agricultural land to his cousins, which he had not returned. On careful calculation he found that the land was equivalent to four hundred dirhams. Thus, he deducted that from his goods and took the remaining portion to 'Uthman b. Sa'id. This time it was accepted from him.[221]

After all these reports about 'Uthman b. Sa'id's honesty and trustworthiness, the respect with which he was held by the tenth and eleventh Imams, and the consensus among the Shi'a about his moral probity and sound character, is it fair to assume that he was a manipulative individual, intent upon deceiving the generality of the Shi'is?

---

[219] Bihar al-anwar, Vol. 51, p. 316

[220] Ibid., p. 335

[221] Ibid., p. 335

'Uthman b. Sa'id, the First Deputy

He was among the most trustworthy and eminent companions of Imam Hasan 'Askari and was his representative among the Shi'a. According to Bu 'Ali and Mamqani, "'Uthman b. Sa'id was thoroughly reliable and highly respected because of his impeccable character. He served as the agent of the Imam Hadi, Imam Hasan 'Askari, and Imam Qa'im (peace be upon them)."[222] Such an opinion of him was universally held by all other authors of biographical dictionaries. Thus, 'Allama Bihbahani, in addition to praising 'Uthman, says that he was actually accredited by the Imams Hadi and Hasan 'Askari.[223]

Ahmad b. Ishaq relates the incident in which he asked the tenth Imam Hadi regarding the person with whom the Shi'a should deal and whose guidance they should accept as coming from the Imams. The Imam said: "'Uthman b. Sa'id is my trusted agent. If he relates something for you then he is telling the truth. Listen to him and obey him because I trust him." When Imam Hasan 'Askari was

---

[222] Minhaj al-maqal (Tehran edition, 1307 AH), p. 219
[223] Bihar al-anwar, Vol. 51, p. 348

asked a similar question he mentioned both 'Uthman and his son Muhammad as his trusted agents. Moreover, he also required his followers to listen to and obey Uthman. These reports were so widespread among the companions of the last Imams that they became the source of the respect and trust with which 'Uthman b. Sa'id was held.[224]

On one occasion Muhammad b. Isma'il and 'Ali b. 'Abd Allah came to Samarra to visit Imam Hasan 'Askari. There was a group of Shi'a visiting the Imam at that time. Suddenly, the servant came and announced that a group of villagers, shabbily dressed, were seeking permission to enter the presence of the Imam. The Imam said: "They are Shi'a from the Yemen." Then he told the servant to ask 'Uthman to be prepared for the visitors. Within a short while 'Uthman was ready. The Imam said to him: "'Uthman, you are our trusted agent. Receive the goods this group has brought." This elevation of 'Uthman, according to the narrators of the report, was done in order to let the Shi'a know the status of 'Uthman. In fact, towards the end of that visit Imam Hasan 'Askari declared to the group saying: "Let it be known to you that 'Uthman b. Sa'id is my agent and his son will be the agent of my son Mahdi."[225]

Imam Hasan 'Askari revealed his son to the group of forty people among his followers, including 'Ali b. Bilal, Ahmad b. Hilal, Muhammad b. Mu'awiya, and Hasan b. Ayyub and said: "This is your Imam and my successor. Obey him! Know that after this time for a while you will not see him. Listen to what 'Uthman b. Sa'id says and follow his instructions because he [Uthman] is the successor of your Imam. The management of the affairs of our people will be in

---

[224] Bihar al-anwar, Vol. 51, p. 346

[225] Bihar al-anwar, Vol. 51, p. 346

his hands."[226]

---

[226] Bihar al-anwar, Vol. 51, p. 316

His Miraculous Acts

In addition to these favorable statements from the Imams accrediting 'Uthman b. Sa'id, there are miraculous acts (*karamat*) ascribed to him. These acts actually provide further evidence to bolster the truthfulness of his statements. For instance, Shaykh Tusi in his *Kitab al-Ghayba*, relates the following story from a number of persons belonging to Nawbakht family, including Abu al-Hasan Kathiri:

A person brought some goods [belonging to the twelfth Imam] from Qumm and the vicinity to 'Uthman b. Sa'id. When the person wanted to leave 'Uthman b. Sa'id said: "You have been entrusted with something else too. Why have you not delivered it?" The person said: "There is nothing else left." 'Uthman b. Sa'id told him to go back and search for it. After a few days of searching the person returned to report that he had not found anything on him. At that 'Uthman b. Sa'id asked him: "What happened to the two pieces of cloth that were handed to you by so and so?" The person said: "By God, you are right. But I have forgotten about them, and now I do not know where they are."

Once more he returned to his place and searched for the material, but could not nd it. He came and told 'Uthman b. Sa'id about that. 'Uthman said: "Go to so and so, the cotton seller, to whom you delivered two bundles of cotton. Open the bundle on which such and such is written. You will nd that entrusted material in it." The man went and did what 'Uthman b. Sa'id had asked him to do. He found the material and brought it to him.[227]

Muhammad b. 'Ali Aswad, another agent of the Imam, was given a piece of cloth by a woman for 'Uthman b. Sa'id. He took it with some other clothes to 'Uthman. 'Uthman asked him to hand it to Muhmmad b. 'Abbas Qummi. He did so. After that 'Uthman b. Sa'id sent him a message which said: "Why have you not delivered the cloth given by the woman?" Muhammad b. 'Ali Aswad remembered the cloth and searched for it until he delivered it to him.[228]

Shaykh Saduq has narrated another incident in his *Kamal al-din*. He writes:

A man from Iraq brought the Imam's share (*sahm imam*) to 'Uthman b. Sa'id. 'Uthman returned the money and said: "Deduct from it that which you owe to your cousins." The man was surprised to hear that. When he investigated his goods he found that he owed part of the agricultural land to his cousins, which he had not returned. On careful calculation he found that the land was equivalent to four hundred dirhams. Thus, he deducted that from his goods and took the remaining portion to 'Uthman b. Sa'id. This time it was accepted from him.[229]

After all these reports about 'Uthman b. Sa'id's honesty and trustworthiness, the respect with which he was held by the tenth and eleventh Imams, and the consensus among the Shi'a about his

---

[227] Ibid., p. 335

[228] Ibid., p. 335

[229] Manhaj al-maqal, p. 305; Rijal Mamqani, Vol. 3, p. 149

moral probity and sound character, is it fair to assume that he was a manipulative individual, intent upon deceiving the generality of the Shi'is?

Muhammad b. 'Uthman, the Second Deputy

Muhammad b. 'Uthman succeeded his father, 'Uthman b. Sa'id, as the deputy after the latter's death in 260 AH/874 CE. Shaykh Tusi, commenting on both these deputies of the Hidden Imam (peace be upon him), writes that "they enjoyed the highest esteem in the eyes of the Master of the Age."[230]

According to Mamqani, the high status of Muhammad b. 'Uthman among the Shi'is is self-evident. They are in agreement that during the lifetime of his father he was the deputy of Imam Hasan 'Askari, and later on he became the deputy of the twelfth Imam. In fact, 'Uthman b. Sa'id explicitly appointed Muhammad b. 'Uthman as his successor and the deputy of the Hidden Imam.[231] Ya'qub b. Ishaq, a prominent follower of the Imams in Samarra, relates:

I wrote a letter to the Imam of the Age through Muhammad b. 'Uthman in which I asked some questions about religious problems. The reply came in the Imam's own handwriting. In addition to the

---

[230] Manhaj al-maqal, p. 305; Rijal Mamqani, Vol. 3, p. 149
[231] Rijal Mamqani, Vol. 3, p. 149 and Vol. 1, p. 200

responses to my inquiries it included the statement: "Muhammad b. 'Uthman is the trusted one. His letters are my letters."[232]

His Miraculous Acts

Muhammad b. Shadhan, a close companion of Imam Hasan 'Askari, relates that he had four hundred and eighty dirhams that belonged to the Imam (peace be upon him). Since he did not like to send without rounding the gure to ve hundred, he added twenty dirhams from his money and sent it to Muhammad b. 'Uthman, without writing to him that he had added that amount. A receipt came from the Imam in which it was written: "We received ve hundred dirhams, which included twenty dirhams from you."[233]

A similar story is reported by Ja'far b. Ahmad b. Matil. Muhammad b. 'Uthman sent a message calling him to visit. When Ja'far came Muhammad b. 'Uthman gave him some pieces of cloth and a bag of dirhams, and asked him to go to Wasit. There he asked him to hand the bag and cloth to the rst person he would meet. When Ja'far reached Wasit the rst person he met was Hasan b. Muhammad b. Qatah. He introduced himself to Hasan who recognized him and they embraced each other. He related to him Muhammad b. 'Uthman's greetings and handed over to him the goods he had brought. When Hasan heard this he thanked God and said: "Muhammad b. 'Abd Allah 'Amiri has died. I left the house to get a shroud for him." Upon opening the goods that were sent by Muhammad b. 'Uthman they found everything they needed to prepare for 'Amiri's burial. Even the money was exactly the amount that was needed to cover the expenses related to the funeral. Hence, they went ahead and buried

---

[232] Bihar al-anwar, Vol. 51, p. 325

[233] Ibid., p. 325

'Amiri.[234]

According to another eminent follower of the Imams, namely, Muhammad b. 'Ali b. al-Aswad Qummi, Muhammad b. 'Uthman had prepared his burial place while still alive. He asked him for the reason. In response Muhammad b. 'Uthman said: "I have been ordered by the Imam to take care of my affairs in advance." Two months following this event Muhammad b. 'Uthman died.[235]

Muhammad b. 'Uthman remained the Hidden Imam's deputy for almost fty years and died in the year 304 AH/916 CE.

---

[234] Ibid., p. 337

[235] Ibid., p. 352

Husayn b. Ruh, the Third Deputy

The third deputy of the Imam of the Age (peace be upon him), was the most learned and astute leader of his time. Muhammad b. 'Uthman had himself designated him as his successor and deputy of the Imam.

'Allama Majlisi, in his Bihar al-anwar, writes:

When Muhammad b. 'Uthman became seriously ill, a group of prominent Shi'is like Abu 'Ali b. Humam, Abu 'Abd Allah b. Muhammad Katib, Abu 'Abd Allah Baqtani, Abu Sahl Nawbakhti, and Abu 'Abd Allah b. Wajna' came to see him. They asked him about his successor. In reply he said: "Husayn b. Ruh is my successor and the trusted deputy of the Master of the Age. Refer to him in your affairs. I have been commanded by the Imam to designate Husayn b. Ruh in the position of deputyship."[236]

Ja'far b. Muhammad Mada'ini relates that he used to carry the goods that belonged to the Imam to Muhammad b. 'Uthman. One day he took four hundred dinars to him. Muhammad b. 'Uthman asked him to deposit it with Husayn b. Ruh and so Ja'far asked him

---

[236] Ibid., p. 355

the reason he did not accept it himself.

Muhammad b. 'Uthman said: "Take it to Husayn b. Ruh. You should know that I have appointed him as my successor." Ja'far went on to ask if he had done so under instructions from the Imam. He replied: "Yes." Hence, Ja'far took the money to Husyan b. Ruh and from this time on he deposited the Imam's share with the latter.[237]

Among the companions and close associates of Muhammad b. 'Uthman there were a number of people, such as Ja'far b. Ahmad b. Matil, who held much higher position in merits than Husyan b. Ruh. In fact, many thought that the deputyship would be given to Ja'far Matil. However, contrary to the generally held expectation, it was Husayn b. Ruh who became the next deputy. Everyone at that point submitted to Muhammad b. 'Uthman's decision, including Ja'far Matil.[238] Abu Sahl Nawbakhti was asked about this decision:

"How did Husayn b. Ruh get appointed to the position of deputyship, when you were more qualied to assume it?" In response he said: "The Imam knows better about the person who can represent him. I am always in debate with our opponents. If I were the deputy, maybe at the time of heated debate, in order to prove my point, I would have revealed the Imam's whereabouts. But Husayn b. Ruh is not like me. If he had the Imam hidden under his garments, and if he were being cut to pieces, he would not expose him to anyone."[239]

Shaykh Saduq relates the circumstances that led his father to write a letter to the Imam and ask him to pray for a son for him. According to this report, it was Muhammad b. 'Ali Aswad who related that Shaykh

Saduq's father, 'Ali b. Husyan b. Babawayh, sent a message through

---

[237] Ibid., p. 352

[238] Ibid., p. 353

[239] Ibid., p. 359

him to Husyan b. Ruh to ask the Imam to pray for a son for him. That message was delivered to Husayn b. Ruh. After three days he informed Muhammad Aswad that the Imam had prayed for him and that in the near future God would favor him with a son.

That very year Muhammad, that is Shaykh Saduq, was born. After that several other sons were born. But it was Shaykh Saduq who used to pride himself on having been born through the special prayer of the Imam. In fact, whenever Muhammad Aswad saw Shaykh Saduq in the learning sessions with prominent teachers, studying extremely well, he would say: "It is not surprising to see you studying so well. After all you were born through the prayer of the Imam of the Age!"[240]

There was a man who had doubts about the deputyship of Husayn b. Ruh. For clarication of his doubt he wrote a letter to the Imam with a dry pen without ink. After a few days he received a reply from the Hidden Imam (peace be upon him) through Husayn b. Ruh.

Husayn b. Ruh died in the month of Sha'ban, in the year 326 AH/937 CE.[241]

---

[240] Kamal al-din, Vol. 2, p. 502-503

[241] Ithbat al-hudat, Vol. 7, p. 340

'Ali b. Muhammad Samarri, the Fourth Deputy

He was the fourth deputy of the Hidden Imam (peace be upon him). His full name was Abu al-Hasan 'Ali b. Muhammad Samarri. According to Ibn Tawus, he had served under the Imam Hadi and Imam Hasan 'Askari. These two Imams were, moreover, in correspondence with him and had written a number of signed notes for him. He was undoubtedly among the most eminent faces of the Shi'a in Baghdad.[242] Husayn b. Ruh, as reported by Ahmad b. Muhammad Safwani, had appointed 'Ali b. Muhammad Samarri in his place so that he could manage his affairs. When his death approached, a number of Shi'is came to see him and asked him about his successor. His response was that he had not been asked to appoint anyone to that position.[243]

It is related by Ahmad b. Ibrahim Mukhallad that one day 'Ali b. Muhammad Samarri, without any indication, said: "May God have mercy on 'Ali b. Muhammad b. Babawayh Qummi!" Those present

---

[242] Rijal Mamqani, Vol. 2, p. 304

[243] Bihar al-anwar, Vol. 51, p. 360

at that time made note of the date of this pronouncement. Later the news came that 'Ali b. Babawayh had died on the same day. He himself died in the year 329 AH/941 CE.[244]

Hasan b. Ahmad relates that he was with 'Ali b. Muhammad Samarri some days before he died. A letter came from the Imam which he read for the people. The contents were as follows:

In the name of God. O 'Ali b. Muhammad Samarri, may God reward your brethren in your death, which is going to take place in six days' time. So take care of your affairs and do not appoint anyone in your place, since the complete occultation has taken place. I will not appear until God permits me to do so (may His name be exalted) and that will be after a long time and after the hearts become hard and the earth is lled with wickedness. In the near future there will be those among my followers who will claim to have seen me. Beware, those who claim this before the rise of Sufyani and the [hearing of the] voice from the sky are liars.[245]

This was the end of the Short Occultation and the beginning of the Complete Occultation. The deputyship of these four prominent members of the Shi'a community is famous among the believers. There were also some individuals who made false claims about being deputized by the Hidden Imam (peace be upon him). Since they could not prove their claim their falsehood became manifest and they were discredited in the community. Among this latter group were Hasan Shari'ati, Muhammad b. Nusayr Numayri, Ahmad b. Hilal Karakhi, Muhammad b. 'Ali b. Bilal, Muhammad b. 'Ali Shalmaghani, and Abu Bakr Baghdadi.

This was, in brief, the account of the special deputies. From all the sources that speak about them it is reasonable to assert that their

---

[244] Bihar al-anwar, Vol. 51, p. 360

[245] Ibid., p. 361

claim to be the deputy of the Hidden Imam was defensible. There is no rational ground to doubt that they truly held that kind of highly esteemed position in the Shi'a community in the ninth-tenth century.

* * *

Dr. Fahimi: I had many more questions in this connection. However, I shall postpone asking them now, since it is getting quite late. Let us raise these questions when we meet next time.

The group met at Dr. Jalali's house. The session began on time. Everyone was anxious to hear Dr. Jalali's questions.

Dr. Jalali: What was the purpose of the Short Occultation? If the twelfth Imam was going to be in occultation, why did he not do so immediately following the death of Imam Hasan 'Askari? Why did he not become completely cut off from his followers?

Mr. Hoshyar: You must realize that the disappearance of the Imam and the leader of the community for a long time is an uncommon event and would be hard for the people to believe and get used to. It was for this reason that the Prophet (peace be upon him and his progeny) and the Imams decided to make the people aware of such a phenomenon gradually.

Hence, from time to time they related the events connected with the occultation, they spoke about the difculties people would face in the absence of the Imam, and described the condition of those who would reject the idea and the losses they would suffer, and praised the condition of those who would remain rm and the rewards they would reap. At times, through their own inaccessibility they demonstrated a situation which resembled the era when the last Imam would be living an invisible life.

Mas'udi, the famous historian, in his book Ithbat al-wasiyya describes this gradual introduction of the notion of the Imam's occultation. He says that Imam Hadi, the tenth Imam, met very little with the people and, except for some of his special associates, did not maintain contacts with others. When Imam Hasan 'Askari assumed the Imamate, most of the time he spoke with the people from behind a curtain so that his followers would be get used to the idea and be prepared to accept the disappearance of the twelfth Imam.[246]

If the complete occultation had begun immediately following the death of Imam Hasan 'Askari, then, in all likelihood, the fact about the existence of the twelfth Imam would have been ignored and in time people would have completely forgotten that there exists an Imam in occultation. Consequently, it was the Short Occultation with which the event of the disappearance of the Imam occurred.

During this period the Shi'a were able to contact the Imam through his special deputies and were witness to the signs and miraculous deeds that appeared in the hands of these prominent followers of the Imam. When the notion of occultation and the Imam's ability to provide the necessary guidance through his deputies in that state became rmly accepted, the Complete Occultation occurred.

---

[246] Ithbat al-wasiyya, p. 206

Is There Any Time Limit to the Complete Occultation?

Engineer Madani: Is there any time limit xed for the Complete Occultation?

Mr. Hoshyar: No, there is no time limit xed. However, there are many hadith-reports that point to the prolongation of the occultation to such an extent that some people will fall into doubt about the existence of the Imam. For example, Imam 'Ali has related the following about the Qa'im:

His occultation will be so long that an ignorant person will say: "God does not need the ahl al-bayt."[247]

Similarly, Imam Sajjad has related that among the characteristics of Noah that would recur in the Qa'im would be his long age.[248]

---

[247] Ithbat al-hudat, Vol. 2, p. 393

[248] Bihar al-anwar, Vol. 51, p. 217

The Philosophy of Occultation

Engineer Madani: If the Imam of the Age was living among the people, they would have been able to reach him and consult with him in times of need to seek solutions to their problems. That would have been better. In spite of such a need among his followers why did he go into occultation?

Mr. Hoshyar: To be sure, if there had been no obstacles to his being present among the people, it would have been more expedient and benecial to have him around. However, since God has chosen a state of invisible existence for him, and since God's acts are founded upon what is in the best interest of humanity, one should also believe, as one does in other instances, that in this case also the reason for occultation is also based on divine wisdom, about which we have simply an overall knowledge, the details being unknown to us. The following hadith corroborates the point we are trying to make, namely, that the actual reason for occultation was not explained for the people, and except for the Imams themselves no one knew anything about it.

The hadith is reported by 'Abd Allah b. Fadl Hashimi. He relates: Imam Sadiq said: "The one entrusted with the command will necessarily live an invisible life. This will lead those who are already astray into doubt." So I asked the Imam the reason. He said: "I am not permitted to reveal the reason." I went on to seek the philosophy behind the invisible life [of the Imam of the Age].

He said: "It is the same wisdom that existed in the prior situation when other proofs of God also went into occultation. However, the true understanding behind this occurrence will not take place until after he has reappeared, just as the wisdom behind making the boat defective, killing the boy, and repairing the falling wall [in the story of Moses and Khidr in the Qur'an] were revealed to Moses only after the two had decided to part company.

O the son of Fadl! The subject of occultation is among the divine secrets and a concealed matter whose knowledge is only with God. Since we regard God to be wise we must also afrm that His acts are based on that perfect wisdom, even when the detailed understanding is not accessible to us."[249]

The hadith certainly points to the fact that the main reason for the occultation was not explained to the people either because it was not suitable for the people or because they had no preparation to grasp it. But there are other traditions in which three benets are given for the occultation of the Imam:

1) The benet of being tested and puried: There are some who do not have strong faith. Through the requirement of believing in such a phenomenon as the invisible existence of the Imam their true inner self is made manifest. Then there are those who do have strong faith in hidden things, but because of the prolonged concealment and their awaiting for the deliverance so long, they have suffered a lot. Such people should receive proper recognition and should reap rewards for their steadfastness and patience. Imam Musa Kazim has related

---

[249] Bihar al-anwar, Vol. 52, p. 91

this situation in the following hadith:

When the fth descendant of the seventh Imam disappears watch out for your faith. God forbid, if someone may drive you away from your religion. O my son! Undoubtedly, the Master of the Command will have such an occultation that a group of believers will turn away from religion. God will test the believers with the occultation [of their Imam].[250]

2) The benet of being relieved from having to pay allegiance to unjust rulers. There is a tradition reported by Hasan b. Faddal from Imam Rida, who said:

"I see my followers in the aftermath of the death of my third descendant [i.e., Imam Hasan 'Askari) looking for their Imam everywhere and not nding him." I asked him the reason for that. He said: "Because their Imam will have entered the state of occultation." I went on to ask the reason for the occultation. He said: "This will be so that when he reappears he will have paid no allegiance to anyone."[251]

3) The benet of being immune from murder. Zurara reports the hadith from Imam Sadiq, who said:

"The Qa'im must live an invisible existence." I asked for the reason. He said: "He is afraid of being killed," and pointed to his stomach.

These three benets are reported in various ways in a number of traditions, especially those reported from the ahl al-bayt.

---

[250] Ibid., Vol. 52, p. 113

[251] Ibid., Vol. 51, p. 153

What Danger Faced the Imam If He Were Visibly Present?

Engineer Madani: If the Imam of the Age were visibly present among people, he would have been living in one of the cities of the world, guiding and directing the religious lives of the Muslims, and continuing to full his obligations until the conditions of the world became favorable. At that time he would have been able to launch his revolution and destroy the power of disbelief and injustice. What is wrong with this supposition?

Mr. Hoshyar: I do not see any problem with the supposition. However, we should evaluate its overall impact. Let me try to analyze the situation under ordinary circumstances.

It is important to keep in mind that the Prophet and the Imams had time and again informed the people regarding the major function of the awaited Mahdi, namely, the destruction of the tyrannical powers and the rectication of injustices committed by them. Because of this, two kinds of people were bound to pay particular attention to the presence of the Imam:

First, those who were wronged and persecuted and, unfortunately, whose number has always been large. This group would have rallied around the Imam and put enormous pressure on him to redress the wrongs committed against them and defend their rights. In other words, there would have been endless turmoil and chaos resulting from the rising and revolutions.

Second, those who were in power and were the source of corruption and ill treatment of the people. These tyrants were not afraid to employ any unjust means to remain in power and protect their interests. In fact, they were willing to sacrice their entire population as long as they retained power. Since they saw the presence of the Imam as a threat and an obstacle to their own interests, they were bound to remove him at any cost so that they could continue to rule. In fact, at times the rulers were united in their elimination of the major threat to their power, namely, the awaited Mahdi. Hence, they were determined to annihilate the source of justice and equity among the people.

Why Is the Mahdi Afraid of Being Killed?

Dr. Jalali: What would be wrong with the Imam suffering death in the path of reforming society and disseminating the true religion and defending the oppressed? Is his blood more dear than that of his forefathers who also suffered martyrdom in defending the religion of God? My question is why at all should he be afraid of being killed?

Mr. Hoshyar: The Imam of the Age, like his forefathers, is not afraid of being killed. Nevertheless, his being killed is not in the interest of the society or the religion. The reason is that whereas when his forefathers were killed they had their offspring to succeed them, the twelfth Imam does not have a son to succeed him should he be killed, and surely the earth cannot remain without God's Proof on it. It is well established that it is God's will that truth shall become triumphant over falsehood and that through the existence of the twelfth Imam the world will become the abode of godfearing people.

Does Not God Have the Power to Protect the Imam?

Dr. Jalali: Does not God have the power to protect the Imam from the threat posed by his evil enemies?

Mr. Hoshyar: To be sure, God's power is unlimited. However, generally God does things in the most normal fashion, using the regular channel of causation. Moreover, God does not want religion or the messengers and leaders of religion to be protected in an extraordinary way, to deprive people of their freedom of choice and of facing the consequences of their choices. Coercion in these matters would divest human beings of their dignity. On the other hand, as free agents, human beings would face the testing and purication that becomes possible by accepting to follow the guidance of truth provided in the religious teachings of the Prophet and the Imams (peace be upon them).

Is It Not Likely That the Unjust Rulers Would Have Submitted to Him?

Dr. Jalali: If the Imam were visibly present then the oppressors would have access to him and would have heard his teachings and probably would have given up on the idea of killing him. On the contrary, they would have probably been guided and would have abandoned their unjust ways.

Mr. Hoshyar: Not everyone submits to the truth. From the beginning of human history till our own times, there has been a group on earth that has vehemently opposed truth and been the enemy of justice.

Moreover, they have tried with all their might to destroy both truth and justice. Did not the Prophets and the Imams teach the truth? Did not the oppressors and unjust rulers have access to their miracles and teachings? In spite of all that, they never hesitated to silence these voices of justice and put out these rays of guidance by the means that were available to them. If the twelfth Imam had not disappeared because of the fear of these tyrants, he too may have suffered the same fate as his forefathers.

He Should Remain Silent So That He Would Be Safe

Dr. Jalali: In my view, if the Imam had entirely withdrawn from politics and had remained silent in the face of these tyrannical rulers' conduct, while continuing to provide moral and religious guidance, he would have been spared from the evil of his enemies.

Mr. Hoshyar: Since the oppressors had heard that the promised Mahdi is their enemy and that, through him, their palaces of injustice would be razed to the ground, they would not have been satised with his silence and non-critical approach to their unjust rule. They would have deemed it necessary to get rid of the potential danger to their power. Moreover, when the followers of the Imam saw the silence of the Imams endlessly, year after year, in the face of all the injustices inicted upon them and their followers, they would have lost hope in the reform of the world and the victory of truth, and would have doubted in the truthfulness of the promises contained in the Prophet's hadith-reports and the Qur'an. In addition, it is inconceivable that the oppressed and the downtrodden would have permitted the Imam to remain silent.

He Could Have Negotiated a Treaty of Non-interference with the Rulers

Engineer Madani: Would it not have been possible for the Imam to negotiate a treaty of non-interference with the rulers, assuring them that he would not interfere in the workings of their government? In that way he would have established his credibility and truthfulness in observing the terms of his treaty and, in return, the rulers would have left him alone.

Mr. Hoshyar: You must keep this in mind that the function of the awaited Mahdi is different from that of the other Imams who preceded him. The other Imams were under obligation to "command the good and forbid the evil" to their best ability. But they were not required to undertake warfare. On the contrary, from the beginning the role of the Mahdi was to be different. The Mahdi would rise against oppression and injustice. He would not keep silent in the face of corruption; rather, he would undertake warfare (jihad) to uproot oppression and ungodliness. He would actually destroy evil forces. These functions were part and parcel of the signs of the appearance of the Mahdi.

All other Imams were asked by their followers at different times:

"Why do not you rise against the oppressors?" They used to answer: "That task is upon our Mahdi." Some Imams were asked: "Are you the Mahdi?" The answer was: "Mahdi will rise with a sword and will ght injustice. But I am not like that, nor do I have the power to do so." Some of them were asked: "Are you the Qa'im?" The reply was: "Yes, I am the one entrusted with truth (qa'im bi-haqq). However, I am not that promised Qa'im who will cleanse the earth of disbelief and injustice." Sometimes the hope was expressed by some in the community: "I hope that you are the Qa'im!"

The answer was: "I am the Qa'im. But the Qa'im who will purify the earth of disbelief and oppression is other than me." When people used to complain about the social and political turmoil and the tyranny of the unjust government and the mistreatment and hardship suffered by the followers of the Imams, the consolation was offered by saying: "The rise of Mahdi is certain. At that time the situation in the world will improve and the revenge against the tyrannical people will be exacted." At other times people would talk about the large number of their enemies and their power compared to their own small number and powerlessness.

The Imams used to comfort their followers and assure them: "The government of the Prophet's rightful successor is a certainty. The nal victory belongs to the followers of truth. Be steadfast and pray and expect deliverance through the descendant of Muhammad (peace be upon him and his progeny)." The believers and the followers of the Imams were waiting for this deliverance to come and willingly accepted adverse and painful situations created by their opponents.

Now let me ask you, in all fairness, with all these expectations of deliverance through the promised Mahdi that the believers had, do you think that he would have negotiated a treaty of non-interference with the unjust rulers of his time? If he had done that, would he not have shattered all the hopes of his followers and caused them to blame him for selling out to the enemies? In my opinion, such a compromise on the part of the Imam is impossible. Actually, the adverse impact of such a compromise would have led these followers of the Imam to abandon their faith and even pursue injustices to combat persecution.

Moreover, if the Imam had signed a non-intervention and friendship treaty with the unjust authorities, he would have been inevitably bound to the terms of such a document. As a result, at no time would he have undertaken to ght, because Islam regards a treaty binding on those who have agreed to its terms.[252] It is for this reason that many hadith-reports make it explicitly clear that one of the purposes of the occultation and the secrecy surrounding the birth of the last Imam is that he should not become obliged to pay allegiance to the rulers so that whenever he wishes to rise there should be no such obligation on him. In the following tradition Imam Sadiq said:

The birth of the Master of the Command will remain a secret so that when he rises he will have no obligation to abide by any agreement. God will bring about his task in the matter of one night.[253]

Besides all that we have said so far, the oppressors and unjust rulers could never have felt secure with such an agreement, mainly because of the perceived danger to their power. Hence, they regarded murdering him as the only solution for assuring their continued control over the affairs of humanity. They would have, as a consequence, rendered the earth devoid of God's proof.

---

[252] There are a number of passages in the Qur'an that require Muslims to abide by the terms of the treaty to which they are signatories. See, for instance, Sura Ma'ida, 1; Mu'minun, 8; and Isra', 34

[253] Bihar al-anwar, Vol. 52, p. 96x

Why Did He Not Appoint Special Deputies During the Complete Occultation?

Dr. Jalali: We accept in principle the necessity of occultation for the Imam. But, the question arises as to why did he not appoint his special deputies during the Complete Occultation as he had done during the Short Occultation? Such an appointment would have enabled the Shi'a to establish contact with him and ask for his assistance in solving their problems.

Mr. Hoshyar: The enemies did not leave the deputies in peace either. They were imprisoned and tortured so that they would reveal the whereabouts of the Hidden Imam (peace be upon him).

Dr. Jalali: Well, in that case perhaps it was possible for him not to appoint specic individuals as his deputies. However, from time to time he could appear for some of his followers through whom he could convey his injunctions for the community.

Mr. Hoshyar: Even this approach was not feasible because in all likelihood that very person to whom the Imam had appeared would have revealed his domicile to the enemy, leading to the arrest and murder of the Imam.

Dr. Jalali: Such a danger would have been possible if he had appeared in front of any unknown person. But if he had appeared for some trustworthy persons among his followers, the probability of impending danger would have been absent.

Mr. Hoshyar: Your supposition can be refuted on several grounds:

First, if the Imam had decided to appear for anyone he would have needed to perform a miracle to introduce himself. In fact, for a cynical individual he might have been required to perform several miracles so that, that person would accept him as his Imam. Among these individuals there was a possibility that there would be some who would resort to trickery and fraud through magic to deceive and mislead the ordinary believers and even claim to be the Imam himself! By the way, it is not possible for everyone to distinguish between a miracle and an act of magic. This very difculty would have led to further corruption among the people, leading to a disastrous situation.

Second, there were actually some shrewd impostors and fraudulent individuals who had abused such incidents for their own personal ambitions. They used to claim to have seen the Imam and spread laws contrary to the Shari'a on his authority so that they could achieve their evil designs. Whoever intended to do something against the law and further his own ends used to claim that he had reached the presence of the Imam of the Age and that the Imam had come to his house the previous night and had told him that he should do such and such or that the Imam approved what he was doing, and so on. The dangerous consequences of such claims is too self-evident to require any further elaboration.

Third, we do not have any unequivocal proof that the Imam of the Age does not appear for anyone highly trustworthy among his followers. Rather, it is quite likely that his pious and godly followers might reach his presence and might be under oath to keep that secret, without revealing it to anyone. In such cases, everyone is bound to their own experience and has no right to judge any one else.

What Is the Benefit of Having the Imam in Occultation?

Engineer Madani: If the Imam is the leader of the people he should be present among them. What is the benefit of having an Imam who lives an invisible life? What is the use of having an Imam who lives in the state of occultation for centuries without fulfilling any of the functions that he normally undertakes: such as propagating religion, solving the problems of society, responding to the attacks of his opponents, commanding the good and forbidding the evil, helping the poor and redressing the wrongs committed against the downtrodden, upholding the ordinances of God by instituting proper penalties and explaining the lawful and the unlawful to the people, and so on.

Mr. Hoshyar: The people are surely deprived of the benefits that you have enumerated during the occultation. However, the benefits of the Imam's presence are not limited to these. In fact, there are other benefits that are available during the occultation. The following two are among those many other benefits that you have not enumerated:

First, in accord with all that we have said previously and the proofs that were derived from the writings of Muslim scholars, including the hadith-reports that spoke about the necessity of the Imamate, the existence of the Imam as a perfect and unique embodiment of humanity serves as a link between the material and the spiritual world. If the Imam is absent the human species will be extinct. If there is no Imam then God cannot be known or worshipped perfectly. Without the Imam the link between the material and the spiritual become severed.

The heart of the Imam is like the source of electricity that distributes light to numerous lamps. The illumination and energization of the hidden universe rst mirrors on the heart of the Imam and then from there it reects on the hearts of humankind. The Imam is the heart of the created universe and the leader and guide of humankind. It is evident that his presence and absence have an impact upon these actualities. After all these, can one ask what benet accrues from the invisible existence of the Imam?

I think that you are raising this objection on behalf of someone else who does not have a real understanding of the meaning of wilayat and the Imamate and who does not see the Imam as more than a legal expert and an administrator of justice, whereas the responsibilities of the wilayat and the Imamate are much more than these external functions.

In a long tradition reported from Imam Sadiq it is related that Imam Sajjad said:

We are the leaders of the Muslims, God's proofs for His creatures, masters of the believers, guides for the godfearing, and those invested with discretionary authority over the affairs of Muslims. We are the security for the dwellers of the earth, just as the stars are the security of the dwellers of the heavens. It is because of us that the heavens descend on the earth whenever God permits. It is because of us that the rain descends and blessings of earth come out of it. If we had not been on earth its dwellers would have been consumed in it.

He then went on to say:

From the day God created Adam until today He has not left the earth without a competent authority (=proof=hujjat). But this authority is sometimes manifest and well known; at other times he is in occultation and in concealment. The earth will not be void of such an authority until the Day of Judgement. If there is no Imam, God will not be worshipped.

Sulayman, the narrator, asked Imam Sadiq: "How can people benet from the existence of an Imam who is in occultation?" The Imam said: "In the same way as they benet from the sun behind the clouds."[254]

In this and other traditions of this kind the existence of the twelfth Imam and the benet derived from him are compared to the benet derived from the sun hidden behind the clouds. To elaborate on this imagery let us remind ourselves of the way natural science explains the phenomenon. It is established in natural science and in astronomy that the sun is the center of our solar system. The laws of gravity protect the earth from falling into an abyss, and permit the earth to revolve around the sun, generating the distinction between day and night and different seasons according to its position in relation to the sun.

The thermal energy produced by the sun is the source of life on earth and its light illuminates the otherwise dark earth. This benet accrues to the earth regardless of the fact of whether the sun is shining directly or from behind the clouds. In other words, all its functions (illumination, providing energy, growth, etc.) are intact even when it shines from behind the clouds. In fact, whether it is from behind the dark clouds or at night when we think the sun is not present, we are still recipients of the sun's thermal energy and all other benets that are critical for our survival on earth.

---

[254] Yanabi' al-mawadda, Vol. 2, p. 317

The existence of the Imam is like the sun behind the clouds that benets the dwellers of the earth. He is the heart of humankind and its existential guide. In order for his benets to reach humanity it does not matter whether he is manifest or in concealment. Let us recall our previous discussions about the necessity of the Prophethood and Imamate and review all their aspects so that we can appreciate the true meaning of wilayat. This review will help us to understand the most important benet of having an Imam from the progeny of the Prophet (peace be upon him and his progeny), whether manifest or in concealment. As we ponder this matter, we are actually enjoying the blessings of this Imam's invisible existence.

As for other benets enumerated by you, Engineer Madani, of which people are deprived, actually, both from the direction of God and from the existence of the Imam, there is no obstacle to these benets reaching the people. The problem is with the people themselves. If these obstructions could be removed and if the people worked towards creating the just order and toward preparing to launch God's government by spreading the right information and strengthening the character of the people to receive the Imam's leadership, then the Imam would appear to lead humanity towards the creation of the divine order on earth.

It is possible that someone might say: Under the circumstances when the overall situation is not favorable to the appearance of the Imam, why should we put ourselves in the dangerous situation of trying to prepare for his return? In response to this it must be pointed out that a Muslim's actions in this connection should not be motivated by the personal gain of some individuals; rather, it should become the goal of each and every person to endeavor for the social reforms affecting all people. Seriousness of purpose in improving the conditions of the people and in removing causes of injustice and tyranny in society are regarded as the most meritorious act of worship in Islam.

Again, it is possible that someone might say: The endeavors of one or a few individuals trying to change the conditions in society may come to nothing. Hence, one should not even try to do anything. Moreover, in principle, it might be asked what wrong have I done to be deprived of meeting my Imam? In response to this one can point out the benet that accrues to an individual and to the society in general when we endeavor to raise the standard of thinking and moral awareness among people, informing them about the lofty goals of Islam and bringing them closer to the goals of the Imam (peace be upon him). By doing so we have actually fullled our obligation as a follower of the Imam. In return, we have attained the highest reward of having furthered the realization of an ideal society, even if merely by a step. Any rational person can attest to this benet of striving to further the divine purposes for human society. It is for this reason that there are numerous traditions that speak about the merits of awaiting deliverance through the appearance of the twelfth Imam, and which regard this awaiting as a form of serving God.[255]

Second, faith in the Hidden Imam and awaiting deliverance through his return is a source of hope and peace for the hearts of the believers. Such a hope is one of the major causes of the success and advancement of the Islamic ideal. Any group of people that becomes bogged down by pessimism and despair also suffers from self-imposed negativism that leads to the defeat of the purpose.

There is no doubt that the social and political turmoil in many parts of the world, the decline of moral and ethical vision, the deprivation and poverty suffered by the downtrodden, the spread of tools of various forms of imperialistic intervention in the affairs of the weaker societies, the arms race among the powerful countries –all these –

---

[255] Bihar al-anwar, Vol. 52, p. 122-150

have led sensitive and conscientious thinkers around the globe to become concerned and even, to a certain extent, pessimistic about the ability of human society to deliver itself from its self-cultivated gradual destruction.

The only door that has remained open for humanity is the door of hope in the darkness of despair. That hope lies in the divine intervention in human affairs by the sending of a divinely guided leader, the Mahdi, to establish a godly society founded upon the divinely ordained laws. Indeed, it is this hope that gives solace to the disturbed hearts of those who have suffered injustices. It is the hope of seeing that government based on the acknowledgement of the Unity of God which has safeguarded the faith of the people, and has made them rm in their commitments to God. It is faith in the ultimate victory of truth that has made these people seek an active role in working towards social reforms and other related matters.

Seeking the help of God under these circumstances helps human beings to avoid becoming hopeless in the face of continued atrocities and wrongs committed against the innocent. The Prophet (peace be upon him and his progeny) laid the foundation of this positive attitude by introducing the universal program of reform under the divinely guided leadership that will undertake to unite human resources in creating the ethical order proclaimed in the Qur'an.

Imam Zayn al-'Abidin has conveyed this positive aspect of the hope of deliverance in the tradition in which he says: "To hope for deliverance and release in itself functions as the most profound form of deliverance."[256]

To conclude our discussion at this point, faith in the promised Mahdi has made it possible for the Shi'a community to hope and work for the ideal. It has eliminated the negative spirit of pessimism,

---

[256] Ibid., p. 122

engendering in it the positive spirit of condence in the human ability to work for its betterment. The belief has, furthermore, required the followers of the twelfth Imam to ght against the forces of disbelief, materialism, corruption, and injustice, and to work for the government of God, the perfection of the human intellect and the establishment of true peace through justice on earth, and to further human knowledge and technology. It is for this reason that the hope for deliverance during the occultation has been regarded as the best form of divine worship and martyrdom in the path of truth in the numerous traditions reported from the ahl al-bayt.[257]

---

[257] Ibid., p. 122-150

The Twelfth Imam Endeavors to Defend Islam during the Occultation

One of the orations of the Nahj al-balagha points to the fact that the Imam of the Age during the occultation also is engaged in furthering the cause of Islam and solving the problems faced by the Muslims as much as he can. Imam 'Ali b. Abi Talib said:

They (i.e., Muslims) took to the right and the left piercing through to the ways of evil and leaving the paths of guidance. Do not make haste for a matter which is to happen and is awaited, and do not wish for delay in what the morrow is to bring for you. For, how many people make haste for a matter, but when they get it they begin to wish they had not got it. How near is today to the dawning of tomorrow. O people, this is the time for the occurrence of every promised event and the approach of things which you do not know.

Whoever from us (i.e., ahl al-bayt) will exist during these days will move through them with a burning lamp and will tread on the footsteps of the virtuous, in order to unfasten knots, to free slates, to divide the united and unite the divided. He will be in concealment (sitra) from people. The stalker will not nd his footprints even though he pursues with his eye. Then a group of people will be sharpened like the sharpening of swords by the blacksmith. Their sight will be brightened by the revelation (tanzil, i.e., the Qur'an), the interpretation will be put in their ears and they will be given drinks of wisdom, morning and evening.[258]

The apparent sense of this oration suggests that during the time of 'Ali b. Abi Talib, people were awaiting events about which the Prophet had informed them. In all probability, it was information related to the occultation. The presumable sense of the oration suggests the Imam during the period of concealment would live an extremely veiled life. But he will endeavor to solve the problems facing the community with deep insight and will vindicate the sanctity of Islam. He will remove the difculties and will come to the aid of the wronged ones. He will disperse the group that would have come together to destroy the Islamic foundations. He will eliminate all the organizations that he would identify as being detrimental to the purposes of God. He will provide the necessary preliminaries needed for bringing about a benecial society. With the blessed presence of the Imam of the Age a group of people will be trained to defend the religion, and will be inspired by the Qur'anic sciences in their resolutions about the ideal Muslim society.

Dr. Fahimi: I wanted you to explain to me the reason as to why in our traditions, that is the Sunni hadith, the existence of the Mahdi, especially his other names like Qa'im and Sahib al-'amr (the Master of the Command = the one entrusted with the command), is not mentioned. However, since it is getting very late in the night, I should keep this question for our next session.

* * *

---

[258] Nahj al-balagha, Vol. 2, Sermon No. 146

To be sure, it was quite late at night. The meeting was adjourned with the next date announced. It was decided that we should meet at Dr. Fahimi's house.

The session began on time at Dr. Fahimi's house. Dr. Fahimi welcomed the group and without wasting much time formulated his question with a brief introduction outlining the problem as he saw it.

Dr. Fahimi: The personality of the Mahdi in the Shi'i traditions is prominent and clear. However, in the Sunni traditions it is mentioned briey and that also with much ambiguity. For example, the story of his occultation which is recorded in the majority of your traditions, and which is regarded as the fundamental aspect of his attributes, is entirely absent in our traditions. The promised Mahdi in your hadith has different names such as Qa'im, Master of the Command and so on, which, in our sources, is lacking and he is mentioned only by one name, that is, Mahdi. More particularly, the Qa'im is totally missing in our hadith. Do you regard this as something normal, or do you see a problem with such an absence?

Mr. Hoshyar: Apparently, the reason could be that during the Umayyad and 'Abbasid periods the subject of Mahdiism had assumed a political dimension. As such the recording and dissemination of the traditions about the promised Mahdi, especially the signs of his appearance and all the details dealing with his occultation and revolution, was suppressed. The rulers were extremely fearful of the spread of the hadith about the occultation and subsequent emergence of the Mahdi. They were certainly sensitive about the terms 'occultation', 'rise', and 'insurrection'.

If you refer to the historical sources and study the social and political conditions that prevailed under the Umayyad and the 'Abbasid caliphate, you will agree with my explanation as to why such information was suppressed by these caliphs and their administrators. In this short time we cannot go into any detail to investigate the major events of the period. However, to prove our point we have to direct our attention to two important issues:

First, since the story of Mahdiism had deep religious roots and since the Prophet himself had given the information that when disbelief and materialism become widespread and injustice and tyranny become the order of the day, the Mahdi will rise and will restore the pure religion and ethical order. It was for this reason that Muslims always regarded this prophecy as a source of great consolation and awaited it to be fullled. Under adverse conditions when they had lost all hope for the restoration of justice, the prophecy was even more in circulation, and those who sought reform, including those who had the ambition to abuse the simple faith of the people, took advantage of this prediction.

The rst person who took advantage of the people's faith in Mahdiism and its religious underpinnings was Mukhtar. Following the tragic event of Karbala in 61 AH/680 CE, Mukhtar wanted to avenge the martyrs of Karbala and overthrow the Umayyad government. But he realized that the Hashimites and the Shi'is had lost hope in seizing the caliphate for themselves.

Consequently, he saw the belief in Mahdiism as the only way to awaken the people and make them hopeful. Since Muhammad b. Hanayya's name and patronymic were the same as that of the Prophet (peace be upon him and his progeny) (this was one of the recognized signs of the Mahdi) Mukhtar decided to seize the opportunity and introduced Muhammad b. Hanayya as the promised Mahdi and himself as his vizier and envoy. He told the people that Muhammad b. Hanayya was the promised Mahdi of Islam.

At the time when the oppression and tyranny were increasing and Husayn b. 'Ali, his family, and companions were killed mercilessly at Karbala, the Mahdi had decided to rise in order to avenge the martyrs of Karbala, and restore justice on earth as it had been lled with wickedness. He then introduced himself as the Mahdi's representative. In this manner Mukhtar launched an insurrection and killed a group of murderers who had participated in killing Imam Husayn. This was, by the way, the rst time that an insurrection had been launched against the caliphate.

The second person who manipulated the faith in the Mahdi for his own political ends was Abu Muslim of Khurasan. Abu Muslim organized a widespread movement against the Umayyads in Khurasan with the pretext of avenging the blood of Imam Husayn, his family and companions who were killed in the tragic event of Karbala. In addition, he rose to avenge the cruel murders of Zayd b. 'Ali during the caliphate of Hisham b. 'Abd al-Malik and of Yahya b. Zayd during the caliphate of Walid.

A group of people regarded Abu Muslim himself to be the awaited Mahdi. Others saw him as a forerunner of the Mahdi and as one of the signs that preceded the nal revolution under he who would appear with black banners from the direction of Khurasan. In this insurrection the 'Alids, 'Abbasids and all other Muslims formed a united front against the Umayyads that nally overthrew their rule over the empire.

Although these movements were heavily based on restoring the usurped rights of the ahl al-bayt and avenging the unjust murders of the 'Alids, the 'Abbasids and their supporters manipulated the insurrection to their own advantage. With treachery and treason they distorted the actual direction of the movement and seized power from the supporters of the 'Alids, thereby establishing themselves as the ahl al-bayt of the Prophet and as the new caliphs of Islam.

In this revolution, which was founded upon Shi'i ideals of justice and equity, the people had succeeded in proving their ability to overthrow the tyrannical rule of the Umayyads. They were pleased that they had eliminated the source of Umayyad corruption and had helped to return the right to rule to its rightful leaders among the ahl al-bayt. After all, they had at least succeeded in getting rid of Umayyad oppression. The success had led them to aspire to a better life and a more equitable society. In fact, they had congratulated each other in those terms.

However, within a short period they were awakened to the cruelty of the new dynasty, the 'Abbasids, and realized that the new rulers were not very different from those they had replaced. There was no change in their living conditions, no justice, no equity, and no peace. Their lives and property were not secure from the worldly rulers and administrators of the new state. The promised reforms and promulgation of the divine ordinances were far from being realized. Gradually, as people became aware of the failure of the revolution they had helped to launch, they became conscious of their error in judgement regarding the 'Abbasids and their deception in the name of the promised Mahdi.

The 'Alid leaders also found the 'Abbasid behavior towards them and towards Islam and the Muslims not very different from that of the Umayyads. In fact, the 'Abbasids proved themselves to be even more manipulative and brutal towards the descendants of 'Ali b. Abi Talib. They were left with no alternative than to launch their resistance anew and ght the 'Abbasids also. The best persons among them to lead such resistance were undoubtedly the descendants of 'Ali and Fatima (peace be upon them).

The reason was that there were a number of their descendants who were known for their piety, wisdom, knowledge and courage. In fact, they were regarded as more qualied candidates for the caliphate. Moreover, they were the true descendants of the Prophet and their direct lineage to him generated a sense of loyalty and love for them. In addition, because their rights had been usurped and they had suffered wrongs at the hands of the Umayyads, the masses had a natural inclination and sympathy for the ahl al-bayt.

Consequently, as the 'Abbasids persisted in committing atrocities against the ahl al-bayt the people were, more than ever before, drawn towards them and rallied to their cause in opposing the rulers and in rebelling against them. In addition, they made use of the notion of the Mahdi that had from the time of the Prophet taken deep roots in the minds and hearts of Muslims and introduced their revolutionary leader as the promised Mahdi. This required the 'Abbasids to confront some of the most popular, highly respected, and very learned rivals to their power.

The 'Abbasid caliphs knew the 'Alawid leaders well, being fully aware of their personal qualities and honorable family lineage and the prophecies that were foretold by the Prophet about the future coming of the Mahdi, the restorer of Islamic purity. They knew that in accordance with the traditions reported from the Prophet the awaited Mahdi would be one of the descendants of Fatima (peace be upon her). He would be the one to rise against tyranny and oppression and establish the rule of justice on earth.

Moreover, they knew that his victory was guaranteed.

The promise of justice through the appearance of the Mahdi had an enormous spiritual impact upon the people and the caliphal authority was fully informed about its potentially explosive repercussions in the empire. It is probably correct to say that the most formidable challenge to 'Abbasid authority was from these 'Alawid leaders, who had caused them to loosen their grip on the regions under their control and face the consequences of their corrupt rule.

The strategy that was adopted by the 'Abbasids in the light of this growing opposition to them was to divide the followers of these 'Alawid leaders and prevent them from rallying around them. The leaders themselves were kept under constant surveillance and, the famous ones among them were either imprisoned or eliminated. According to Ya'qubi, the historian, the 'Abbasid caliph Musa Hadi tried his utmost to arrest the prominent descendants of 'Ali b. Abi Talib. He had even terrorized them and had sent instructions all over his realm demanding that they be arrested and sent to him.[259] Similarly, Abu Faraj Isfahani writes: "When Mansur became the caliph all he was concerned about was the arrest of Muhammad b. 'Abd Allah b. Hasan [b. 'Ali b. Abi Talib] and nding out about his plans [regarding his claim to being the Mahdi]."[260]

---

[259] Ta'rikh (Najaf edition, 1384 AH), Vol. 3, p. 142

[260] Maqatil al-talibiyyin, p. 233-234

The Occultation of the 'Alawid Leaders

One of the issues that was extremely sensitive and worth investigating was the claim to invisible existence or occultation of some of the 'Alawid leaders. Any one among them who had the personal ability and qualities to become the leader immediately attracted the people who then rallied around him with dedication. This attraction took an extreme and intense form if that person happened to possess one of the signs of the expected Mahdi. On the other hand, as soon as a person became the rallying point for the people, the caliphal authority became fearful of the opposition and undertook to keep a close watch over its underground activities and even to curtail its growing popularity among the masses by using terror as a means of repressing revolutionary fervor. Under these circumstances, the leader had to live in concealment to protect himself. A number of these 'Alawid leaders lived a life of concealment for a number of years. Among them are the following examples cited by Abu Faraj Isfahani:

1. During the time of Mansur, the 'Abbasid caliph, Muhammad b. 'Abd Allah b. Hasan and his brother Ibrahim lived an invisible

life. Mansur had tried several times to arrest them. A number of the Hashimite leaders were imprisoned and they were grilled to reveal the whereabouts of their messianic leader Muhammad b. 'Abd Allah. At the end of the day the prisoners were tortured in various ways and killed.[261]

2. 'Isa b. Zayd lived in retreat and concealment during Mansur's caliphate. Mansur made every effort to arrest him, but he failed. Following him, his son Mahdi also tried, but without any success.[262]

3. During the caliphate of Mu'tasim and Wathiq, Muhammad b. Qasim 'Alawi lived an invisible life in concealment and was regarded as being in occultation by the establishment. He was, however, arrested during Mutawakkil's caliphate and died while in prison.[263]

4. During the caliphate of Harun Rashid, Yahya b. 'Abd Allah b. Hasan lived in concealment. But he was nally discovered by the caliph's spies. At rst he was given amnesty, but later he was arrested and incarcerated. He died in Rashid's prison of hunger and other forms of torture.[264]

5. During the caliphate of Ma'mun, 'Abd Allah b. Musa lived in concealment and because of him Ma'mun lived in constant fear and anxiety.[265]

Musa Hadi appointed one of the descendants of 'Umar b. Khattab by the name of 'Abd al-'Aziz as the governor of Madina. 'Abd al-'Aziz

---

[261] Ibid., p. 233-299

[262] Ibid., p. 405-427

[263] Ibid., p. 577-88

[264] Ibid.,p. 463-483

[265] Ibid., p. 519

used to treat the 'Alids very harshly. He kept them under constant surveillance, watching their movements very closely. He used to force them to appear in his audience every day so that they would not disappear. He actually exacted promises from them to that effect and made each one of them answerable for the other.

Thus, for instance, Husayn b. 'Ali and Yahya b. 'Abd Allah were made responsible for Hasan b. Muhammad b. 'Abd Allah b. Hasan. On one of the Fridays when the 'Alawids were all gathered in his presence he did not allow them to return until it was time for Friday prayer service. At that time he permitted them to perform their ablutions and prepare for the worship. After the prayer was over he ordered all of them arrested. During the late afternoon prayer he asked them to attend the court and later dismissed them. It was then that 'Abd al-'Aziz noticed that Hasan b. Muhammad b. 'Abd Allah was not present. So he called Husayn b. 'Ali and Yahya b. 'Abd Allah, who were answerable for him, and informed them that for the past three days Hasan b. Muhammad had not appeared in his audience.

As such, he had either revolted or disappeared. Since they were answerable for him they had to nd Hasan and bring him to 'Abd al-'Aziz, otherwise they would be imprisoned. To this Yahya replied: "He

must have been occupied and, therefore, did not show up. It is not possible for us also to bring him back. Justice is a good thing. Just as you keep a check on us making sure who is present and who is not, why do not you ask the descendants of 'Umar b. Khattab also to appear in the audience? See how many are present, and if their absentees are not more than ours then we have no objection to your decision. Do as you please and take any decision regarding us." 'Abd al-'Aziz was not satised with their response. He swore that if they did not nd Hasan and bring him to him he would demolish their homes, set their goods on re and whip Husayn b. 'Ali.²⁶⁶

Episodes like this reveal that the topic of invisible existence or occultation of the 'Alawid leaders was one of the regular issues during the 'Abbasid era. As soon as one of them disappeared from public life he became the center of attention from two directions: on the one hand, the masses, who knew that occultation was one of the signs of the Mahdi, were attracted towards him; on the other hand, the caliphal authority had developed an extreme sense of anxiety because of the explosive ramications of such a disappearance for the security of its power.

After all, it was one of the signs of the Mahdi, and when the people were told of the disappearance of these 'Alids they speculated of their being the promised messianic leader who would overthrow the tyrannical government of the 'Abbasids. Hence, the authorities were worried about the ensuing chaos and political turmoil unfolding in front of their eyes which the caliphal power would have difculty in repressing.

Now that you have familiarized yourself with the critical social and political conditions that existed during the 'Abbasid period and during which the hadith books were compiled and composed, it is important to bear in mind that the authors of these works and the transmitters of the hadith did not possess the freedom to record all the hadith-reports dealing with the promised Mahdi, and more particularly, traditions dealing with the occultation and the rise of the awaited Mahdi.

Is it possible to maintain that the 'Abbasids did not have any involvement or inuence over the events in which Mahdi'ism had taken a political form? Or, that they would permit the transmitters of the traditions about the messianic role of the Mahdi and his

---

²⁶⁶ Ibid., p. 294-296

occultation to freely record and publicize the traditions that would have actually been to their own detriment?

It is possible that you may contend that the 'Abbasids knew at least this much: that it was not in the interest of the society to impose restrictions over the scholars and to interfere with their scholarly work. Rather, the scholars and the transmitters of the hadith-reports should be left alone to present the truth to the people and make them aware of their responsibilities. Well, we should cite some examples in which the 'Abbasids and their predecessors, that is the Umayyads and the early caliphs, restricted free expression and hence suppressed traditions that were against their political domination.

Violations of Free Expression under the Caliphs

Ibn 'Asakir has related a tradition in which, according to 'Abd al-Rahman b. 'Awf, 'Umar b. Khattab sent for some of the prominent companions of the Prophet, including 'Abd Allah b. Hudhayfa, Abu Darda', Abu Dharr Ghiffari, and 'Uqba b. 'Amir, and reproached them saying: "What are these traditions that you are relating and spreading among the people?" The companions said: "Apparently, you want to stop us from transmitting the traditions." 'Umar said: "You have no right to step outside Madina, and as long as I am alive do not distance yourselves from me. I know better which hadith should be accepted and which should be rejected." The companions had no choice but to stay in Madina as long as 'Umar lived.[267]

Ibn Sa'd and Ibn 'Asakir have related that Mahmud b. 'Ubayd heard 'Uthman b. 'Affan telling people from the pulpit: "No one has the right to relate a tradition that was not narrated during Abu Bakr and

---

[267] As cited by Mahmud Abwar, Adwa' 'ala-al-sunna al- Muhammadiyya, p. 54

'Umar's time."²⁶⁸

During his reign Mu'awiya had sent ofcial directions that his security was removed from anyone who reported a tradition in praise of 'Ali b. Abi Talib and his descendants. At another time he sent a written command that whereas the people should narrate the merits of the companions and the caliphs, they should be forced to relate for all the other companions merit a similar to that which was attributed to 'Ali.²⁶⁹

In the year 218 AH/833 CE, Ma'mun ordered all the scholars and jurists of Iraq and other places to attend an audience. He then went on to question them about their beliefs and asked them specically regarding their belief about the Qur'an, whether it was the created or eternal Word of God. He condemned those who maintained that it was not created and instructed his governors in all provinces to reject their testimony. With the exception of a few, the decision forced a majority of the scholars to concede to the caliph's viewpoint.²⁷⁰

Malik b. Anas, the great jurist of Madina, had issued a legal opinion contrary to the wishes of Ja'far b. Sulayman, the governor of Madina. The latter required him to present himself in his court where he was rst humiliated and then whipped severely with seventy lashes. This caused him to be bed-ridden for some time. Later on, Mansur sent for Malik. In the beginning he apologized for Malik's having been treated so harshly by Ja'far b. Sulayman. Then he asked him to write a book on law and traditions. "But be careful not to include difcult traditions narrated by 'Abd Allah b. 'Umar, trivial topics related by 'Abd Allah b. 'Abbas, and the rare hadith reported by Ibn Mas'ud. Include only those things on which the caliphs and the companions

---

²⁶⁸ Ibid

²⁶⁹ Sayyid Muhammad b. 'Aqil, al-Nasa'ih al-kafiya, p. 78, 88

²⁷⁰ Ya'qubi, Ta'rikh, Vol. 3, p. 202

had agreed. Write this book so that I can send it to all cities and require people to strictly follow only this book, and none other."

Malik complained that the scholars from Iraq held variant opinions on matters related to law and hence would not accept his opinions. Mansur asked him to write the book anyway and assured him that he would impose it even on the people of Iraq. "If they do not submit, I will behead them and will punish them severely. Hence, be quick in writing this book. Next year my son Mahdi will come to you to get it."[271]

The 'Abbasid caliph Mu'tasim required Ahmad b. Hanbal to appear in the court and tested him about his belief in the Qur'an. When Ahmad refused to submit to the caliph's belief about the created Qur'an, he ordered him to be whipped.[272] Similarly, Mansur enticed Abu Hanifa to come to Baghdad and eventually he poisoned him.[273] Harun Rashid ordered 'Abbad b. 'Awam's house destroyed and prohibited him from transmitting traditions.[274]

Khalid b. Ahmad, the governor of Bukhara, asked Muhammad b. Isma'il Bukhari, one of the major compilers of Sunni traditions, to bring his written traditions to him and read them. Bukhari refused to do so and sent him a message that if he did not wish him to collect traditions he should say so, so that he could have a valid excuse for not doing so on the Day of Judgement. It was for that reason that he was deported from his homeland. He took refuge in a small village known as Khartang where he lived until his death. The narrator relates that he heard Bukhari pray to God in his midnight prayer: "O God, if the earth has turned narrow for me, then take my life away."

---

[271] al-Imama wa al-siyasa, Vol. 2, pp. 177-180

[272] Ya'qubi, Ta'rikh, Vol. 3, p. 206

[273] Maqatil, p. 368

[274] Ibid., p. 241

It was the same month in which he died.[275]

When another traditionist Nasa'i wrote his book Khasa'is, in which he included traditions in praise of 'Ali b. Abi Talib, he was asked to appear in Damascus and was ordered to write a similar book in praise of Mu'awiya. He declined to write such a book because he could not nd any materials praising him except what the Prophet had said about him: "May God never ll his stomach!" Because of this statement Nasa'i was beaten up so badly that he died of it.[276]

---

[275] Ta'rikh Baghdad, Vol. 2, p. 33

[276] al-Nasa'ih al-Kafiya, p . 109

The Implications of the Situation

In view of the political turmoil and social unrest that existed under the 'Abbasids and the activist message of the traditions that deal with Mahdi'ism, especially the disappearance of and eventual revolution under the Mahdi which had taken on a political dimension, the masses were attracted to the promises of a better future that were made in these messianic traditions. Moreover in the unfavorable conditions that existed for the authors and compilers of such traditions, it was almost unthinkable that they would publish traditions dealing with the signs of the appearance of the Mahdi, his invisible existence and his ultimate emergence with the mission of destroying the wicked forces of injustice. More importantly, it is highly improbable that the ruling dynasties would have permitted the publication and dissemination of the information that was available to these scholars. The publication of such ideas was deemed a danger that directly threatened the stability of their unjust and illegitimate power.

Consequently, neither Malik b. Anas nor Abu Hanifa could have recorded any traditions dealing with Mahdi'ism and the occultation in their books. It is worth recalling that it was during this period that

Muhammad b. 'Abd Allah b. Hasan and his brother Ibrahim were living an invisible and fearful life. A large number of people believed that Muhammad was the promised Mahdi who would revolt against the unjust rule of the 'Abbasids and initiate reforms to institute justice. Due to the fact that Mansur was afraid of Muhammad's disappearance and eventual revolt, he had imprisoned a number of innocent 'Alawids to arrest him. After all, he was the same caliph who had killed Abu Hanifa with poison, and whose governor had whipped Malik b. Anas.

Again, it is relevant to bear in mind that it was Mansur who had ordered Malik to write a book in which he should reject any hadith from 'Abd Allah b. 'Umar, 'Abd Allah b. 'Abbas and Ibn Mas'ud. When Malik objected by pointing out that the people of Iraq had their own traditions and opinions, Mansur promised that he would coerce them into accepting Malik's version. Who could have objected to the caliph that he should keep clear of the people's religious matters? Why should the traditions reported by such prominent early gures like Ibn Mas'ud and others be rejected?

There is no reason that can justiably be cited to explain such an irrational behavior on the part of those who were in power. To be sure, these individuals whose traditions were prohibited from being cited were relating traditions that were viewed by these wicked rulers as a threat to their power. Hence, they banned their publication and dissemination. In the case of Malik, it is said that he had heard some hundred thousand traditions of which he published only ve hundred in his book on traditions: Muwatta'.[277]

In other words, it was impossible for the traditionists like Ahmad b. Hanbal, Bukhari and Nasa'i to record traditions that were more favorable to the 'Alawids without suffering torture and deportation

---

[277] Adwa 'ala al-sunna al-Muhammadiyya, p. 271

at the hands of the 'Abbasids.

Concluding Remarks

From all that we have discussed so far, we can draw the following conclusions:

1. Since the traditions dealing with Mahdi'ism, more specically the occultation and revolution of the Mahdi, had assumed a political dimension which was deemed by the rulers a threat to their power but favorable to their rivals, the 'Alawids, the Sunni scholars could not record these traditions in their books because of the limitations imposed upon them by the caliphs and their governors. And, if some succeeded in sidestepping the prohibition and published these traditions, ways were found to suppress them. It may be because the fundamental belief in the Mahdi, in its ambiguous and concise form, posed no threat to the caliphate that it remained immune from eradication. But the information about all the signs of the promised Mahdi and other details were preserved in the traditions that were reported by the Prophet and the Imams (peace be upon them) and were circulated among the Shi'a.

2. In spite of all the obstacles created by the caliphal

authority, the Sunni books of hadith contained numerous traditions on the subject of the Mahdi. One day someone mentioned the following in the presence of Hudhayfa: "You must be very fortunate if the Mahdi appears while the companions of the Prophet are still alive. Is that not true? The Mahdi will not rise until there exists a concealed person dearer to the people than him [the Prophet]."[278]

Here Hudhayfa has hinted at the occultation of the Mahdi. Hudhayfa was among those few companions of the Prophet who had information about the conditions of the time and about some of the hidden matters that were told by the Prophet. He used to say: "Among all the people I am the most informed about the future occurrences, because the Prophet had mentioned those in a gathering [among the members of which] I am the only survivor."[279]

---

[278] al-Hawi li al-fatawa, Vol. 2, p. 159

[279] Ibn 'Asakir, Ta'rikh, Vol. 4, p. 9

How Long Will the Hidden Imam Live?

Dr. Jalali: How Long Will the Hidden Imam Live?

Mr. Hoshyar: The term of his life has not been fixed. But the hadith reported on the authority of the Imams introduce him as the one endowed with a long life. For instance, Imam Hasan 'Askari related:

After me my son is the Qa'im. He is the one in whom two characteristics of the ancient prophets, namely, long life and occultation, will be realized. His occultation will be so much prolonged that the hearts of the people will become hard and dark [with doubt]. Only those who receive God's special favor and whose hearts are made unwavering and who are confirmed by the holy spirit will remain faithful to him.[280]

Dr. Jalali: All that you have explained about the Imam of the Age so far is both rational and appropriate. However, there is one thing that really troubles my mind as well as the minds of those who are here in our gathering, namely, the problem of longevity. Educated

---

[280] Bihar al-anwar, Vol. 51, p. 224. Additionally, there are some 46 other traditions in this section on the same theme

and intelligent people do not nd such a claim of longevity plausible, because the age of the human cell is limited. Bodily organs like the heart, brain, kidney, and abdomen have a precise potential to perform their function. It is logically impossible for me to believe that the heart of a normal person can function for more than a thousand years. Let me be very honest about the fact that you cannot present such a phenomenon to the public in this age of science and space technology.

Mr. Hoshyar: Dr. Jalali, I do confess that the extended age of the Guardian of the Age (peace be upon him) is among the difcult things to believe. I have no knowledge of medicine or biology. However, I am ready to accept the truth. Hence, I request you to share your knowledge about long life with us.

Dr. Jalali: I too should acknowledge that my own scientic knowledge is not sufcient to allow me to solve the fundamental question we are faced with. As such, it is better to get some expert opinion on this subject. I think that Dr. Nasi, the Dean and Professor of the Medical School at the University of Isfahan, would be the most appropriate person to address our concern. Besides his thorough training in the eld of medicine in general, he has lot of interest in the question of longevity.

Mr. Hoshyar: I have no objection to your proposal. I will make the necessary inquiries and write a letter to Dr. Nasi, inviting him to join the group in one of its session. It might be in our interest to wait to hear from him and, therefore, I will suggest that we meet again after getting enough information about longevity so that we can enter our discussions with a better understanding. When Dr. Nasi replies to our invitation I will ask Dr. Jalali to contact you by phone to let you know about our next meeting.

It was almost a month later when Dr. Jalali informed everyone about the next meeting on Friday evening at his residence. The group had come together to resume the discussion. After a brief introduction and some refreshments the session was formally opened by Mr. Hoshyar, who informed the gathering about the letter he had received from Dr. Nasi. He asked Dr. Jalali to read it aloud. Dr. Jalali agreed and read the letter:

Dear Mr. Hoshyar:

Thanks for your letter and your invitation to speak to your group about my research on longevity. Since I am too busy to accept any speaking engagement and since the subject is very dear to me, I thought I would respond to your questions in writing, however brief, for the benet of your colleagues. I hope that my responses will be satisfactory.

Is There Any Fixed Term for Human Age?

Mr. Hoshyar: Is there any term xed for human age in medical science or biology beyond which any transgression is impossible?

Dr. Nasi: There is no such age xed for human life the transgression of which would be impossible. However, ordinarily the longest period for human life is a little less than a hundred years. It appears that in the recorded history of humankind this period has remained without any considerable change.

Nevertheless, average age differs, depending upon the region, climate, race, heredity and life style, and has varied at different times in each historical period. Hence, in comparison to other periods, in the last century the average life span has varied considerably. For example, between the years 1838 and 1854 in England the average age of a man was 39.91 and of a woman 41.85 years. But in the year 1937 this average had increased to 60.18 and 64.4 years respectively.

In the United States the average age for a man in 1901 was 48.23 and for a woman 51.8 years. On the other hand, in 1944 it was 63.5 and 68.95 years respectively. This increase is clearly the result of a better survival age for infants as a result of improved health care and preventive medicine, more particularly immunization against infectious disease. However, cures related to the diseases of old age have not had much success.

Mr. Hoshyar: Is there a general rule or standard to determine the life span of living beings?

Dr. Nasi: The widespread belief is that there is a direct correlation between the size of a body and its life span. For example, it is worth observing the difference between the short age of a moth or a y and that of a turtle, which might live as long as two centuries. However, this correlation is not as constant as it might seem, because a parrot or a crow, more often than not, live longer than birds that are bigger in size, and even longer than the majority of the mammals. Some sh, like salmon, live up to a hundred years; whereas a horse does not live more than thirty years.

From the time of Aristotle, there has been a belief that the life span of each being is in accord with the time it takes to grow. This equation for animals, as estimated by some scholars, was eight times the period that was required for a species to mature, whereas others maintained it to be ve times that period. For human beings, one hundred years is regarded as a normal span. This opinion is widely held even now. However, David, the Prophet, has regarded seventy years as a natural age.

In those ancient periods several individuals are believed to have lived for over a hundred years. However, their identity and the actual scale of their life may not be as accurate as it seems. Among these individuals are Henry Jenkins, who died in December 1670 at the alleged age of 169 years; Thomas Parr, who died in November 1635 at the alleged age of 152 years; and Catherine, countess of Desmond, who died in 1604 at the alleged age of 140 years.[281] Some other names appear in different journals across the world today.

---

[281] Encyclopedia Britannica, Article Growth and Development: section dealing with "Aging and Senescence," p. 428

The Reasons for Longevity

Mr. Hoshyar: What are the factors that lead to longevity?

Dr. Nasi: The following have been considered as probable factors of longevity.

1) Heredity: The signicance and the inuence of heredity in longevity are self-evident. There are families whose members have been observed to live longer than the average human life expectancy, except in cases where death occurs because of an accident.

In this connection it is relevant to mention the research done by Raymond Peril. In a book that he co- authored with his daughter, he studied a family that had a record of longevity going back seven generations. The total number of years going back seven generations in that family was 699 years, including two persons who were killed in an accident. In addition, in more recent statistics conducted by insurance companies it has been proven that longevity in the progenitor has a direct inuence on longevity in the progeny.

The heredity factor can be neutralized by other factors such as environment and bad habits. However, heredity can explain the reason why certain individuals living under unfavorable circumstances, such as alcoholics, can live longer. An offspring inherits strong and healthy body parts and organs from parents, including the nervous system and blood circulation. The famous proverb, "The age of a person can be gauged from the shape of his arteries," is based upon recognition of this heredity factor. In other words, for a number of people, when they reach their old age, their arteries become blocked because of hereditary traits. Moreover, the majority of the people who die before the age of ninety because of a heart attack or stroke have been found to suffer from arteriosclerosis.

2) Environment: This is the second most important factor in longevity. The environment that offers moderate climate and clean air, is free of harmful microbes and poisons, and contains safe and peaceful living conditions has a bearing upon the well being and longevity of its inhabitants.

3) Profession: The type of work and the working conditions as well as the duration in hours, in addition to spiritual and psychological activities, have an impact upon longevity. It appears that when a person enjoys good physical health and mental tranquility, it affects their life span signicantly. On the other hand, a stressful life accompanied by a lack of physical respite and mental peace, even more so than hard physical and psychological labor, reduces life span. It is for this reason that there are more persons enjoying longevity among religious scholars and prime ministers than among ordinary people. This longevity is directly related to their style of working and managing their stress under the constant pressure that is exerted by their profession. It is for this reason that joblessness and early retirement at a younger age might actually lead to the shortening of one's life span.

4) Nutrition: The kinds of food and the amount we consume have an impact upon our life span. The majority of the people whose life span exceeded more than a hundred years have been found to be dieters. There are numerous proverbs that signify the harm caused

by overeating. Among these are: "A person digs his grave with his own teeth." To be sure, overeating requires the entire body to work harder and is a cause of digestive disorders, heart and kidney diseases, and other ailments.

Unfortunately, these overeaters enjoy enormous energy by which they are deceived until symptoms of disorders begin to surface. During World War I, it was observed that death as a result of diabetes had signicantly declined in some countries. The main reason was the shortage of food in those areas.

Hence, it appears that poverty as a cause of reduced intake of food is a blessing in disguise. Moreover, consumption of large amounts of meat after the age of forty is extremely harmful.

Dr. McCay's experiments on mice at Cornell University have demonstrated that thin mice were able to overcome fat ones. A mouse reaches physical maturity at the age of four months; becomes old at two years, and dies before three. Dr. McCay's experiments involved keeping a group of mice under a strict low calorie diet that was enriched with vitamins and minerals. After some time he came to this conclusion: The period of their physical maturity could be prolonged to a thousand days instead of four months.

Further, he observed that the oldest mice who were fed on a regular diet died after 965 days. But the mice who were kept under strict diet remained young and full of energy for a longer than usual time. In relative comparison to a human life span, this latter group had lived a life of a hundred or a hundred and fty years. More importantly, this group remained healthier, suffering no ailments, and smarter than those who were on a regular diet. Such experiments have been conducted on sh and amphibians with similar results.

It is important to bear in mind that just as overeating can become a cause for a shorter life span, poor eating can lead to a surge in illness and a shortening of life span. That is, dieting must be accompanied with proper nourishment, otherwise it could lead to one being aficted with diseases.

Senility and Its Causes

Mr. Hoshyar: What is the meaning of 'senility' or 'getting old'?

Dr. Nasi: 'Senility' is marked by the wear and tear on human organs like the heart, stomach, brain, and internal glands which can no longer perform their functions to their capacity, mainly because they are unable to renew their cells and increase the excretions they need to refurbish themselves. This leads to the inrmity and weakness that become apparent in the human body at this stage.

Mr. Hoshyar: What causes senility?

Dr. Nasi: The signs of old age begin to appear at a certain stage in human life. However, it is not certain that senility is dened by the passage of time and by specic signs in the parts of the body such that one could assert that when a person has lived a number of years he has reached an old age. It is more correct to maintain that the main reason for senility and its manifestation is the onset in of the disturbance of a equilibrium at this age. As such, the main reason for senility is not the passage of time; rather, it is a deciency that appears in the proper functioning of the body parts.

At this age, different bodily functions slow down, and anatomically the tissues become smaller and their blood supply decreases. Digestive and alimental systems become weaker since they are unable to perform their function to the full. This causes an overall weakening of the body. The procreative power becomes less, and the brain slows down. In most people memory power reduces, especially recollection of names or dates becomes difcult. Nonetheless, it is quite possible that while physical functions are reduced, spiritual powers are augmented.

It is important to remember that all these occurrences and weaknesses that set in at a given stage in life are the result of a disturbance of the equilibrium that has occurred. Hence, it is more accurate to say that senility is not the cause; it is the effect. In other words, if a person is found who, despite an advanced age, does not experience any deciency or loss of equilibrium, then he might continue to live much longer with a healthy body and mind. The Opposite has been observed too whereby despite a young age, a person might lose vitality and become old before the age that is ordinarily regarded as senile.

Mr. Hoshyar: What causes the balancing system of the body to become weak and lethargic?

Dr. Nasi: The body's organs from the time of the birth of each person possess the ability to perform their naturally endowed function. This ability in the organs, as we have mentioned earlier in our discussion about the elements that impact upon longevity, is very much affected by the physical constitution of the parents and the kind of nutrition, environment, and climate to which they are exposed. Following that, it appears that as long as no deciency sets in they will continue to provide their natural function as long as a person lives. But, if a deciency affects one or any of them resulting in the reduction of its normal workload, then senility with all its signs peeps through and old age becomes manifest.

In short, the human body is continuously assailed by different kinds of viruses, bacteria, and microorganisms that endlessly attack it, producing toxic substances inside the body which destroy the healthy cells, thereby obstructing the continuation of life. When these things happen, on the one hand, the human body has a greater responsibility for providing the necessary nutrients for its survival and, on the other, it has to put up a defence against the attack of the microorganisms that cause inrmity in it.

Moreover, the body has to restore the healthy state of those organs that were assaulted and get rid of excessive toxic matter in the blood stream while sending help to the inrmed organs.

However, as soon as one enemy is brought under control it is faced with another attack, and so on. Hence, the internal defence system of the body has to remain alert all the time. In order to equip itself with its defenses, the body has to seek help from outside. Unfortunately, humans do not have sufcient knowledge about their own physical constitution and their internal needs. Moreover, in this sacred battle of self preservation, not only do human beings not cooperate with their body, but because of their ignorance and short-sightedness they actually end up assisting its enemy by eating the wrong foods and, as a consequence, open the doors to reducing their health and life span. Evidently, when the body is unable to furnish the necessary tissues, it looses the ability to perform vital functions when attacked by merciless microorganisms. Under these conditions the human body begins to decline and the signs of inrmity become manifest.

Just as the human body becomes tied to the destiny of being senile under the impact of hard work, it also becomes the victim of senility as a consequence of the extremely stressful episodes in life. Some scientists believe that untimely senility is caused by some diseases or harmful habits. According to the ndings of some research, the toxic secretions that are produced by the fermentation of intestinal microbes could be the cause of senility; hence, if these microbes are exterminated age could be prolonged.

The basis for such a conclusion is provided by the empirical data collected in the Balkans, more particularly in Bulgaria, Turkey, and the Caucasus. In these areas, a greater number of people live for over a hundred years. The reason for this longevity has been sought in yoghurt which is consumed in large amounts by these peoples. Scientists believe that since yoghurt possesses lactic acid that kills the microbes in the intestine, the person consuming it is able to live longer.

However, it is evident that the secret of longevity in these peoples living in the mountain regions of the Balkan countries could not be simply attributed to their diet. Rather, it is also to be sought in the climate, their peaceful but hard working life style, and in their inherited genetic composition. All these factors, more or less, have contributed to their long life. Longevity has been observed in other cases of people living in mountainous regions of the world.

Mr. Hoshyar: Is the cause of death and of the termination of the bodily functions, that same longevity and the immense toil that it involves? In other words, is death a necessity and certainty in old age because of longevity and toil, even if the main reason for death might be something else?

Dr. Nasi: The main reason for death is the occurrence of deciencies which set in all the main organs of a body. As long as those deciencies do not occur, death does not result. In fact, if the weaknesses occur before old age, then even a young person dies. But if he remains immune from these death- causing symptoms, then ordinarily as determined by the natural course of life, these symptoms denitely occur in old age. Having said all this, it is important to keep in mind that if an unusual person is born who lives a long life, but because of his unique physical constitution and other social conditions none of his organs has suffered any deciency, then his having lived a long life will not necessarily cause him to die.

Mr. Hoshyar: Is it not possible that a human being in the future might be able to discover a medication by means of which he might be able to increase the vitality of his body and prevent it from getting old and physically decient?

Dr. Nasi: This is entirely possible. On the basis of the insufcient knowledge that we possess today, we cannot reject such a possibility. Scientists have always conducted and continue to do research about the phenomenon of long life. Hopefully, one day they will discover the secret of longevity and human beings will be able to overcome old age and the short life span.

The Long Life of the Twelfth Imam

Mr. Hoshyar: As you know, the Shi'a believe that the promised Mahdi in the Prophet's hadith is identical with Imam Hasan 'Askari's son who was born in the year 255 AH/873 CE or 256 AH/874 CE. He has been alive since that time and continues to be in that state in occultation. Moreover, he may continue to live for centuries in that invisible state. Does the science of medicine regard such a long age strange and impossible?

Dr. Nasi: The question that has remained a mystery for me, insofar as my information and knowledge of the books that I have read goes, is the secret of the longevity of the Qa'im (may God hasten deliverance through him) from the family of the Prophet (peace be upon him and his progeny). However, with the phenomenal advancement made in natural sciences, and with God's endorsement of such endeavors, we might see a breakthrough in this regard and those of us who are seeking to understand this mystery might be able to see God's wisdom in this connection.

The only thing I can say at this stage of human knowledge is that one cannot reject such a possibility on the basis of the analogy that since it has not been empirically observed it cannot exist. The reason is that besides the principle of probability, there is a list of things in nature whose long life span is beyond any doubt.

a) In the world of vegetation, there are species that are known to have long life and are known to be the oldest surviving existents on earth. Among these are the Californian sequoia. These trees are three hundred feet tall and cover one hundred ten feet around the trunk. The life span of some of these trees exceeds ve thousand years. It is possible to conjecture that when the Pharaoh began construction of the largest pyramid in Egypt these trees must have been in the early youth of their existence. And at the time of the birth of Jesus (peace be upon him), the skin of the trunk must have been one foot thick. For example, the cross section of one of the trunks of this species which is preserved in the museum of natural history in South Kensington has 1,335 rings, each ring representing one year.[282]

The oldest surviving species, which is some 4,600 years old today, is a kind of pine tree known as pinus anstata that grows in central and eastern California. The oldest surviving animal is a turtle on the island of Galapagos that is 177 years old, weighs 450 Ibs and measures four feet long.[283]

b) The archeological diggings that were undertaken in Egypt discovered wheat in the pyramid of Tutan Khamen, which I personally saw and read about in the journals, that was sown in some parts and germinated. Wheat grew in these elds, demonstrating the fact that the germ continued to live for some three to four thousand years.

c) Viruses can be regarded as the longest living creatures. The virus is a living being that can be studied to reveal the secret of life. These are the creatures responsible for the development of certain diseases in plants, animals, and humans. The common cold, chicken

---

[282] Encyclopedia Britannica, Vol. 14, p. 346

[283] Encyclopedia Americana, Vol. 17, p. 463

pox, small pox, German measles, are some of these virus-related diseases. In the excavations that were carried out in ancient sites, it has been possible to discover prehistoric viruses and cultivate them in specic areas. In other words, although for all these years these creatures were living a concealed existence and practically were not different from a dead thing, they actually continue to live even after thousands of years.[284]

d) Recently I read in the newspapers that huge frozen animals were found during excavations in Siberia. After they had been placed in warmer conditions vital signs of life returned.

e) One of the ways of prolonging the life of a living being and keeping it half alive in order to observe its life is hibernation. This is also known as a state of "winter sleeping." In some animals hibernation continues throughout winter, whereas in others it continues during the summer. When an animal hibernates, its need for food disappears and the wear and tear on the body decreases between 30-100 to. The thermal function of the body comes to a temporary halt. Since the environment is also cold the hair and skin of the animal does not become stiff and hence it does not shiver.

The temperature of the body becomes like the temperature of the environment, reaching somewhere around 39-41 degrees fahrenheit, some degrees above the freezing point. Breathing becomes slow and irregular; heart beat becomes random and slow. Different reexes stop and nerve impulses in the brain cannot be observed under 52-66 degrees F. Some sea animals, including sh, are capable of living under the extremely cold waters for a long time.

Various living cells like human and animal sperm cells can be conserved in cold temperatures for articial insemination, and red bloods cells for transfusion. Moreover, several species of small

---

[284] Ittila'at

animals can be frozen and brought back to a living condition with a change in temperature, without causing any harm to them. The study of hibernation could lead to a breakthrough in understanding the secret of longevity and humankind can reach its dream of long life.

All the above observations in the medical and biological sciences make it possible for human beings to expect to discover the secret of longevity and overcome old age one day. Moreover, it has prompted them to continue their research until the goal is reached. There is hope that scientic research into understanding the mystery of longevity will also lead to uncovering the secret of the long life of the Qa'im from the Family of the Prophet (peace be upon him and his progeny).

Let us hope that day will come soon.

Dr. Abu Turab Nasi Professor and Chair School of Medicine University of Isfahan

Mr. Hoshyar: During this time when we were waiting to hear from Dr. Abu Turab Nasi I came across an interesting article, translated from French, on the subject under discussion. I thought I would read it to you so that we can all benet from this research.

The Article by Justin Glace

B iologist have been able to determine the life span of living creatures from a range of a few hours to hundreds of years. Some insects live only for a day, some others for a year. In each species, however, there are some who have transgressed the limits of an ordinary life span and have lived twice or thrice the normal age of their kind. In Germany, there is a rose tree that, compared to its own kind, has survived for hundreds of years. Similarly in Mexico there is a pine tree that is two thousand years old. Some alligators have been found to have lived for one thousand and seven hundred years.

In 17th century London, there was a man by the name of Thomas Parr whose age had reached one hundred and fty two years. In contemporary Iran there is a man by the name of Sayyid 'Ali whose age is one hundred and ninety ve years, and his son has lived one hundred and twenty years. In Russia, a man called Louis Poof Pujak is one hundred and twenty years old. A Caucasian by the name of Mikokho Polov is one hundred and forty one years old.

Biologists think that some internal factors are the cause of the unusually long life spans. These factors have resulted in the prolongation of the life span. Century old individuals are the favorite offspring of nature. The chemical composition of their bodies is perfectly in agreement and in accordance with the desirable perfection.

According to the biological theory, the natural life span of each species should be seven to fourteen times their growth period. Hence, for instance, since the growth period of a human being is twenty ve years, his natural age should be in the vicinity of two hundred and eighty years.

By adopting a balanced diet also, one can disturb the order of nature. The proof for this assertion is provided by a honey bee whose life span is only four to ve months. On the other hand, the queen bee, who is born from an egg and a larva like others, because of her special kind of diet, lives for some eight years.

Ostensibly, the matter is not that simple when it comes to human beings. We cannot live in a special place like the queen bee, with the temperature of our dwelling under constant watch to maintain a uniform environment. We are faced by a host of hazards, some of them, according to the biologists, include self poisoning, a lack of vitamins, and arteriosclerosis.

According to one of the experts in London, the disturbance of the equilibrium and the increase in the supply of one of the following in the body may hasten death: iron, aluminum, magnesium, and potassium. What is amazing is the fact that among all these hazards there is no specic mention of senility, because death is not regarded as having been caused precisely by senility.

A Swedish physician, who is life-long chair of the American Scientic Association of Human Aging, believes that old age is caused because of the entanglement of protein molecules with bodily cells. This condition causes the cells to gradually stop functioning, which in turn causes death. This physician is in search of a matter that can disentangle this condition in order to revive the bodily cells to undertake new tasks and thereby defeat senility. In laboratory experiments, the life of some animals, like an Indian pig, has been prolonged by 46.4 by increasing the dosage of vitamin B6, nucleic, and pantonxic acids in their food.

Russian biologist Philatoff is hopeful that he should be able to eliminate old age altogether by utilizing stagnant tissues. These stagnant tissues can be made to function like agricultural fertilizer to revive the human body. Besides, there are certain rules whose observance may lead to the prolongation of life.

These rules include dietary and biochemical regulations, relaxation, breathing and other instructions for a healthy life. Some nutritionists are of the opinion that by merely following proper dietary rules, one can extend the life span to more than a century. We are what we eat.[285]

---

[285] The translation of the French article appeared in the annual number of the journal Shohrat, 1342 AH, p. 289

Research into the Matter of Longevity

There was another article on research on longevity that appeared in an Arabic journal. The following is the translation of that article:

Some reliable scientists have been quoted saying: "Each major organ of an animal body is capable of living for an unlimited period. If human beings do not encounter hazards and accidents then they are capable of living for hundreds of years." This statement given by these scholars is not founded upon speculation; rather, it is based upon prolonged experiments conducted in the laboratories. One of the surgeons successfully preserved a severed part of an animal's body for longer than that animal's life span. On the basis of this he reached the conclusion that the life of the severed part depended upon the nutrients that were prepared for it. As long as it received proper nutrition it was able to continue living.

That surgeon was Dr. Alexis Carl, who was engaged in his research at the Rockefeller Foundation in New York. He had performed this experiment on a severed part of a chicken. The part continued to grow as usual for more than eight years. The team of physicians repeated the experiment on severed parts of a human body, like muscle tissue, heart, skin, and kidney. They observed that as long as the necessary nutrients reached these parts they are able to continue growing and living.

According to the professors of medicine at the Johns Hopkins University, the main organs of the human body are capable of living indenitely. This fact has been proven through repeated experiments, and, at least, is a preponderant opinion. The reason is that the life of the organs that are under the experiment at this time continues uninterrupted. The thesis then is based on clear evidence and carefully supervised scientic experiments.

Apparently, the rst person to embark upon these experiments on the animal organs was Dr. Jack Lobe. He too was engaged in his research at the Rockefeller Foundation. It was while he was studying reproduction in frogs through an unfertilized egg that he suddenly realized that while some eggs live for a long period, others die early. This led him to experiment on the organs of a frog. In this experiment he succeeded in keeping these organs alive for a long period.

Following him, it was Dr. Warren Lewis and his wife who demonstrated that it was possible to preserve a bird's embryo in a saline mixture in such a way that its growth could be revived anytime a part was attached to it. This experiment was conducted repeatedly to ascertain its ndings, including the observation that the living cells of an animal can be preserved in a mixture with the necessary nutrients to allow it to continue to grow and live. However, there was no proof to maintain that it could not die.

Dr. Carl was able to prove through persistent research and experimentation that the parts under experiment do not grow old, and live even longer than the animals themselves. He and his colleagues had begun their research in January, 1912 and had faced difcult problems which they overcame to establish the following points in connection with aging:

1. As long as the living cells under experiment do not face any anomalous condition that could cause their death, such as a decrease in the level of the nutrients in the mixture or an attack by microbes, they can continue to live eternally.
2. These organs are not only living, they have the ability to grow and to proliferate.
3. Their growth and proliferation can be compared and measured in relation to the nutrients that are prepared for them.
4. The lapse of time has no impact on them. Hence, they do not become weak or old; rather, there are no signs of aging in them. They continue to grow and proliferate the same year after year. It is probably right to maintain that as long as these cells are under the watchful eyes of the scientists, who feed them sufciently, they will continue to grow and live.

Thus, it is correct to say that old age - senility - is the effect rather than the cause. Then why does man die? Why is his life span limited? Why is it that with the exception of a few individuals who make it to a hundred or more years, most people live only for seventy or eighty years? The answer to these questions is that the bodily organs of an animal are numerous and different. There is a perfect interrelationship and interconnectedness among them.

The life of some depends on the others. If any of them, for some reason, becomes weak or decient and dies, then the death of the other parts is imminent. It is sufcient to cite a sudden death that occurs because of an attack by microbes. This has also become the main reason that human life has not increased beyond the average of seventy, eighty, or even less. This is also true with respect to infant mortality.

In the nal analysis, that which has been proven so far is that the reason for death is not the number of years a person has lived;

rather, it is the anomalous conditions that attack the body and render its major organs decient and incapable of defending it under adverse situations. Consequently, one can say that when medical science becomes capable of subduing these anomalous conditions or bringing them under some kind of control, then there will remain no obstacle for life to continue beyond a number of centuries, as is the case with some trees, for instance. Such a breakthrough in the advancement of medical science does not seem possible within the foreseeable future. Nevertheless, it is not far-fetched to expect that the present average life span may increase to two or three times.[286]

---

[286] The Arabic article is cited by Ayatullah Sadr, Kitab al-Mahdi from the journal al-Muqtatif, Vol. 59, Number 35, pp. 141-143

Further Research on Longevity

An English physician has written a detailed article on aging in which he maintains that some scientists have been able to increase the life span of a fruit y nine hundred times the normal life of others in the same species. This success was due to the fact that they had protected the y from poisons and other enemies, creating a favorable environment for it.[287]

Engineer Madani: Even I have come across several scienti c and interesting articles in which scholars have discussed their ndings about the secrets of long life, and the causes and factors that lead to old age and death; and the ways of combating that. However, since it is already late, we should take up these articles next time.

* * *

The following week the meeting took place at Dr. Fahimi's house. Mr. Hoshyar requested Engineer Madani to share the information he had gathered from his readings on longevity.

---

[287] Muntakhab al-athar, p. 278, citing the journal al-Hilal, Vol. 38, Number 5

Engineer Madani: I would like to present the articles that I read some time ago which should help resolve some of the questions that we have about the possibility of longevity.

New Research on Longevity

According to Professor Metalinkef, an expert on studies about death, the human body is made up of thirty trillion different cells of which not all can die at once. As a consequence, death occurs only when the human brain goes through irreparable chemical changes. On August 3, 1959, Dr. Hans Sealy, a researcher on the subject of death in the city of Montreal, Canada, showed a cellular tissue of an animal to the newsmen and claimed that the tissue was alive and would never die. In other words, the animal cellular tissue never dies and is, technically speaking, eternal. In addition, he claimed that if a human cellular tissue could be brought under the same conditions, human beings could live up to a thousand years.

Theoretically Professor Sealy regards death as a kind of gradual illness. According to him, no one dies of old age because if that were the case then under the impact of old age the entire cellular system of the body should deteriorate. Moreover, all the organs should stop functioning. On the contrary, following death, many cells and parts of the body of an old person are in good shape. In fact, the majority of people die a sudden death because one of the vital organs has stopped functioning. Since bodily parts are interconnected, the collapse of one leads to the failure of the other parts. Professor Sealy announced that one day when medical science has advanced to the point where it can inject new cells into the decient and worn out organs, it should be able to revive the human body and prolong human life as one desires.[288]

Some scientist have suggested that physiologists should make a distinction between an old age which is the result of natural processes of growth and an old age which occurs prematurely as a consequence of a destructive effect upon the organism, such as poison, diseases and other deciencies. Further, they maintain that old age must be considered as an inrmity and, accordingly, treated. Human life can be much longer and should move forward. However, it has been caught up in the midstream. As such, it is necessary to take all the possible steps to restore its natural physiological longevity without a decline in its energy and ability to run its natural course.[289]

---

[288] Based on some foreign journals, translated into Persian in Danishmand, Vol. 3, Number 7

[289] Danishmand, Vol. 4, Number 45. The section is based on a Russian work translated into Persian, entitled: Vaqti ki insan pir mishavad (When a human being turns old), tran. by Abu al-Fadl Azmudeh

Longevity

Following a series of lengthy experiments Professor Sealy and his colleagues have reached the following conclusion: The uctuation in the level of calcium is the reason for old age and changes that attend old age. Is there any compound that can prevent the occurrence of anomalous manifestations of old age? Dr. Sealy, with his repeated experiments with a chemical known as iron- dextran, discovered that calcium deposits in the tissue were the preventive agent. Consequently, the anomalous manifestations of inrmity connected with old age are the effect of a self-cultivated human condition that was reproduced and controlled in laboratory experiments upon animals. Dr. Sealy maintains that it is improbable that one can turn a ninety year old person into a sixty year old. However, it is entirely possible to stop the progression of a sixty year old to the deciencies and anomalous condition of a ninety year old.[290]

In one of his lectures Professor Ottinger reminded the younger generation that one day they might realize the reality that the

---

[290] Danishmand, Vol. 3, Number 5

question of the eternity of the human species must be admitted just as people today have accepted the fact of space travel. With the advanced technology and research pioneered today, it is probably correct to maintain that in the next century a human being will be able to live up to a thousand years.'[291]

---

[291] Danishmand, Vol. 6, Number 6

A Summary of a Russian Study on the Subject of Old Age

Longevity has been an aspiration as old as human existence on earth. According to the famous Russian scientist Michnikoff, until now human beings have not found any reliable method of prolonging life.

Evidently, death is the natural end of life, and there is no being that can escape that fate.

The Cause of Old Age:

The human body is made up of some sixty trillion cells. These cells gradually become old and when this occurs they are barely able to provide for the basic necessities of the body. Their proliferation is interrupted, and, hence, they die. The nerve and muscle cells that have died gradually increase and turn into a sturdy tissue. This change to hard muscle and nerve tissue as a result of the dead cells is known as sclerosis. Thus we have heart sclerosis, blood vessel sclerosis, nerve sclerosis, and so on.

Ellia Michnikoff, the famous Russian physician and physiologist, used to think that this phenomenon occurs because of the poisonous toxins created by the microbes that had placed themselves into the bowels of an animal and gradually caused the death of the tissues by poisoning them. Pavloff was of the opinion that a series of nerve cells that applied pressure on the brain from outside played a dominant role in aging. Psychologically stressful conditions like depression, despair, fear and so on render the nerve cells worn out and weak. This nervous wearing out is the cause of many inrmities which ushers in old age and subsequently death. The dream of an everlasting life is nothing more than an imagination. However, an increase of the human life span and a triumph over old age, is regarded as a possibility.

The Science for the Study of Aging and Death:

Some three centuries ago a new branch of biology known as 'gerontology' was born. The goal of gerontology is to investigate and discover practical laws that govern aging in order to conquer them. This branch of scientic inquiry is closely related to another offshoot of the same discipline, namely, thanatology, that is, the study of death. Discovering and studying the laws related to death, and to an extent delaying it, is the scope of this new branch of biology. According to these scientists death is always caused by the disruption of the ow of life, whereas the end of life is known as physiological death.

At present time scientists are engaged in nding ways of prolonging life to its logical and natural limit. This limit, as postulated by these scientists, varies. Pavloff xed the limit of natural human life to a hundred years. Michnikoff pushed it up to between one hundred fty and one hundred sixty. Gofand, the famous German physician, and scientist regarded the natural life span to be two hundred years. On the other hand, the nineteenth century physiologist, Dr.

Floger, maintained that it was six hundred years. Finally, Roger Bacon speculated it to be a thousand years. None of these scientists produced hard evidence to support their theory about the natural life span for human beings.

The Theory Proposed by the Frenchman, Dr. Boufon:

The famous natural scientist, Dr. Boufon, believed that the life span of any creature was ve times the period of its maturation to adulthood. The period of maturation for an ostrich is eight years, and, hence, its average life span is forty years. The maturation period for a horse is two years, and, as such, its average life span is fteen to twenty years. Consequently, as Boufon maintained, the average life span for human beings is one hundred years, because human maturation continues for twenty years.

However, there are many exceptions to Boufon's general formula. It is for this reason that it has been almost ignored. For example, a sheep matures at ve, but lives for ten to fteen years. A parrot completes its maturation at two, but lives up to a hundred years. In the case of an ostrich, although its maturation is complete at the age of three, it lives for thirty to forty years. In other words, scientists have not been able to determine the limit of the human life span with any certainty. But most of them believe that by eliminating the deciencies and anomalous conditions that actually lead to the shortening of life, it is possible to prolong the human life span to two hundred years. And, although this scientic belief remains at the theoretical stage, it cannot be dismissed as nonexistent and fanciful.

Average Human Life Span:

In ancient Greece the average human age was 29 years; whereas in ancient Rome it was a little longer than that. In sixteenth century Europe the average age was 21 years, in the eighteenth century it was 26, and in the nineteenth century it was 34. In the beginning of the twentieth century this average suddenly jumped to 45-50 years. Of course, these gures are from Europe. The reason for the upsurge in the average age today is the decrease in the number of infants dying. There is, however, a noticeable discrepancy between the developed and developing countries in this regard. For example, the average age in Russia is 71 years; whereas in India it is less than 30.

The average life span of other animals compared to human beings does not show any remarkable difference. For comparison with the average human life span, that is 60 to 80 years, it is interesting to note that a duck has an average life span of 30 years, an ostrich 35-40 years, a crow 70 years, a horse 20-30 years, a dog 16-22 years, a frog 16 years, a parrot 90 years, a cat 10-12 years, an eagle 162 years, and so on. It is remarkable that although the human being is regarded as the most perfected species in the animal kingdom, he seems to possess a shorter life span than many other lower creatures.

Michnikoff's View:

A careful evaluation of Michnikoff's theory explains the reason for such a radical variance between the average human age and that of the lower animals. He has conjectured that the reason for aging and untimely death is the infection of the body's cells and tissues which is caused by the secretion of toxic matter by the intestinal bacteria. It is important to bear in mind that the mere position and length of the intestines makes them an attractive habitat for these microorganisms.

An average of 130 trillion microbes are assumed to be born everyday and the majority of them in the intestines are harmless. But some are deadly, producing poisons that cause the body to become ill. In all probability, the resourceful cells and tissues of the body are infected by these microbes which leads to premature aging. By comparison, as indicated above, reptiles live longer than mammals. Reptiles do not have large intestines. Among the birds, only the ostrich has a large intestine and, hence, its average age is lower. Among the animals, cattle seem to live the shortest period. Apparently, the reason again may be their well developed large intestine. A bat also has a small sized large intestine and its life span is longer than that of other insect eating animals who are of similar size in growth. It seems that there is a connection between the development of a large intestine and longevity in human life. However, its importance is not as great as Michnikoff appears to indicate. Some individuals have lived long even after their large intestine was removed. To be sure, the existence of this organ is not necessary for the body. There are also individuals who have lived long with a large intestine. A goal of the scientists who study aging is to identify these individuals and keep them under scientic observation.

The Future Human will live longer:

People who have lived for more than 150 years are few and far apart. Some of those whose names have been mentioned in the books, include:

A Hungarian farmer lived to be 185 years old in 1724. He was reported to have worked until his last moment as if a young person. Another person by the name of John Rawl was 170 years old when he died. His wife was 164 of age years at that time and they had lived together for 130 years. An Albanian by the name of Khude also lived for 170 years. At the time of his death he was survived by 200 children, grandchildren, and great-grand-children. Some time ago a newspaper article reported that a man in South America had died at the age of 207 years. In Russia there are some 30,000 people whose life span has extended beyond a century. Presently, Russian scientists are engaged in investigating the factors that lead to aging and in discovering ways of prolonging life. There is no doubt that human knowledge will overcome aging in the future and that the future generations will be able to live longer lives.

A Little Known Theory about the Cause of Death

At the end of this discussion, it is not a bad idea to keep in mind that there is no doubt that death is associated with the separation of the soul from the body. However, there is another subject worth pursuing, namely, whether inrmity in the body causes the soul to depart and therefore the body is responsible for bringing about death. Or is it the soul which is the main reason for death? Is it the soul that at the time of death is unable to scrutinize the body, which then makes it vulnerable to weakness, aging, and various types of disease?

The majority of scientists and physicians accept the rst thesis by maintaining that when the organic energy of the body ends, the entire physical system falls apart. The organs and their ability to perform their function become weak; the main parts become worn out, giving up on the techniques of survival. Since the soul becomes tired and worn out in managing and maintaining the body, it becomes helpless and inevitably leaves the body, causing it to die:

The soul made the intention of leaving. I told it do not leave.
It said: "What can I do? The house is falling apart! "

Contrary to this there is an opinion held by the great philosopher Mulla Sadra. In his book *Asfar* he maintained that the management and protection of the body is upon the soul. It is the soul that manages the body in the way it wishes. As long as it needs the body it strives to maintain and protect it. But when it attains more independence and no longer depends upon the body to fulll its needs, the soul becomes less interested in its body and pays little attention to it. As a result, the body experiences inrmity and has worn out. By the time the soul has completely withdrawn from governing the body, death has set in.

Now, friends, you are aware that if this latter theory is proven and if it is established that the decision to die is in the hands of the soul, then the question about the long age of the twelfth Imam (peace be upon him) becomes easier to explain. In the light of Mulla Sadra's theory one can say that since the holy spirit of the twelfth Imam feels that its existence is a necessity for the betterment of humanity, then it would continuously engage in protecting the body of the Imam and in keeping it young, fresh and energetic.

Let me make it clear in conclusion that I am not in the process of proving or disproving this theory. I am simply introducing it as an unknown theory for the friends at this gathering. I do concede that the subject is unfamiliar and original. We should not be hasty in treating it supercially or in rejecting it because it does not make sense to us. One can judge its merit with certainty only when one is fully informed about the reality of the soul, its impact on and complex relationship with the body. To be sure, this is not an easy task, because it needs to analyze a series of philosophical and psychological matters and to undertake numerous, lengthy and complex biological experiments to understand the soul- body relationship. So far, human knowledge has not reached sufciently far as to allow one to deduce a valid opinion. Psychology as a science of the mind is still in its early stages of understanding the function of the human soul. Certainly, if human knowledge had paid attention to the human body and soul, our world would have been a totally different place today.

Dr. Alexis Carl, in his book entitled: "The Human, a being unknown," writes: "We do not know about anything about our own existential constitution, except in a limited and imperfect way. If Galileo, Newton, and others like them, had spent their intellectual energy studying the human body and mind, our world view would have been very different than what it is today."

Conclusion

Mr. Hoshyar: Several points can be surmised from what has been discussed so far:

1) Human life has no limit in the sense that any traversing beyond it would be regarded as impossible. No scientist has ever said that a certain number of years marks the maximum to which human life can reach and that when one arrives to that point then death is inescapable. On the contrary, all the scientists, from west and east, ancient and contemporary, have explained clearly that there is no limit to human life, that the future human can conquer death, or can hold it back for a long time and acquire a long life span. It is this very scientic possibility and the hope for success that has driven the researchers to continue to investigate and experiment, and until now their achievements in this regard have had considerable success.

These experiments have demonstrated that, like other inrmities, death is caused by natural factors and reasons which, if they are identied and if their inuence is brought under control, can delay death and allow human beings to live longer and free from its fear.

Just as scientic investigation has been able to discover many reasons and factors that cause illnesses and have been able to control their consequences for human well being, it is reasonable to presume that science will continue to succeed in identifying the causes of death and to prevent their effects in shortening life span.

2) Among the living species of plants, animals, and humans there are some which are observed to possess particular distinction in living longer than others of the same species. The existence of such exceptional entities points to the fact that there is no specic limit to their age which cannot be exceeded. While it is true that most humans die before reaching the age of one hundred, our familiarity with that quantity does not constitute a proof that life beyond a hundred is impossible. For there are many individuals who have lived longer than a hundred years. The existence of persons with 150, 180, and 250 years of age is a clear proof that there is absolutely no limit to human age. What does it matter if a human lives for two hundred or two thousand years? Both these gures are ordinarily unfamiliar and unknown.

3) Old age is not a non-preventive defect. Rather, it is a kind of disease that can be cured. Just as medical science has so far discovered reasons and factors that cause different ailments and has provided remedies for their cure and prevention, it is reasonable to expect that it will also nd the causes for aging and will provide the means to contain these. A group of scientists are diligently working to discover the miracle drug for preserving youth. So far these academic endeavors have produced relatively successful results, on the basis of which it is conceivable to expect that in the near future the research will lead to a preventive remedy to overcome aging and to provide a cure for this inrmity. In this case, human beings will be able to preserve their youthful age for a long time.

I am sure you will agree that based on the ndings of the researchers and the afrmation of the scientists studying the phenomenon of aging and longevity, it is conceivable to expect that a person who enjoys a perfect genetic constitution and an impeccable organic structure would live a long life. This is even more plausible when it is known that all the physical parts and organs of that person are free from any inrmity or deciency, and that he follows all the good habits of a healthy life and avoids anything that causes harm or disturbs his existential equilibrium. Moreover, he is free from any hereditary defects, from an immoral life, from stressful conditions. Undoubtedly, such a person enjoys the perfect balance between his bodily and his spiritual requirements which allows him to live a life free from any threat, internal or external, which would cause him to age or to die. Not only do science and wisdom not regard such a long life impossible, they actually have demonstrated its possibility through persistent research.

It is for this reason that one should not regard the extended age of the Imam of the Age (peace be upon him) as an unresolvable problem that dees nature. To the contrary, science and wisdom regard longevity through the preservation of youthful energy and vitality, as an absolutely possible occurrence. If the existence of a particular person was necessary for the universe and if it became imperative that this person should have a long life span, God the Almighty is capable of controlling the system of creation and the series of causation in such a way as to allow this perfect individual to benet from sciences and other sources of knowledge to further Divine goals for humanity.

Dr. Fahimi: What you have said simply proves the possibility of the existence of such a distinguished person. But how do we know that such a person does exist in reality?

Mr. Hoshyar: We have already demonstrated, both rationally and revelationally, that the existence of an Imam is necessary for the survival of humanity. Moreover, on the basis of numerous authentic traditions, the number of the Imams does not exceed twelve. In addition, we also proved that the son of Imam Hasan 'Askari, the twelfth Imam, is the promised Mahdi, who was born of a mother and who lives an invisible life in occultation. There are numerous *hadith*-reports to that effect. Now, in support of what we have said about the subject of long life and the conrmation provided by the experts in religious sciences, it is possible to prove such unusual and unknown long life spans.

Those Who Lived a Long Life in History

*E*ngineer Madani: How can one explain that God endowed only the twelfth Imam with a uniquely long life span that was not given to others?

Mr. Hoshyar: Incidentally, the world has seen the likes of this rare individual. Among them one should mention the name of the Prophet Noah (peace be upon him). Some historians have attributed 2,500 years of age to him. In the Torah 950 years are mentioned. The Qur'an clearly states that he struggled to spread the message of God among his people for 950 years. In the Sura 'Ankabut God says:

> "Indeed, We sent Noah to his people, and he tarried among them a thousand years, all but fty; so the ood seized them, while they were evildoers." (The Holy Qur'an, 19:14)

Even when we doubt the historians, we cannot doubt the Qur'an. That heavenly book describes the days of Noah's preaching to his people, namely, 950 years. Now this age is utterly unusual.

Engineer Madani: I have heard that this verse from the Qur'an is among the ambiguous passages that is open to interpretation.

Mr. Hoshyar: Where is the ambiguity in it? Is the ambiguity because of the meaning and the intention which is obscure or brief? Anyone who is minimally familiar with the rules of the Arabic language can explain the verse without any difculty. If this is regarded as an ambiguous verse in the Qur'an, then there is no clear verse in the Book of God! I cannot agree with the assessment of these people except that I think they are fundamentally opposed to the information contained in the Qur'an, but are afraid to say so.

Mas'udi has mentioned a number of historical gures who lived a long life. Among them are:

Adam, who lived for 930 years; Seth, 912 years; Anush, 960 years; Lot, 732 years; Idris, 300 years; Noah, 950 years; Abraham, 195 years; Jamshid 600 years; 'Umar b. 'Amir, 800 years; 'Ad, 1,200 years.[292]

If you refer to the books on history, hadith, and the Torah you will nd numerous persons of this kind mentioned there. However, it is necessary to keep in mind that the main sources for these examples of long age are either the Torah and its histories, whose reliability is not faultless; the 'single' traditions, which do not establish certainty in what they inform; or the books on history that have not been regarded as authentic and which are not free from exaggeration.

Since their authenticity was not clear to me I did not produce them as proofs in my discussion and, in fact, I limited myself only to the long age of Noah, as stated in the Qur'an. If you are interested in investigating the matter further you might read a book on persons who lived long lives, by Abi Hatim Sijistani, al-Mu'ammarun wa al-wasaya. Another book that treats the subject is Abu Rayhan Biruni's al- Athar al-baqiya. In addition, there are other historical sources that discuss the matter of the longevity of certain famous people in history.

---

[292] Muruj al-dhahab, Vol. 1 and 2

Dr. Fahimi: Where does the Imam of the Age live during the occultation?

Mr. Hoshyar: His residence is not established. Probably he does not have a xed residence, and lives invisibly among the people, interacting with them. It is also possible that he may have selected a far away place for his domicile. In some hadith-reports it is stated that the twelfth Imam comes to Mecca during the pilgrimage season and participates in the hajj rituals. He sees and knows the people, whereas people do not see him.[293]

Dr. Fahimi: I have heard that the Shi'is believe that the Imam disappeared in the city of Samarra, in that cellar which is ascribed to him and is a place of visitation (ziyarat). It is here, they say, that the Hidden Imam lives, and he will reappear also from this spot. If he is there in that cellar why cannot he be seen?

Who brings food and drink for him? Why does he not go out from there? One of the Arab poets has composed a poem about this subject. He says:

Has not the time come for the cellar to bring out what you, out of your conjecture, believe to be a human being?

Shame on you, for creating a third ctitious being, other than a legendary bird and a ghost.

Mr. Hoshyar: This ascription is nothing more than a falsehood which has been circulated out of obstinacy. The Shi'is do not maintain such a belief. There is absolutely no report that says that the twelfth Imam lives in the cellar and will rise from there. No Shi'i scholar has mentioned such a thing. On the contrary, many hadith-reports narrate that he lives among the people and associates with them.

Sadir Sayra has related a tradition from Imam Sadiq (peace be

---

[293] Bihar al-anwar, Vol. 52, p. 152

upon him) which says:

That which makes the condition of the Master of the Command (i.e., the twelfth Imam) resemble Joseph is that in spite of being mature and wise, and in spite of having associated with him before, Joseph's brothers could not recognize him when they came to him [in Egypt] until he introduced himself to them. Moreover, in spite of the fact that the distance that existed between Joseph and Jacob was no more than eighteen days, Jacob had no information about him. Then why are these people denying that God can do a similar thing for His Proof, the Master of the Command? He too can interact with people, walk around their market place, sit on their carpets and still they would not recognize him! He would continue to do that until God permits him to introduce himself.[294]

---

[294] Ibid., p. 154

The Story about the Countries that Belong to the Sons of the Imam

*D*r. Jalali: I have heard that the Imam of the Age has numerous sons, who live in large well developed countries whose capital cities are known by names such as Zahira, Rathiqa, Saya, Zalum, and 'Anatis. Five of his well respected sons by the name of Tahir, Qasim, Ibrahim, 'Abd al-Rahman, and Hashim rule these countries. Some of the description of these countries includes their likeness to paradise where the climate is perfect and the blessings are countless. In these places there is such a total peace that a wolf and a sheep live together. Wild animals do not bother humans.

The inhabitants of these countries are the righteous followers of the Imam who have received their instruction from the Imam's school. Falsehood and deception have not found their way in these places. From time to time the Imam visits these ideal places. Such are the agreeable things reported about these countries that belong to the Imam's sons.

Mr. Hoshyar: The story of these unknown countries is undoubtedly a legend. The only source for it is the anecdotal account related in Hadiqat al-shi'a, Anwar nu'maniyya and Jannat al-ma'wa. In order to elucidate this we should look at the source of the anecdote. The story has been related in the following form:

It is related by 'Ali Fath Allah Kashani that Muhammad b. 'Ali b. Husyan 'Alawi has narrated in his book from Sa'id b. Ahmad who said: Hamza b. Musayyib narrated for me a story on the eighth day of Sha'ban, 544 AH (1149 CE), that 'Uthman b. 'Abd al-Baqi related on the seventh day of Jamadi al-Thani, 543 AH (1148 CE), who in turn related from Ahmad b. Muhammad b. Yahya Anbari on the tenth day of Ramadan, 543 AH (1148 CE) to me, saying: "I was with some people in the gathering of the vizier 'Awn al-Din Yahya b. Hubayra. In that gathering there was also a respectable person whose identity was not known. The person was engaged in relating the story in which he described one of his sea journeys.

That year the ship lost its way and took them to the mysterious island about which no one knew anything. 'We had to disembark and we landed in that island.'"

At this point Ahmad b. Muhammad relates the fantastic story about those countries from this unknown narrator in great detail, and at the end of the story he appends the following:

After hearing the story the vizier entered his special chamber and asked all of us to come in. He then said: "No one has the right to transmit the story for anyone, as long as I am alive." We too, as long as the vizier was alive, never related the event for anyone.[295]

We have taken care to mention the source of the story so that the readers should realize the weakness of the transmission and its unreliability. For the detail of the story you may refer to the book itself. It is obvious for the scholars that the existence of such countries cannot be proven on the basis of this narrative. First, the reporter of the important story is an unknown person whose identity

---

[295] al-Anwar al-nu'maniyya (Tabriz edition), Vol. 2, p. 57

is unclear.

Hence, his report has no credibility. Second, it is not possible that such places exist when no one has any information about it.

This is particularly so in this age when all corners of the world have been mapped out and studied by the scholars. However, some people have defended the existence of these places as vehemently as if they were defending some fundamental Islamic principle. These people say that perhaps such places are present even now, but God has concealed them from strangers and non-believers! I do not believe that such opinions require any response. Actually, I do not understand what has prompted these people to offer such a whimsical and conjectural explanation of a story whose reliability and credibility is itself questionable!

It has been asserted that even if it is assumed hypothetically that such countries are non-existent now, one can still maintain that they did exist in the past and are now in ruins and their inhabitants extinct.

Such an assertion is also baseless, because if such prosperous and large countries with Shi'i population had existed, there would have been many who would have known about them and would have related, however speculatively, the amazing things about them in history books.

Ordinarily, it is improbable that such major countries could have existed and no one ever recorded anything about them. It is equally implausible that such a thing would have been known to only one unidentied person whose report about these places forms the basis of this fantastic narrative.

Moreover, it is unthinkable that the evidence about their existence would be so thoroughly wiped out that there would remain no archeological or historical trace of those places and their inhabitants!

The great scholar 'Allama Agha Buzurg Tihrani has critically evaluated the story and has doubted its reliability. In his comprehensive bibliographical study of books that were written by Muslim scholars about various Islamic subjects, he writes the following about the source that reports the incredible story about these prosperous countries that belong to the sons of the twelfth Imam:

This story appears at the end of one of the manuscripts of the book Ta'azi, written by Muhammad b. 'Ali 'Alawi. Hence, 'Ali b. Fath Allah Kashani assumed that the story is part of that book. He has certainly made an error since it is not possible that the story could be part of the book.

The reason is that Yahya b. Hubayra, the vizier in whose house the story took place, died in the year 560 AH (1164 CE), whereas the author of Ta'azi lived two centuries before that. In addition, there are inconsistencies in the text of the story because the narrator of the story, namely, Ahmad b. Muhammad b. Yahya Anbari, says: "The vizier exacted a promise from us that we would not relate the story to anyone. We too have fullled our promise and as long as he lived we did not disclose it."

In that case the narration of the story must be placed after 560 AH (1164 CE), that is, subsequent to the vizier's death. On the other hand, 'Uthman b. 'Abd al-Baqi in the story says: "Ahmad b. Muhammad b. Yahya Anbari related the story to me in 543 AH (1148 CE)."[296]

In another place, says Agha Buzurg, the story relates: ". . . 'Uthman b. 'Abd al-Baqi related to me on the seventh of Jamadi al-Thani, 543 AH (1148 CE) that Ahmad b. Muhammad [Anbari] related to me on the tenth of Ramadan, 543 AH . . .!" Since the month of Ramadan falls two months after the month of Jamadi al-Thani how can it be possible for anyone to report in Jamadi Thani something that occurred in Ramadan?

---

[296] Tihrani, al-Dhari'ah ila tasanif al-shi'a, Vol. 5, p. 108

In short, we are not religiously or rationally required to speculate and produce weak arguments to speak about the place of the twelfth Imam's residence and try to prove that Jaza'ir Khadra' (Evergreen Islands) or the city of Jabulqa or Jabursa are the places of his residence. Or declare that the Imam has chosen the Eighth Clime as his residence!

Dr. Fahimi: Then what is this story about the Jaza'ir Khadra'?

Mr. Hoshyar: Since it is getting late, shall we discuss the rest of the subject next week? If you all agree, we can meet in my house.

* * *

Jazira Khadra' (The Evergreen Island)

The session began on time at Mr. Hoshyar's residence.

Dr. Jalali: If I remember correctly Dr. Fahimi had a question regarding Jazira Khadra' in the previous meeting.

Dr. Fahimi: I have been told that the twelfth Imam (peace be upon him) and his sons live in Jazira Khadra'. What is your opinion about this belief?

Mr. Hoshyar: This story about Jazira Khadra' is no more than a legend. 'Allama Majlisi has narrated the entire story in his Bihar al-anwar, the summary of which is as follows. Majlisi says:

I found a manuscript in the Amir al-Mu'minin library of Najaf which was a treatise on the story of Jazira Khadra'. The author of this manuscript is Fadl b. Yahya Tayyibi. He has written that he heard the story of Jazira Khadra' from Shaykh Shams al-Din and Shaykh Jalal al-Din in the shrine of Imam Husayn [in Karbala] on the 15th night of Sha'ban, 699 AH (1299 CE). They related the story on the authority of Zayn al-Din 'Ali b. Fadil Mazandarani. Thus I decided to hear the story from him myself.

Fortunately, in the beginning of the month of Shawwal of the same year, it so happened that Shaykh Zayn al-Din travelled to the city of

Jazira Khadra' (The Evergreen Island)

Hilla. I met with him in the house of Sayyid Fakhr al-Din. I asked him to tell me the story he had related for Shaykh Shams al-Din and Shaykh Jalal al-Din. He said:

I was engaged in studying with Shaykh 'Abd al-Rahim Hana and Shaykh Zayn al-Din 'Ali Andalusi in Damascus. Shaykh Zayn al-Din was a pious man, and held good opinion about the Shi'a and their scholars, and used to respect them. I stayed with him for a while and benetted from his lectures. It so happened that he had to travel to Egypt. Since we liked each other, he decided to take me with him. We travelled together to Egypt and he chose to live in Cairo. We lived in the most favorable condition there for nine months. On one of the days he received a letter from his father, requesting him to return because he was seriously ill and wished to see him before his death.

The shaykh wept upon reading the letter and decided to travel to Andalusia. I also accompanied him in this journey. When we arrived in the rst town of the peninsula, I became seriously ill and could not move at all. The shaykh became troubled over my condition. He entrusted me to the preacher of the town, asking him to take care of me and he continued on his journey to his city. My illness lasted for three days and gradually I started getting better. I came out of the house and strolled in the streets.

There I saw some caravans that had come from the mountainous region with goods to sell.

I engaged in conversation with them and they told me that they had come from the Berber region which is close to the islands of the Radis (Shi'is).

When I heard about the islands of the Radis I became eager to visit them. They told me that the distance between this town and the islands was twenty-ve days of journey, of which for some two days there is no water or person to be found. To cross those two days I hired a donkey, and the rest of the journey I travelled on foot. I went on until I reached the islands of the Radis which were fortied with a strong wall and tall, sturdy watch towers. I entered the mosque of the city and it was a spacious mosque. I heard the muezzin calling the faithful to prayer in the way the Shi'is do, and following the call he prayed for the deliverance of the community through the immediate return of the Imam. I was crying with happiness.

The people started coming to the mosque and following the Shi'i practice they performed their ablutions and entered. A handsome man entered the mosque and went towards the mihrab (the niche). The congregational prayer began and after it was over they offered their supplications. Then they saw me and inquired about me. I told them my story and informed them that I was originally from Iraq. When they found out that I was a member of the Shi'a, they respected me and xed me a place in one of the rooms in the mosque. The leader of the prayer showed his respect to me and never left me alone at any time.

On one of the days I asked him as to where the food and other needs of the people come from. He replied that their provision comes from Jazira Khadra', which is located in the middle of the White Sea. Twice every year their food comes by ship from the Jazira. I asked him about the time when the ship was due to return and he said that it would be in four months. I was sad to learn that it would take that long. However, after forty days seven ships anchored off shore. From the largest vessel a handsome looking person emerged. He came to the mosque and performed his ablutions in accordance with Shi'i teachings and offered his noon and afternoon prayers. After the prayers were over he came towards me, greeted me – mentioning my and my father's name.

I was surprised and said: "Did you learn my name during the journey from Damascus to Cairo or from Cairo to Andalusia?" He replied, "No. Rather, your name, and your father's name, as well as your features and characteristics have reached me. I will take you to Jazira Khadra' with myself." He sojourned there at the island for a week and after completing his work we set off. After some sixteen days had passed on the sea, my attention was drawn by the clear waters in the middle of the sea. That man whose name was Muhammad, asked me as to what had drawn my attention. I said that the waters of this region had a different color. At that he told me that this was the White Sea and that the Jazira Khadra' was there. "These waters are a life fortication surrounding us and protecting us in such a way that, by God's help, if the ships belonging to our enemies try to get closer to this point, through the blessing of the Imam of the Age, they are drowned."

I drank some of the water in that region. It was as sweet as the water of the Euphrates. After having crossed the white waters we arrived at the Jazira Khadra'. We disembarked from the ship and went to the city. The city was prosperous and full of fruit trees. It had a number of market places lled with goods and the inhabitants of the city lived most happily. My heart was lled with joy.

My friend Muhammad took me to his house. After we had rested for a while we went to the congregational mosque. Large crowds had gathered in the mosque. In the midst of all these people was a prominent and awe-inspiring person whose imposing features I cannot describe. His name was Sayyid Shams al-Din Muhammad. People were gathered around him studying the Arabic language, the Qur'an and other religious sciences. When I came into his presence he welcomed me and made me sit close to him. He enquired about my health and told me that it was he who had sent Shaykh Muhammad to fetch me. Then he ordered one of the rooms in the mosque to be prepared for my stay. I remained there and ate my meals with Sayyid Shams al-Din and his companions. Eighteen days passed in this way.

The first Friday that I was there I went to offer the special service of the jum'a. I saw Sayyid Shams al-Din reciting the two units of the Friday service as an obligatory act.[297] I was surprised to observe this and when everything was over I asked Sayyid Shams al-Din in private: "Is it now the period of the presence of the Imam that you offered the jum'a as an obligatory act?" He said: "No, the Imam is not present, but I am his special deputy." I went on to ask: "Have you ever seen the Imam of the Age?" He said: "No, I have not seen him, but my father used to say that he used to hear his voice but could not see him. But my grandfather would hear his voice and see him too." So I asked him: "O my master, what is the reason that some people can see him and some others do not." He said: "This a special favor that God grants to some of His creatures."

Then the Sayyid took me by the hand and we went out of the city. I saw lush trees, and fruit and flower gardens, the like of which I had not seen in Syria and Iraq. While we were strolling we met a handsome looking man who greeted us. I asked the Sayyid if he knew the man. He said: "Do you see this tall mountain?" I answered, "Yes." "In the middle of this mountain there is a beautiful home, with a sweet water spring under the trees, and," he continued, "there is a dome made of bricks there. This man and his other companions are the servants of this dome and the court. Every Friday morning I go there and meet with the Imam of the Age. After saying two units of prayer I find the paper on which all the problems that I need a response for are written. It is appropriate that you too should go there and meet the Imam in that dome."

---

[297] As a rule, during the absence of the twelfth Imam, since there is no directly appointed deputy of the Imam, the Friday service is offered as a recommended act, which is immediately followed by the noon prayer as the obligatory act. In this case Sayyid Shams al-Din, as the deputy of the twelfth Imam, in the context of this narrative offers the Friday service as an obligatory act. Tr

Hence, I began to walk towards the mountain. I found the dome as he had said, and saw the two servants I had seen before. I requested to see the Imam (peace be upon him). They said it was not possible and that they had no permission to admit anyone. So I said to them: "Pray for me." They agreed, and prayed for me. I descended the mountain and went to the house of Sayyid Shams al-Din. He was not at home.

I went to the house of Shaykh Muhammad with whom I had been on the boat, and related to him my experience on the mountain and told him that the two servants did not permit me to see the Imam.

Shaykh Muhammad told me that no one except Sayyid Shams al-Din had permission to go to that place because he was one of the sons of the twelfth Imam. Between him and the Imam of the Age there was a distance of ve generations of the Imam and that he was his special deputy.

After that I sought permission from Sayyid Shams al-Din to ask him about his rulings on some religious problems which I could then cite on his authority. I also asked him if I could read the Qur'an with him so that he could teach me the correct pronunciation. He agreed and told me that we should start with the Qur'an rst. During my recitation I would mention the differences in the reading among the Qur'an reciters. The Sayyid told me that we do not recognize those variations, and added: "Our recitation is in conformity with the Qur'an of 'Ali b. Abi Talib (peace be upon him)."

At that point he told me the story of how the Qur'an was compiled by 'Ali b. Abi Talib. I asked him why some verses of the Qur'an had no connection with what was being said before and after. He agreed that the situation was as I described then related the story of how the Qur'an was compiled by Abu Bakr and how the caliphs rejected the compilation that was made by 'Ali b. Abi Talib. "It is for this reason that you see some verses not being related to those before or after," he said.

I asked the Sayyid's permission and reported from him some ninety rulings, which I cannot permit anyone to see except some very special individuals among the followers of the Imam . . .

At this juncture the narrator introduces another story which he had witnessed:

I asked the Sayyid about a tradition from the Imam of the Age that has been related to us that anyone who claims to have seen the Imam during the occultation is telling a falsehood. "How is this hadith compatible with what some of you are able to see?" He replied: "This is true. The Imam has said thus. However, it was said for that time when he had many enemies among the 'Abbasids and others. But at this time when the enemies have become disappointed and since our cities are distant from them where no body can get close to us, meeting the Imam does not pose any danger to him."

I then asked him if he knew about another tradition which is reported by the Shi'i scholars from the twelfth Imam regarding the khums – that the Imam has made it lawful for the Shi'is. He replied: "The Imam has given the permission in regard to the khums to his Shi'a."

Then the narrator quotes some more rulings given by the Sayyid, who tells him: "Until now you too have seen the Imam twice without recognizing him." The story ends with his declaration: "The Sayyid imposed upon me the duty of not extending my stay in the Maghreb and of returning immediately to Iraq. And I obeyed his command."[298]

Mr. Hoshyar: The story of Jazira Khadra' is as I have narrated for you in brief. Let me hasten to add that this story has no credibility and that it resembles a legend and a ction for the following reasons:

First, its chain of transmission (sanad) is unreliable. The story has

---

[298] Bihar al-anwar, Vol. 52, p. 159-174

been taken from an unidentied manuscript. 'Allama Majlisi himself says thus: "Since I have not found this story in any authentic book, I created a special section to report it [so that it does not get mixed up with the other reliable contents of Bihar al-anwar]."

Second, there are a number of inconsistencies in the narrative. I am sure you noticed that in one place Sayyid Shams al-Din tells the narrator that he was the deputy of the Imam, but he had not seen him. Moreover, he says: ". . . but my father used to say that he would hear his voice but could not see him. But my grandfather used to hear his voice and see him too." The same Sayyid later on says that he sees the Imam every Friday morning and encourages the narrator to do the same. The Shaykh who brought the narrator to that island also tells him that the Sayyid and those like him are the only ones who can meet with the Imam. As you have noticed this is a contradictory statement. The interesting part of the story is that if the Sayyid knew that he was the only one who could meet with the Imam, why did he propose to the narrator that he should go to the mountain and see the Imam?

Third, the story makes reference to alterations in the Qur'an, and such a view is impossible to maintain. Muslims scholars have unanimously rejected such a contention about the Holy Book of God.

Fourth, the lawfulness of the khums has been touched upon in the story, which, according to the jurists, is unacceptable.

At any rate, the story has been created like a ction, and seems strange and far from the truth. A person by the name of Zayn al-Din leaves his home in Iraq for education in Syria. From there he accompanies his teacher to Egypt, and from Egypt to Andalusia in Spain. He travels all this distance, becomes ill, his teacher leaves him and after getting well he hears the name of the Jazira of the Radis. He becomes so desirous of visiting this place that he forgets his teacher and takes off until he reaches the island.

The island appears to be without any vegetation because he asks about the people's food and where it comes from. In response he hears that it comes from Jazira Khadra'. Although he is told that the next ship with food would arrive after four months, it arrives in forty days! After a week's sojourn he is taken to sea. In the middle of the White Sea he observes clear, white waters . . . and nally arrives at Jazira Khadra'. Well, you know the rest of the story!

It is remarkable that a person from Iraq would travel all that distance through the different countries and would speak the languages of the people everywhere. Did the people in Spain also speak Arabic?

Another fantastic point is that part which deals with the White Sea. As you all know the White Sea is located in the northern part of Russia. The story as related takes place in a different region. Of course, the Mediterranean Sea, where the story takes place, is also known as the White Sea. However, the entire sea is called the White Sea, and not only a spot in it, as the narrator indicates.

Any person examining the story closely would realize that it is fabricated. In the nal analysis, let me point out that we have previously noted that the hadith-reports mention that the Imam of the Age (peace be upon him) lives among the people and associates with them. He also participates in some important occasions, including the annual pilgrimage to Mecca, and helps people in trouble.

In the light of these traditions, to introduce a distant place, dicult to access and in the middle of the sea, as the Imam's domicile – the Imam who is the hope of the downtrodden and the redresser of the wrongs committed against them, is, to say the least, unfair and unreasonable. Finally, let me apologize to you for taking your valuable time to analyze and discuss such an unreliable story.

Dr. Jalali: Does the Imam of the Age have any offspring or not?

Mr. Hoshyar: We do not have convincing proof supporting or rejecting the subject of the Imam's marriage and the existence of offspring for him. It is quite likely that he has been married and does have offspring without anyone knowing about it. He can do whatever is in his interest, which, in the view of some, might suggest that he already has offspring or that they will be born for him later.[299]

---

[299] This is the point of the prayer mentioned in the Mafatih al-jinan in which a believer prays to God: "O God, give him (i.e., the twelfth Imam), his family, his children, his descendants, his community and his subjects in their entirety, that which is pleasing in his eye." Also, in another supplication, received from the twelfth Imam himself, he says: "O God, grant him in himself, in his descendants, his followers, his subjects, his associates, his general supporters, his enemies, and all the inhabitants of the world that which will be pleasing in his eye." However, it is important to keep in mind that such prayers can not serve as hard core evidence to prove that the twelfth Imam (peace be upon him) has offspring. At the same time, one cannot rule out altogether that he does not have any offspring. Imam Sadiq has related a tradition in which he says: "As if I am seeing the Qa'im descending in the mosque of Kufa with his relatives and his family." See Bihar al-anwar, Vol. 52, p. 317

When Will He Appear?

Dr. Jalali: When is the promised Mahdi expected to appear?

Mr. Hoshyar: No time has been fixed for his appearance (zuhur). As a matter of fact, the Imams have regarded those who fix the time of the Mahdi's appearance as liars. Thus, for instance, Fudayl, a companion of Imam Baqir, asked the latter whether there was any specific time when the Mahdi would appear. The Imam in his response said three times: "Any one who fixes the time of the appearance is telling a falsehood."[300]

Another companion by the name of 'Abd al-Rahman b. Kathir was with Imam Sadiq when Mahzam Asadi came to visit the Imam and asked him: "When will the Qa'im from the family of the Prophet rise and establish the just government that you are expecting, for it has been delayed? When shall this be realized?" The Imam replied: "Those who fix the time of the appearance are certainly telling a lie. Those who become hasty in this matter will definitely destroy themselves. Those who are patient will be delivered and will return

---

[300] Ibid., Vol. 52, p. 103

to us."³⁰¹

A prominent and well trusted companion of Imam Sadiq by the name of Muhammad b. Muslim was told by the Imam: "Any one who xes the time of the appearance for you – do not hesitate to falsify him, because we do not x the time for the appearance." There are ten other traditions on the same theme.³⁰²

These and many other traditions on this subject provide evidence that neither the Prophet nor any of the Imams ever xed the time of the Mahdi's advent. Hence, if a tradition on this subject xes the time and the tradition is attributed to the Imams and if the text is open to some exegetical explanation, then it should be explained. Otherwise, it should either be ignored or else falsied. An example of such an explanation of a weak and unreliable tradition is provided by the example of Abu Walid Makhzumi, who had attributed to the Imam a statement that said: "Our Qa'im will rise in ALR."³⁰³

---

³⁰¹ Ibid., Vol. 52, pp. 104 and 117

³⁰² Ibid., Vol. 52, pp. 104 and 117

³⁰³ Ibid., Vol. 52, p. 106.

The Signs of His Appearance

Engineer Madani: How reliable are the signs of the appearance of the Mahdi?

Mr. Hoshyar: There are numerous signs of the appearance of the Master of the Command (may God hasten deliverance through him!) mentioned in the books on hadith. We cannot undertake to discuss each one of them because we do not have that much time. It will require several sessions to cover even the most important of these. Nevertheless, some observations are in order, however brief.

1. The hadith-reports coming from the ahl al-bayt have divided the signs of the appearance into two parts: rst, those reports that mention the signs that will occur without any question and which are unconditional. These signs must occur prior to the appearance of the Mahdi. Second, those signs that are introduced without their being absolute occurrences. These are the events that are not in any way denitely the signs of the Imam's appearance; rather, they are conditional. If the conditions are fullled, so too will be the signs; and if the conditions are not fullled, so it is with the signs. It was because

of some exigencies that they have been mentioned as part of the signs of the appearance.

2. The signs of the appearance are those things without which the twelfth Imam will not appear. The fulllment of each of these signs indicates that the days of restoration and deliverance are to some extent close by. However, this does not mean that after the signs are fullled, without any delay, the Imam will appear. In the case of some of these signs it is mentioned that proximate with their fulllment, the Imam will appear.

3. Some of the signs of the appearance will occur as a kind of miracle, so that the claim to Mahdiism is conrmed and the extraordinary situation of the world is conveyed to the people. The status of these signs is the same as with other miracles, which, even when they do go beyond the world of natural and normal phenomena, should not be regarded as unacceptable.

4. There is a kind of sign that is mentioned in some books and which seems customarily improbable, such as the saying that when the Mahdi appears the sun will rise from the west, and that the solar eclipse will occur in the middle of the month of Ramadan, whereas the moon eclipse will occur towards the end of the same month. All rational people know that the occurrence of these signs means that the natural order will have fallen apart and that the solar system will have changed. It must be pointed out that the traditions that report such events at the End of Time are no more than 'single' (ahad) transmission.

In other words, they do not generate certainty as to the substance that is being reported. If anyone probes into their chain of transmission (sanad), he may quickly discover that these were fabricated and circulated during the Umayyad and the 'Abbasid periods under their patronage. That period in history saw many individuals who claimed to be the awaited Mahdi and challenging the de facto governments by rallying the support of the people against the unjust rulers. Since the Umayyads and the 'Abbasids understood that it was not possible to falsify the traditions about the Mahdi that were reported uninterruptedly for several generations, they used a trick on the people to discourage them from revolting under 'Alawid leadership.

Consequently, they fabricated and put into circulation traditions that carried impossible signs for the appearance of the Mahdi. In this way they sought to dissuade people from following the 'Alawids in their rebellion against the injustices of the ruling house. However, if these traditions are true, then there is nothing problematic in visualizing catastrophic events preceding the advent of the Mahdi to inform the people about the importance of the event, and to arouse in them a sense of urgency to work for the government of God on earth.

The Story of Sufyani

Engineer Madani: What is the sign about the appearance of Sufyani towards the End of Time when the Mahdi is to emerge?

Mr. Hoshyar: On the basis of numerous traditions it appears that before the rise of the Master of the Command, the twelfth Imam (peace be upon him), a man from the descendants of Abu Sufyan will rise. He has been described as an outwardly pious person who will take care to remember God at all times. But in reality he will be the most wicked person on earth.

He will deceive a large number of people and will rally them around himself. He will gain control over ve regions: Damascus, Hims, Palestine, Jordan and Qinnasrin, and the 'Abbasid's power will be permanently destroyed by his hand. He will kill a large number of Shi'is. Then he will learn of the emergence of the Imam and he will dispatch an army to ght him. But the army will be unable to get close to him and will sink into the earth in the area between Mecca and Medina.

Dr. Jalali: As you know the 'Abbasid empire saw its downfall a long time ago. There is no trace of it left that Sufyani could destroy!

Mr. Hoshyar: In a hadith reported from Imam Musa Kazim (peace be upon him) he says: "The 'Abbasid dynasty is founded upon fraud and deception. It will also vanish in such a way that no trace of it will remain. However, it will revive itself again in such a way that it would seem as if it never saw that decline."[304]

The apparent sense of this hadith suggests that 'Abbasid power will recur and that the nal blow to it will be dealt by Sufyani. It is possible to maintain that although the rise of Sufyani could be regarded as one of the denite signs of the Imam's appearance, the manner and time of his emergence does not seem to be absolute. For example, it is possible that the destruction of 'Abbasid power at the hands of Sufyani may not be among the absolute signs of the appearance and it may take place at the hands of someone else.

Dr. Fahimi: I have heard that since Khalid b. Yazid b. Mu'awiya b. Abi Sufyan had the wish of gaining the caliphate which he saw in the hands of the Marwanids, he coined the tradition about the Sufyani to console himself and to boost the morale of the Umayyads. The author of the book Aghani says the following about Khalid: "He was learned and a poet. It is said that he fabricated the tradition about Sufyani."[305]

According to Tabari, the historian, 'Ali b. 'Abd Allah b. Khalid b. Yazid b. Mu'awiya arose in the year 159 AH/775 CE in Damascus saying that he was that awaited Sufyani. In this manner he used to call people to join his movement.[306] From this historical evidence it is clear that the tradition about Sufyani is among the fabricated hadith.

---

[304] Bihar al-anwar, Vol. 52, p. 250

[305] Abu al-Faraj Isfahani, al-Aghani, Vol. 16, p. 171

[306] Bihar al-anwar, Vol. 52, p. 193-197; Muslim, Sahih, Vol. 18, p. 46 to 87; Abu Dawud, Sunan, Vol. 2, p. 212.

Mr. Hoshyar: The traditions about Sufyani have been reported by both the Sunni and the Shi'i scholars. It is likely that the tradition is among the uninterruptedly (mutawatir) transmitted ones. Hence, by the mere fact of the appearance of a false pretender one cannot rule the tradition to be fabricated and, hence, spurious. Rather, one should say that since the tradition about Sufyani was well known among the people, they were awaiting him. Some took advantage of this and revolted against the rulers claiming to be the awaited Sufyani, thereby deceiving their followers.

The Story of Dajjal

Dr. Jalali: The rise of Dajjal is regarded as one of the signs of the appearance of the Mahdi. He has been described in the traditions as a disbeliever who does not have more than one eye which is located on his forehead and shines like a star. On his forehead is written the following: "He is a disbeliever," which every person, literate or illiterate will be able to read. There will be an abundance of food and a river of water with him at all the times. He will ride a white donkey whose each step will span a mile. At his command the sky will rain and the earth will grow vegetation. The earth will be at his discretion. He will bring the dead back to life. He will cry out in a loud voice that will be heard all over the world saying: "I am your almighty god who created you and who sustains you. Run towards me!"

It is said that there was a person during the Prophet's time who was called 'Abd Allah or Sa'd b. Sayda. The Prophet and his companions went to visit him in his house. He claimed to be a god. 'Umar wanted to kill him but the Prophet restrained him. He is still living and at the

End of Time will emerge from Isfahan in the village of Yahudiyya.[307]

It is reported from Tamim al-Dari, a Christian convert to Islam in the 9 AH/630 CE, who said: "I saw Dajjal in chains and fetters on one of the islands in the west."[308]

Mr. Hoshyar: In English, Dajjal is known as the 'Antichrist', that is the one 'against' or the 'enemy' of Christ. The name Dajjal is not a proper noun of an individual, In Arabic any impostor or a deceiver is called 'Dajjal'. In the Bible also the word 'dajjal' can be seen in the same sense. In the First Letter of John 2:22 it is written:

Who is the liar but he who denies that Jesus is the Christ? This is the antichrist, who denies the Father and the Son.

In another place in the same letter, 2:18, it is written:

Children, it is the last hour; and as you have heard that antichrist is coming, so now many antichrists have come, therefore we know that it is the last hour.

And in 4:3, it says:

And every spirit which does not confess Jesus is not of God. This is the spirit of antichrist, of which you heard that it was coming, and now it is in the world already.

In the Second Letter of John, verse 7, it is written:

For many deceivers have gone out into the world, men who will not acknowledge the coming of Jesus Christ in the esh; such a one is the deceiver and the antichrist.

From these references in the Bible it is evident that the word dajjal ('antichrist') is used in the meaning of a 'deceiver' and a 'liar.' Moreover, the story of the rise of the antichrist was well known among the Christians who awaited his rise.

---

[307] Ta'rikh Tabari, Vol. 7, p. 25

[308] Bihar al-anwar, Vol. 52, p. 193-197; Muslim, Sahih, Vol. 18, p. 46 to 87; Abu Dawud, Sunan, Vol. 2, p. 212.

It appears that Jesus (peace be upon him) had mentioned the emergence of the antichrist and had warned people about his sedition. Accordingly, Christians awaited him. In all probability, the antichrist mentioned by Jesus was the false messiah, a certain man named Dajjal, who appeared some ve centuries following Jesus Christ and falsely claimed to be a prophet. It was he who was crucied and not Jesus, the Prophet. In Islam also there are a number of traditions about the existence of Dajjal. The Prophet used to warn people against the sedition of Dajjal, saying: "All the Prophets who came after Noah used to warn their community about the sedition of Dajjal."[309]

The Prophet is reported to have said: "The Day of Judgement will not take place until thirty Dajjals emerge claiming to be a prophet."[310]

'Ali b. Abi Talib said: "Be afraid of the two Dajjals who will be born of the descendants of Fatima. A Dajjal ('imposter') will arise from Dijla at Basra who is not from me. He will be the forerunner of a number of Dajjals ('deceivers')."[311]

In another tradition the Prophet said: "The Day of Judgement will not commence until thirty liars and Dajjal-like persons appear and ascribe falsehood to God and His Prophet."[312]

In still another tradition the Prophet is reported to have said: "Before the rise of Dajjal, more than seventy Dajjals ('impostors') will precede."[313]

From all these traditions it appears that 'Dajjal' is not the name of a specic person. Like the word 'antichrist' it is generally applied to any deceiver, imposter, and fraudulent person. In short, the roots

---

[309] Muslim, Sahih, Vol. 18, p. 79; Abu Dawud, Sunan, Vol 3, p. 214

[310] Muslim, Sahih, Vol. 18, p. 79; Abu Dawud, Sunan, Vol 3, p. 214

[311] Bihar al-anwar, Vol. 52, p. 197.

[312] Abu Dawud, Sunan, Vol 2, p

[313] Majma' al-zawa'id, Vol 7, p. 333

of the story of Dajjal must be searched in the Bible and among the Christians. Thereafter, most of the hadith-reports on the subject, with all of their details, are to be found in the Sunni books and were transmitted by their narrators. It is quite possible that the actual events concerning Dajjal, as foretold in some traditions, might be true. However, all the details about his features and character do not have the stamp of authenticity on them, since the majority of these descriptions, published in Bihar al-anwar and other books, are reported by unidentied narrators.[314]

Consequently, even if it is hypothetically admitted that the actual instance of the appearance of Dajjal is authentic, the details that are provided have certainly been colored by ctitious stories. We can maintain this much without difculty: that in the Last Days and close to the emergence of the twelfth Imam, a man will be found who will be singularly a deceiver and an imposter, surpassing in wickedness all the previous Dajjals. He will mislead a group by his nihilistic claims. He will present himself to the people as if he is in control of their bread and water. People will become so delinquent in moral discernment that they will begin to believe that the entire universe is within his control. In his deceitful communication he will introduce good works as bad and bad as good. He will show hellre as paradise, and paradise as hellre. But his disbelief will be evident to all literate and illiterate persons.

However, there is no evidence to regard Sa'id b. Sayd as the promised Dajjal or to believe that he continues to live since the time of the Prophet. For, apart from the weakness in the chain of transmission, the Prophet is reported to have said this about Dajjal:

---

[314] For the detailed chain of transmission and the problem of unknown reporters in that chain see: Bihar al-anwar, Vol. 52 where the traditions are reported with full documentation made up of some unidentified narrators

"He will not enter the two cities of Mecca and Medina." On the contrary Sa'id b. Sayd had entered these cities. He died in Medina and some people were witness to his death.[315]

If it is hypothetically accepted that the Prophet did name Sa'id as Dajjal, he must have used the word in its common meaning as a 'deceiver' and a 'liar' rather than as the Dajjal who is part of the signs of the appearance of the Mahdi. In other words, when the Prophet met Sa'id he introduced him as a personication of an antichrist to his companions. Following that, when he informed the people about the emergence of Dajjal in the Final Days, those who heard him thought the reference was being made to Sa'id b. Sayd whom he had called a Dajjal, and it is this Dajjal who would appear as one of the signs of the Last Days, akhir al-zaman. The tradition about Dajjal being alive and possessing a long age comes from this incident.

The session began exactly on time. Dr. Jalali opened the meeting with his question.

Dr. Jalali: The reality of human life today reveals a diversity of opinions, beliefs, and religions. It also reveals the factors which breed differences among human beings in everything you can imagine. With the existence of a plurality of every sort, how can we imagine that the entire humanity will come under one government and one power when the earth is directed by the government of the Mahdi?

Mr. Hoshyar: If the general conditions of the world and the degree of human knowledge, perceptions, and intelligence remain at the same level as before, then it is certainly farfetched to think about a unied world government under the Mahdi. On the other hand, just as the degree of human reason and civilization, and the level of human knowledge in the past centuries were not at the present level – having through changes and transformations that are very much

---

[315] Bihar al-anwar, Vol. 52, p. 199

a part of human history gradually reached this higher point, it is plausible to maintain that the present level will not remain stagnant.

Rather, it can be said with much condence that with the passage of time humanity will reach even higher stages, allowing a better understanding the social good and the general interests of society. To comprehend this fully we must understand the past age and compare it with the present to formulate our vision of the potential future.

It has been established with abundant evidence that selshness and self-interesteds are natural instincts in human beings. These natural traits are responsible for much of the energy that has propelled human advancement towards perfection and the acquisition of happiness and other self-serving ends. Every individual tries his utmost to further his own interests, and to overcome any obstacles that might hamper this personal gain. In this movement towards one's own interests there is very little attention paid to the interests of others in society. However, when an individual realizes that his advantage is better served by preserving the interests of others, then he accepts that idea and willingly gives up some of his own advantage for others.

It was probably this recognition of a personal interest in the preservation of the common good that prompted the institution of marriage to develop. Every man and woman realized that they needed each other and that sense of need and dependency strengthened their marital relationship. The need to balance one's own selshness with the advantages that are accrued through relationships has been a

key element in the development of a healthy family and other mutually benecial social relations. In reality each member of a family does not have any other purpose than the realization of their own happiness. However, since the attainment of personal happiness was dependent on the happiness of others in the family, the attainment of collective happiness through a sense of cooperation and interaction quickly became the cornerstone of an ideal human relationship.

For a long time human beings lived as an extended family in tents. Following incidents of hostility, conict and skirmishes that disturbed their sense of security, the families came together to form a society in order to consolidate their resources to defend themselves against other families and groups. This development led to the reformation of kinship groups into tribes and nations. Members or evolution coalescence of these new groups, through mutual agreement gave up some of their individual and familial rights in order to function as a tribe with a sense of the common good and were willing to put up a defense to protect their common interests against any external threat. This advancement in collective thought and recognition of a critical need to coexist, both within the tribe and in relation to other tribes, moved the society to create villages and cities to further and to defend its common good.

The progression from village life to city and national life was gradual and prompted by a pragmatic decision to further the common good that was very much dened by the need for security and peaceful relations with those societies that were more numerous and powerful. The birth of a nation was the logical outcome of the human need to provide the maximum benet of corporate existence within a dened territory. It was in many ways an extension of familial structure in which citizenry provided the new basis for social and political cooperation. More importantly, it transcended racial and other forms of distinctions that converged under a national culture.

Ultimately, their development served to remove causes of conict and hostility and to demonstrate the benet of unity in furthering the purposes of a good society. With the cumulative experience of hundreds of centuries of living together, an absolute egocentric individualism and human pettiness were to a considerable extent brought under some ethical scrutiny. In spite of all the benets that accrued through a mutually recognized social contract, the need to work even harder to improve living conditions had to be guaranteed through the creation of a social and economic infrastructure.

The role played by technology in improving the quality of life was underscored by the state's endeavors to ensure that these scientic advancements were regulated through proper institutions and human rational control. Today, we are witness to the technicalization of societies around the world which has led to phenomenal breakthroughs in global relations through the technology of telecommunications.

Things that had appeared to previous generations as scientic ction have become a reality. Of all the things, national and cultural boundaries that seemed to have been dened in terms of an "iron curtain" separating the nations into eastern and western blocs have been overshadowed by electronic super- highways of ideas. The revolution of communication has changed the ideological conguration of the world. No nation can afford to live in isolation. In the midst of all this advancement, however, there remains the troubling question of how to make an individual responsive to the ethical and spiritual values which function as the backbone of a healthy society. Could the democratization of the nations guarantee the preservation of this unquestionably fundamental inner need of humanity?

The world community has experimented with different philosophies and ideologies to strengthen the common vision that would guarantee harmony and justice among peoples of different races and creeds. Nationalism, communism, socialism, capitalism, and so on have alternatively divided the nations, united them partially under one or another -ism, brought them to the brink of destructive nuclear warfare, and forced them to work with each other under international organizations like the United Nations. The human search for harmony and peace with justice remain the most precious prize for the global community. At the same time, the lingering memory of two World Wars with their disastrous outcomes have provided a grim reminder of how far humanity seems to be from that lofty ideal of peace on earth.

International organizations are marred by the power politics of stronger nations against the weaker ones. Different forms of imperialism and colonization are rampant even in the post-colonial era. In spite of all the experiences with wars and conicts, the world's nations are engaged in accumulating weapons of mass destruction that could wipe out the entire human race in a matter of seconds. The very foundation of human global community, namely interconnectedness, is at stake.

If human history in the recent past can be taken as indicative of the future direction of the global human enterprise, it is not difcult to surmise that humanity is at a crossroads marked with basically two choices: to pursue a pure materialism its moral and social accompaniments; or, to respond to the moral- spiritual challenge of accepting God as the sole guide.

In other words, with materialistic consumerism at its height, and individualism and secularism functioning as the two wings that make this kind of blind dedication to it possible, God and God's ethical and spiritual directives have been practically trivialized and systematically removed from the public life of a nation. At the same time, there is this natural urge in human beings to seek out their Creator, to worship the Merciful, Compassionate God. Until and unless that is satised human beings can not nd peace and harmony. No material or secular ideology can substitute for this simple, natural faith that provides the inner peace and a sense of cosmic harmony and total integrity to humankind.

The Abrahamic religions have, in particular, emphasized this natural religion of humanity founded upon an innate disposition to worship One God and implement the Will of God on earth by creating an ethical and spiritually-oriented society. These revealed religions also promise that God will empower those who respond to their innate nature by making them role models and leaders for humanity. Moreover, all false beliefs and gods are prone to provoke conict and must be eliminated for God's order to be realized. It is only when humanity acknowledges this God-centered universe that it will be able to further the ideal global community. Such a community will naturally respond to the call of Islam and the Prophet of Islam (peace be upon him and his progeny) whose invitation to the Peoples of the Book, that is, the Jews and the Christians, to abandon differences and concentrate on One Lord, the Almighty God, is enshrined in the Qur'an in Sura Al 'Imran, verse 64 as follows:

> *"People of the Book! Come now to a word common between us and you, that we serve none but God, and that we associate not aught with Him, and do not some of us take other as Lords, apart from God." (The Holy Qur'an, Surah al-'Imran 3:64)*

The Qur'an presents this revolutionary program of creating an ethical order that will reect the divine will on earth through God's righteous servants who have submitted themselves to God's will, the Muslims.

The Prophet has also informed us that the uniquely qualied person to lead humanity to become united under One God by abandoning all forms of idolatry and concentrating on the divine purposes for humanity will be the promised Mahdi, a descendant of his. Imam Baqir has related: When our Qa'im arises he will place his hands on the heads of God's servants, bringing together disparate minds and thoughts to form a unied opinion and will lead them to pursue a singular goal, making them excel in their moral life.³¹⁶

In another tradition Imam 'Ali b. Abi Talib has conveyed the essence of al-Qa'im's role in the future of humanity. He says:

When our Qa'im rises hostility and resentment will be eliminated from the hearts of the people, and general security will be established all over the world.³¹⁷

Finally, Imam Baqir says: When our Qa'im takes the command in his hands, all the public wealth, mines and treasures on the earth will be at his disposal [for fair distribution among people].³¹⁸

The Final Victory of the Downtrodden (mustad'an)

Dr. Jalali: In every part of the world there are oppressors and tyrants who rule over the helpless downtrodden people. These oppressors hold everything under their control and have used their power to terrorize ordinary people. With this in mind, how shall the Mahdi take the command into his hands and succeed in overthrowing these tyrants?

Mr. Hoshyar: Actually the triumph of the Mahdi is the triumph of the downtrodden people of the world over their oppressors. After all, they are in the majority and all power in reality stems from them; whereas the oppressors, however powerful they may be, are in the minority and do not possess the real power. This is the sense in which the universal victory of the twelfth Imam is conceivable. Let me elaborate at this juncture so that what I am asserting becomes clear.

On the basis of some passages of the Qur'an and several hadith-reports it is correct to suggest that in the nal analysis the oppressed people of the world, as a united bloc in a single revolution against

---

³¹⁶ Bihar al-anwar, Vol. 52, p. 336

³¹⁷ Ibid., p. 316

³¹⁸ Ibid., p. 351

the oppressors, to be led by the promised Mahdi (peace be upon him), will be victorious. They will permanently defeat the forces of tyranny and injustice and will assume the administration of the world. God, the Exalted, says:

"Yet We desired to be gracious to those that were abased in the land, and to make them leaders, and to make them the inheritors, and to establish them in the land." (The Holy Qur'an, Surah al-Qasas 28:5)

The passage explicitly gives the glad tidings that the nal control over the power and administration of the world will be in the hands of those 'that were abased.' Hence, the victory of the twelfth Imam, the Mahdi, is the same as the victory of the downtrodden peoples of the earth. To further clarify the matter let me emphasize the following points:

1. What is the meaning of being 'abased' or 'downtrodden' (istid'af) and who are the 'abased' (mustad'an).
2. What are the characteristics of the 'tyrants' or 'oppressors' (mustakbirin)?
3. Why is it that the tyrants have got an upper hand over the downtrodden?
4. How is it possible for the downtrodden to overpower the tyrants?
5. Who is the leader of this world movement?

In the Qur'an the term 'downtrodden' is juxtaposed with 'oppressor.' For this reason, it is necessary to examine these two terms together. According to the Qur'an, 'oppressors' have certain characteristics. In a passage where Pharaoh, an oppressor, is mentioned the Qur'an says:

> "Now Pharaoh had exalted himself in the land and divided its inhabitants into sects, abasing one party of them, slaughtering their sons, and sparing their women; for he was of the workers of corruption." (The Holy Qur'an, Surah al-Qasas 28:4)

Three characteristics of the oppressor are identied in the above passage. First, exalting oneself; second, dividing people into sects; third, working corruption.

In another verse the Qur'an says:

> "Pharaoh was high in the land, and he was one of the prodigals." (The Holy Qur'an, Surat Yunus 10:83)

In this verse prodigality or wastefulness is regarded as a characteristic of an oppressor. In another passage the Qur'an says:

> "So he (i.e., Pharaoh) made his people unsteady, and they obeyed him; surely they were an ungodly people." (The Holy Qur'an, Surat az-Zukhruf 43:54)

Here the verse points to making people 'unsteady', that is, humiliating them and then making them obey him, as another characteristic of a tyrant.

In another passage the Qur'an says:

> "And Korah, and Pharaoh, and Haman; Moses came to them with clear signs, but they waxed proud in the earth, yet they outstripped Us not." (The Holy Qur'an, Surat

al-'Ankabut 19:39)

In this verse, refusing to accept the truth is regarded as a trait of oppression. In yet another verse the Qur'an says:

Said the Council of those of his people who waxed proud (alladhina-stakbarü) to those that were abased (alladhina-stud'ifü), to those of them who believed,

> "Do you know that Salih is an Envoy from his Lord?' They said, 'In the Message he has sent been with we are believers.' Said the ones who waxed proud, 'As for us, we are unbelievers in the thing in which you believe.'" (The Holy Qur'an, Surah al-A'raf 7:76)

In another place the Qur'an identies the tyrants as those who spread disbelief and the setting up of compeers to God (shirk):

Those that were abased will say to those that waxed proud, 'Had it not been for you, we would have been believers.' . . . And those that were abased will say to those that waxed proud, 'Nay, by devising night and day, when you were ordering us to disbelieve in God, and to set up compeers to Him.'

Several traits of the oppressors become evident from the above citations from the Qur'an:

1. Waxing proud, that is, regarding oneself as superior;
2. Creating differences and conicts among the people in order to divide them;
3. Immoderation and extravagance;
4. Humiliation and persecution of the people;
5. Spreading corruption;
6. Refusal to accept the truth; and,

7. Propagation of disbelief and setting up compeers to God.

Oppressors are a group of people who without any grounds introduce themselves as superior to others. They tell the people that they are statesmen and intelligent experts able to manage their affairs better than they can do for themselves, thereby implying that the people neither possess the maturity nor the ability to realize their own good. Hence, in order to become prosperous and happy, they should obey these so-called 'experts.'

One of the most important strategies that they employ in controlling the people is to divide and rule. Moreover, to perpetuate their power they actively engage in spreading corruption through disbelief and in encouraging sinful deviation and wickedness among the masses. Through manipulation and exploitation of the people's wealth they are able to gain complete domination of their political and social life.

In the name of the defense of the land and people they engage in the accumulation of destructive armaments which they ultimately use against their own subjects. All in all, these individuals are engaged in wholesale exploitation of their people in order to amass wealth and use it for their personal benet with absolutely no accountability. In reality, these individuals, in the Qur'anic phraseology, are 'those who wax proud' through trickery and through misappropriation of the power that stems from the people.

The downtrodden people, in contrast to these oppressors, are not truly the weak and disabled ones. They are those who have suffered at the hands of the oppressors who have denied them their human dignity and have exploited them thoroughly to serve their own material and wicked goals. In this process of exploitation these downtrodden people have forgotten their own real worth and have fallen into mental slavery to those who have colonized them. After all, everything in the form of national wealth, good land, water, and so on belongs to the people.

Natural resources, power of labor, knowledge, industry, and discovery of new sources of generating wealth – all these belong to the people. The power that comes from a laborer, an industrialist, a soldier, an army, an administrator of justice and other organs of government is produced by the people. As such, it is the people who are the source of power and not the oppressors. If people stop cooperating with the tyrants, where will their power come from? Nevertheless, it is through false promises and fraudulent advertising of their goals that the oppressors are able to alienate the people from their pure and original selves and bring them under their unjust charge. They use the people against the people. In other words, oppressors throughout history have been a minority who have endeavored to keep the people ignorant of their true selves and eternally downtrodden so that they can perpetually dominate them.

Here we come to understand the missions of the Prophets who were sent to humanity to pull the people out of their ignorance and enable them to realize their true worth. The Prophets became the leaders of the downtrodden in order to guide them to free themselves from the yoke of slavery to the tyrants whose falsehood and arrogance they exposed openly, challenging these tyrants to abandon their wickedness and exploitation of the peoples. In a sense, the mission of the Prophets has been to empower ordinary human beings to realize the divinely ordained goal of creating a just and equitable society on the earth.

The Qur'an documents for us the history of this struggle of the Prophets against the tyrants of their time. Thus, Abraham arises against Nimrod, Moses stands rm against the domination of Pharaoh, Jesus perseveres against those who exercised authority invested in them unjustly, and the Prophet Muhammad (peace be upon him and his progeny) rises up against the Abu Jahls, Abu Sufyans, emperors and other rulers of his age to engage in jihad to liberate people from the shackles of oppression and the tyranny of the powerful in the society.

An extremely important feature which distinguishes the mission of the Prophets from that of the tyrants is the Prophet's cardinal attempt at awakening the people to their true nature, the state in which God created humanity. This distinction of the Prophetic mission is captured in the following verse of the Qur'an:

"Indeed, We sent forth among every nation a Messenger, saying: 'Serve you God, and eschew idols (taghūt).'" (The Holy Qur'an, Surah an-Nahl 16:36)

So whoever disbelieves in idols (taghūt) and believes in God, has laid hold of the most rm handle, unbreaking.

The Qur'an regards warfare in the path of God as permissible and as a Muslim's duty, because it is undertaken to save and protect the downtrodden. Thus, it says:

How is it with you, that you do not ght in the way of God, and for the men, women, and children who, being abased, say, 'Our Lord, bring us forth from this city whose people are evildoers, and appoint to us from Thee a helper'?

"The believers ght in the way of God, and the unbelievers ght in the idol's way. Fight you therefore against the friends of Satan; surely the guile of Satan is ever feeble." (The Holy Qur'an, Surah an-Nisa' 4:76)

Let us draw some conclusions from what we have discussed so far:

1. The oppressors who exercise power over the people are no more than a handful. They themselves do not posses the power; rather, they are using the power that stems from the downtrodden whom they enslave by weakening and exploiting them.
2. The downtrodden are the majority who possess the real power. They are neither as weak nor as disabled as they appear under the impact of the brainwashing strategies of the tyrants. These rulers have implanted these negative ideas in them about their weakness.
3. The most important element in the unfortunate situation of the downtrodden peoples is the self- cultivated sense of helplessness and weakness. Since they regard themselves weak and the tyrants strong and powerful, they unconsciously become the vehicle of domination, obeying orders and acquiescing to all sorts of humiliation and deprivation, without feeling the courage to confront their oppressors. Perhaps the most signicant obstacle to their taking any action to improve their lot, is the negligence of their own power. In the long process of tyrannical rule, the colonized people usually become overwhelmed by demonstrations of the colonizer's power and are oblivious to the fact that such demonstrations are no more than a fraud.
4. The only way for the downtrodden to salvage themselves from this miserable condition is to engage in self-realization. This requires a revolution in thought and attitude to overcome many years of brainwashing carried out by the oppressive regimes and their supporters. It takes a revolution to free them from the shackles of unjust domination. That such a power is within a people's reach needs to be discovered and employed to achieve the good of the entirety of humanity. If all sectors of society – the scholars, professionals, workers, soldiers, and so on – come to this self-realization they can overcome even the most

powerful oppressive regime on earth.

However idealistic and impractical this proposal may sound, there is little doubt that this is what the Qur'an expects from human beings while promising its realization:

> *"Yet We desired to be gracious to those that were abased in the land, and to make them leaders, and to make them the inheritors, and to establish them in the land." (The Holy Qur'an, Surah al-Qasas 28:5)*

Such a universal revolution to free human beings from the shackles of tyrants and wicked powers will be launched by the twelfth Imam, the Mahdi. His companions, followers, and supporters will become the inheritors, as promised in the above passage. Imam Baqir (peace be upon him) has related the following hadith:

When our Qa'im emerges with the command, God, the Exalted, will make him place his hand over the heads of the people so that their consciences and their intellects will be perfected [to accept his lead in launching his universal revolution].[319]

From the message contained in the Qur'an and the hadith it is evident that this revolution will be universal and for the sake of the religion of God and the implementation of the divinely ordained scale of justice. Its leader will be the twelfth Imam, the promised Mahdi (peace be upon him), and his true and worthy supporters will conduct the struggle, the legitimate and just jihad, in the way of God. The Qur'an says:

God has promised those of you who believe and do righteous deeds that He will surely make you successors in the land, even as He made

---

[319] Bihar al-anwar, Vol. 52, p. 336

those who were before them successors, and that He will surely establish their religion for them that He has approved for them, and will give them that He has approved for them, and will give them in exchange, after their fear, security:

"They shall serve Me, not associating with Me anything."
(*The Holy Qur'an, Surah an-Nur 24:55*)

In the hadith-reports it is related that the above-cited verse refers to the twelfth Imam and his associates and followers. It will be through them that the religion of God, Islam (islam in the basic meaning of 'submission to the will of One God'), will spread in every corner of the earth, replacing all other religions. The Qur'an and the hadith from the Imams promise a day when the downtrodden people of the world will wake up from the deep slumber of heedlessness and ignorance concerning their own worth and realize the emptiness of the claims made by the arrogant, powerful tyrants about their own power.

At that time, under the leadership of the Mahdi will rally under the ag of the Unity of God, al-tawhid, and gaining power from their faith in God, they will confront the unjust rulers. With a single collective blow of powerful faith they will defeat their oppressors for ever. This will be the time when the rule of justice and equity becomes established and forces of disbelief and wickedness are permanently wiped out. There will be no more ghting among the people, since the justice of God will rule and will remove any reason for conict and warfare. This will be the golden age of peace and harmony, under the government of God.

Why Does the Mahdi Not Appear?

Dr. Jalali: Now that injustice, oppression, disbelief and materialism have become so widespread everywhere, why does not the promised Mahdi appear so that he should put an end to the tumultuous conditions of the world?

Mr. Hoshyar: Any insurgent or revolutionary movement for a specic goal requires certain background preparation for it to succeed. One of the important prerequisites for its success is that the people should feel the need to launch the revolution and they should be psychologically prepared to endorse and support it. Otherwise the revolution could face a defeat. The revolution of the Mahdi is not free of this general prerequisite for it to achieve its goal. It could succeed only when the conditions are favorable.

The Mahdi's movement is not an ordinary reform movement within a small community. It is a comprehensive movement that will engulf the entire world. Its mission is global and will include all humankind. By the same token, it is extremely difcult to implement this mission without rst preparing the grounds for it. To gauge this challenging aspect of the revolution let us recall that one of the goals of the appearance of the Mahdi is to eliminate all kinds of discrimination – racial, creedal, cultural, linguistic, and so on – that human societies have created in their relationships with each other.

In order to create a global community based on peace and harmony through the implementation of justice and fairness, the Mahdi will have to correct the situation from its origins so that all kinds of conicts that have marred human society should be resolved. Such a task, even today with the creation of a world body like the United Nations, has not been easy to achieve. As long as human beings are not brought back to their spiritual origins, and as long as materialism and extreme forms of selsh behavior in the name of individualism are not corrected, it is impossible to imagine how a God-centered human society can materialize. The God-centered human society can be erected on the divinely ordained laws and the divine blue print provided by the Islamic faith.

The Mahdi's revolution aspires to provide a religious focus to the confused mental situation of humanity. It desires to destroy all the false and beguiling gods created by human minds, including: geographic boundaries, races, nations, creeds, political parties, false prophets, and so on, and to replace them with purity of thought, sincerity of action, and all those values that contribute towards the betterment of humanity.

Of course, talking and writing about such things is not difcult; but to implement them through a revolution is certainly not an easy task. Such an international movement would have to do a tremendous amount of work to prepare people in every way to respond adequately to ensure its success. The religious nature of the revolution demands that it should arise from the depths of the people's souls. In particular, since Muslims have to assume the leadership role in the revolution they need to prove their worthiness in being entrusted to undertake such a major responsibility. The Qur'an posits the condition of being worthy and righteous as a prerequisite to assuming charge of the affairs of humanity:

> *"For We have written in the Psalms, after the Remembrance, 'The earth shall be the inheritance of My righteous servants.'" (The Holy Qur'an, Surah al-Anbiya' 21:105)*

Consequently, the promised Mahdi will not appear so long as human beings have not attained the level of perfection that is necessary to accept the government of truth. To be sure, mental maturity is not an overnight development. It is a process that feeds upon events and experiences in order to become perfect. Human beings have to continue ghting over this or that piece of land until all their energies are exhausted and the truth about the articiality of these human-invented national boundaries becomes as clear as the daylight.

Only then will they stop thinking in those narrow terms and disputing over matters that do not deserve all that bloodshed and violence. When human beings begin to think in terms of their interconnectedness and when a brown or white or black person begins to think in terms of the common humanity that he or she shares with others, then it will be time for the nal revolution to occur.

This situation of desperation has to occur in all other elds until that time when human beings are left with no other choice but to turn to an alternative provided by God. Even in a eld like law, human experience has been one of perpetual revision to make the laws more fair and just. Hence, generation after generation of legal scholars are engaged in promulgating new laws and abrogating old ones so that they can reect the changing times in the process of legislation. This process will continue until people realize that man made laws serve the vested interests of those who are in power; and that the time has come to discover the immutable divine laws which have been sent through the Prophets, God's representatives on earth.

Human beings today are still not ready to submit to God's plans for them. They believe that through science and technology they shall create means of acquiring happiness. It is for this reason that they have put aside spiritual and moral values and have attached themselves to godless materialism. They will run after this materialism until such time that they realize that these scienic and technological advancements, although capable of carrying human beings to the farthest possible points in space and conquering it for them, or of creating the deadliest nuclear weapons for the preservation of their power, are utterly helpless in solving international problems of injustice and in removing the vestiges of imperialism and colonialism to establish an ethical and just global society.

From the time humans founded rulers, governors, and commanders and accepted their authority, they have also held some expectations of them. They have always hoped that the stronger and cleverer individuals would restrain the oppressors and would work towards the prosperity of all. But this hope has rarely been fullled and seldom have a people seen their ideal government come to power. In every age human government has appeared in different forms and shapes; but invariably it has fallen into the same pattern that was described as inadequate, unjust, corrupt and that was replaced by the new form. It seems that these forms of government need to exhaust themselves for humans to realize that enough is enough, and that it is time for God's government founded upon the principle of *tawhid* (belief in the Unity of God) to take over the reins. Hisham b. Salim has related a tradition from Imam Sadiq, who said:

The Master of the Command will not assume the government until all kinds of people [with all forms of government in mind] have ruled. The reason is that when his government becomes instituted no one will be able to say: 'Had we reached power we too would have ruled with justice.'[320]

In another tradition Imam Baqir says:

Ours will be the nal government. All families with an aptitude to rule will have reached power before us. This will be to forestall any claim after seeing our government: 'Had we reached power, we too would have acted like the progeny of Muhammad.' This is the meaning of the verse which declares: "The nal result is for the godfearing."[321]

In the light of the above discussion it is evident that human nature has not sufciently matured to become the receptacle for the government based on the belief in the Unity of God. However, there is no reason to despair because this condition will not remain forever, and ultimately God's mercy and favor will encompass humanity. In order to further the divine purposes God will endow human beings with the necessary wisdom and faith to fulll the goal of creation.

No human can deny the aspirations shared by all generations, from time immemorial, that human beings should be happy and prosperous in their life on the earth; that there should be justice and equity in the society; that there should be a complete sense of security from any internal or external threat to human existence. This aspiration is part of God's creation impressed in the nature of human beings and, therefore, God will guide and assist them in fullling it.

This will happen when all human ideologies and -isms have utterly failed to further good of human society.

At such a time of despair there will be a renewed hope in the teachings of the Prophets and in the divinely ordained laws of justice and equity that these seless and sacricing messengers of God came to

---

[320] Bihar al-anwar, Vol. 52, p. 244

[321] Ibid., p. 332

promulgate. There will surely be a recognition that human society, in order to become spiritually and morally sound and prosperous, is in need of two things: one, a clear and perfect blueprint from God that would set forth a program for reform and revival; and two, a divinely protected (ma'süm) leader who can execute the divine blue print without any error of omission or commission. God, in His Divine Wisdom, has prepared the Mahdi for such a highly sensitive time as that so that he can implement the program that Islam came to teach under the Prophet (peace be upon him and his progeny).

Another Reason for the Delay in the Appearance of the Mahdi

Another reason mentioned in the traditions is reported in a hadith from Imam Sadiq in which the Imam said:

In the loins of disbelievers and hypocrites God has deposited a seed for believing persons. It was for this reason that Imam 'Ali b. Abi Talib refrained from killing the fathers of disbelievers so that believing children could be born of them. After that whenever he met them he would endeavor to kill them.

Similarly, our Qa'im will not rise until God's trust from the loins of the disbelievers has been delivered. After that he will appear and will eliminate disbelievers.[322]

The program that will be followed by the twelfth Imam is that he will offer the religion of Islam to the non- believers. Anyone who accepts that call will be saved from being killed. All those who refuse to accept Islam will be killed. On the other hand, we know that history is replete with cases of believing children born of non-believing and hypocritical parents. Was it not the case of the early

---

[322] Ithbat al-hudat, Vol. 7, p. 105

Muslims who were born of non-believing parents in the pre-Islamic age?

If the Prophet had killed all the non-believers during the conquest of Mecca, the Muslims then born of their generation would never have come into existence. God's grace and benevolence necessitates that human beings should be left alone to their beliefs so that in time those believers among their children will be born. It is necessary that the earth should produce believing humans, in accordance with its potential and capability, and that God grants them life. As long as a human being procreates and brings forth a believer and worshipper of God, he or she should remain on earth. This situation will continue until people's understanding becomes receptive to God's unity and worship. At that time the Imam of the Age (peace be upon him) will appear.

A large number of disbelievers will accept faith at his hands. Those who persist in their disbelief in those circumstances will be the people from whom there will be no believing offspring.

The meeting started on time. Dr. Jalali welcomed the group and opened the session with his question.

Dr. Jalali: How will the Imam of the Age know that the time for his emergence has arrived? If it is said that at that moment he will receive the information from God, then it becomes necessary that he too, like the Prophets, receives revelation. In that case there would be no difference between a Prophet and an Imam.

Mr. Hoshyar: First of all, it must be pointed out that both the rational arguments and hadith that speak about the Imamate regard it possible that the sacred existence of the Imam has contact with the hidden world. At times of dire necessity the Imam is empowered to know such religious truths. In some traditions it is reported that the Imam can hear the voice of an angel, although he does not see him.³²³

Consequently, it is possible that God, the Almighty, might inform the twelfth Imam through inspiration. Imam Sadiq has related:

One of us, the Imams, is victorious although in concealment. When God wills to make his task public He will impact his heart with a hint, and he will emerge and take charge of the affairs with God's command.³²⁴

It is reported by Abu Jarud, who came to meet with Imam Baqir and asked him to tell him about the Master of the Command. The Imam said:

At night he would appear to be one of the most fearful persons, whereas in the morning he will turn into one of the most condent and secure persons. His program will be revealed to him in a matter of one night and a day.' Abu Jarud went on to ask: "Will he receive revelation?" The Imam said: "Yes, he will receive revelation. But it will not be the revelation Prophets receive. Rather, it will be a revelation similar to the one ascribed to Maryam, the daughter of 'Imran, to the mother of Moses and to a honey bee. O Abu Jarud, the Qa'im of the family of the Prophet is more respectable than Maryam, the mother of Moses and a honey bee!"³²⁵

These and other similar traditions suggest that the Imams too receive revelation and inspiration, while the difference between the two divinely ordained ofces of the Prophet and the Imam remains intact. After all, the Prophet is the lawgiver and received the norms and the injunctions of the Shari'a through revelation. On the other hand, the Imam is merely a protector of the law who does not receive the injunctions and the laws through revelation.

---

[323] Kulyani, Kafi, Vol. 1, p. 271

[324] Ithbat al-hudat, Vol. 6, p. 364

[325] Ithbat al-hudat, Vol. 7, p. 172; Bihar al-anwar, Vol. 52, p. 389

Moreover, it is possible that the Prophet has informed the Imams about the actual time of the Mahdi's appearance, through his provision of some indications about the signs of appearance that shall occur at the time. The Imam of the Age is also awaiting the fulllment of these signs. For instance, in the following tradition the Prophet is reported to have predicted the emergence of the Mahdi. He said:

When the time of the zuhur arrives, God will bring the sword and the standard of the Mahdi to a sound calling out: 'O God's friend, rise and kill the enemy of God!'[326]

One piece of probable documentation that is provided in the hadith is the tradition that describes God's sealed instructions given for each Imam about their role by means of a revelation to the Prophet who handed that scroll to 'Ali b. Abi Talib. When 'Ali assumed the caliphate he opened the scroll and read the instructions for him and followed them during his public mission. Similarly, each Imam following him did the same thing during their period of Imamate. At present the sealed scroll with the instructions for the twelfth Imam is with him.[327]

---

[326] Bihar al-anwar, Vol. 52, p. 389

[327] Kulayni, Kafi, Vol. 1, p. 279

The Preparation for the Emergence Will Take Place Overnight

There are many traditions from the Imams that describe the events in the last days before the rise of the Mahdi which will actually prepare the way for his revolution and its ultimate success. Moreover, these events will occur overnight, advancing his plans and ushering in the nal advent. For instance, in a tradition reported by 'Abd al-'Azim Hasani, he cites Imam Jawad saying:

'Our Qa'im is that Mahdi who should be awaited during his occultation and should be obeyed when he appears. He will be my third descendant. I solemnly declare by swearing upon God who selected Muhammad to be His Prophet and favored us with the Imamate that if there remains only one day in the life of this world, God will prolong it so much that the Mahdi will appear and ll the earth with justice and equity as it is lled with tyranny and wickedness. God will carry out His reform work overnight just as He accomplished the task He assigned to Moses overnight when he went to fetch re for his wife and returned with the crown of Prophethood.'

He then added: 'One of the best deeds of our followers is to await for deliverance [through our Qa'im].'[328]

Similarly, the Prophet declared that the Mahdi is among his descendants and that God will accomplish his task overnight.[329] Imam Sadiq related a tradition in which he explained the reason for keeping the birth of the twelfth Imam concealed and then added: 'God will help him accomplish his task overnight.'[330] Finally, in a tradition from Imam Husayn, he says: 'In my ninth descendant a tradition from Joseph and a tradition from Moses will recur. He will be the Qa'im from the ahl al-bayt. God will help him accomplish his task overnight.'[331]

---

[328] Ithbat al-hudat, Vol. 6, p. 420

[329] Suyuti, Kitab al-hawi li al-fatawa, Vol 2, p. 78

[330] Suyuti, Kitab al-hawi li al-fatawa, Vol 2, p. 78

[331] Bihar al-anwar, Vol. 51, p. 133

Awaiting Deliverance through the Appearance of the Imam

Dr. Jalali: What are the Muslims supposed to do during the period of occultation? In other words, what are their obligations during this period?

Mr. Hoshyar: Our scholars have identied and written in their books certain things Muslims ought to do during the occultation: to pray for the twelfth Imam; to do charitable works for him; to perform hajj and to appoint someone to do that on his behalf; to seek his help and assistance in times of difculty, and so on. There is no doubt that all these suggestions are praiseworthy and there is no need to enter into any discussion about them. However, the most important obligation mentioned in the sources and that which needs further elaboration is awaiting deliverance through him (intizar faraj). To some extent, this obligation has been neglected and no detailed discussion about it has been undertaken. There are many traditions from the Imams, both recommending the awaiting and enumerating its merits and excellences, during the occultation. Let us cite some examples:

Imam Sadiq (peace be upon him) says:

Any one who dies with the love (wilayat) of the ahl al-bayt while awaiting deliverance [through the appearance of the Qa'im], resembles the one who will be in the Qa'im's tent.[332]

Imam 'Ali Rida (peace be upon him) reporting from his forefathers and from the Prophet relates the hadith from the latter, who said: 'The best deed of my community is to await for the deliverance.'[333]

Imam 'Ali b. Abi Talib (peace be upon him) says:

Any one who awaits our government, resembles the one who, in the way of God, has rolled in his own blood.[334]

In another tradition Imam Rida praises the one who awaits the deliverance, and says:

How praiseworthy are patience and awaiting for deliverance! Have you not heard that God says in the Qur'an: "You await, and We too are awaiting?" So be patient because deliverance will come after despair. Those who were before you were even more patient than you.[335]

There are numerous traditions on a similar theme. The Imams always used to advise their followers to await deliverance. They reminded them that the mere act of awaiting for deliverance is a kind of emancipation. The one who awaits is like the one who ghts against the disbelievers on the battleeld and has rolled in his own blood. As such, there is no doubt that the most weighty obligation for Muslims during the occultation is to anticipate deliverance. Let us now consider the meaning of this awaiting or anticipating deliverance.

How can a person who anticipates deliverance acquire the greatest reward that accrues to the one who does good? Is it sufcient for

---

[332] Kamal al-din, Vol. 2, p. 644

[333] Ibid

[334] Ibid

[335] Ibid., p. 645

the one awaiting the deliverance to materialize to just say with their tongue that they are awaiting the appearance of the Imam of the Age? Or, perhaps, from time to time, he should cry out and pray: "O God, send the deliverance through the Imam of the Age!" Or, after the daily prayers or in the holy shrines he should beseech God to hasten the deliverance! Or, following the blessing on the Prophet and his family he should add: allahumma 'ajjil farajahu-shsharif, meaning, "O God, hasten the deliverance through this noble [Imam]!" Or, maybe he should read the special prayer of nudba (lamentation) on Friday mornings with a loud lament and sob.

All these recommendations are in their own place tting. However, I do not think that by merely saying these things a person can attain the true benet of awaiting the deliverance, whose excellences are enumerated in several traditions on the subject. Especially the comparison of the one awaiting the deliverance with the one dying on the battleeld ghting against the enemy of God, as related in one of the hadith above, cannot be just an exaggeration, since it is coming from the Imam to whom no false statement can be ascribed.

Imagine a person or persons who escape from every kind of social responsibility, from the moral responsibility of commanding the good and forbidding the evil, from taking a stance against corrupt and sinful behavior, from doing anything to stop injustices, by simply saying: 'O God, let the deliverance through the Imam of the Age be imminent so that he can prevent this corrupt behavior!' Can your conscience accept that this person's status is comparable to the status of the who is killed defending his religion? Can he be equal to the one who has sacriced all his wealth, his family, and his comfort and security in the way of God and attained the status of a martyr?

To be sure, there is a deeper meaning and signicance to the act of awaiting the appearance of the Imam. In order to understand that let me preface the discussion with two general observations:

First, in the light of the traditions dealing with the function of the Mahdi, it is possible to suggest that the program that the Imam intends to implement is ideal, comprehensive and, of course, difcult. It has as its target the reform of the entire world, the defeat of the forces of tyranny and wickedness in their entirety, the raising of Islam as the ofcial religion of all the inhabitants of this world, the removal of prejudices and wrong attitudes from the minds of the people so that they can all live in peace and harmony under the government of God. In addition, the Mahdi's revolution aspires to found a global community under one God, one religion, and one ideal system of law, and to bring all other communities under the united ag of Islam.

Obviously, such a goal is not easy to accomplish. This program is practicable only when the human mind is prepared to accept those goals and to go beyond the narrow connes of materialistic ideologies to realize the value of God's guidance for humanity. The need for the revolution and the desire to promulgate the divine blueprint for an ideal human society have to come from the people who have actively participated in preparing the way for the twelfth Imam to launch his program for the new world order.

Second, in view of several traditions reported from the Imams, it appears that the Imam of the Age and his supporters will overcome the forces of disbelief and godless materialism by undertaking jihad. It will be with the power of just warfare that the forces of God's enemy and the supporters of disbelief and injustices will be exterminated. There are numerous traditions that speak about the impending use of force to achieve the goal. For example, Imam Baqir said:

The Mahdi resembles his grandfather Muhammad (peace be upon him and his progeny) in the way in which the latter began his struggle with the sword. He will kill the enemies of God, His Prophet, and those who have oppressed the people and have led them astray. He will gain victory through sword and creating fear [in the enemy]. None of his army will face defeat.[336]

---

[336] Bihar al-anwar, Vol 51, p. 218

A companion of Imam Baqir by the name of Bashir told the Imam:

People say that when the Mahdi launches his revolution his tasks will become easy for him and there will be no bloodshed even to the smallest measure of a wound made for the purpose of cupping.

The Imam said: 'By God, that is not the case. If such a thing were possible it would have taken place for the Prophet. On the contrary, his teeth were wounded and his forehead injured on the battleeld. I solemnly declare that the revolution of the Master of the Command will not take place without our endeavors on the battleeld and without our blood being spilt.' He then wiped his forehead with his hand.[337]

The traditions suggest that the victory of the Mahdi's revolution will not simply be the result of God's endorsement and endowment of some hidden power to the Imam. It is not expected to succeed without manifest forces like a miracle that brings to fruition its program of reform and revival; victory does not depend on the

---

[337] Bihar al-anwar, Vol. 52, p. 358

ordinary course of events. Besides this divine endorsement the revolution will rest upon a well-equipped army that is capable of handling the most advanced weaponry in the contemporary arsenals.

With these observations derived from different traditions about the nal revolution under the Mahdi we can begin to understand the preconditions for the advent of the Imam. This will also help us in grasping the responsibilities Muslims have towards this revolution, and then in judging whether Muslims today are ready to actively support this difcult task and whether their awaiting for the establishment of the ideal rule under the Qa'im has any merit.

My own understanding, which is based on the traditions from the ahl al-bayt, indicates that the most important duty of the Muslims during this period when the twelfth Imam lives a life of invisible existence (ghayba) is, rst of all, to work diligently at reforming ourselves from within and with all the necessary seriousness. Muslims should adorn themselves with Islamic virtues, perform all the duties that are made obligatory on them, and apply the directives provided by the Qur'an in their daily lives. Second, they should extract the social teachings of Islam from the teachings of the Qur'an, the Prophet and the ahl al- bayt, in order to execute those perfectly in their societies.

By implementing the Islamic economic programs they should resolve their economic problems and ght against poverty, unemployment, and concentration of illicit wealth. By adopting the divinely ordained laws they should rid themselves of injustices and corruption. In short, they should commit themselves to set in motion the realization of an Islamic political, social, economic, and legal system, and present this to the world as a viable alternative.

More importantly, Muslims should learn modern sciences with extreme seriousness in order to not only benet themselves but also other societies around the world. They should, in fact, seek to be the leaders in all fields of human knowledge. Through their own religious and scientific progress they should demonstrate to the entire world that Islamic laws and ethics can serve as the ideal global system that strikes the balance between this and the next world. Moreover, by combining the concerns of a complete legal codex with the spiritual and moral concerns of the Islamic system, Muslims can become the source of emulation for a humane political, social and economic system.

In other words, Muslims have the obligation of excelling in every possible field related to the betterment of human society in order to provide each discipline with the moral and spiritual dimensions that Islam seeks from its followers. It is only then that they can expect to lead and to establish an ideal Islamic system under the leadership of the Mahdi.

Those who are engaged in these endeavors to make the revolution of the Mahdi possible and successful are the ones who are truly awaiting for deliverance through the appearance of the twelfth Imam (peace be upon him). These hard-working, self-sacrificing individuals are the soldiers of the twelfth Imam and can be compared with those who are actually on the field of battle fighting the forces of evil and wickedness.

As for those people who expect their problems to be solved by the political, social, and economic system created by those who have no commitment to the faith or to its moral and spiritual components, have so far created systems which give rise to inequalities, immoderation in spending, injustices in distribution of resources, and the many other evils with which humanity is confounded today. The situation is so desperate that it is hard to imagine the level of exploitation, corruption, and conflict that is generated by the new wealth and power, the byproducts of scientific and technological advancements.

The rich countries intend to dominate; the poor countries have shamelessly submitted to the overbearing compromises negotiated by their own rulers, the majority of whom are corrupt and morally bankrupt. In order to remain in power, they have sold out their own peoples and countries to their powerful masters, who make for them their decisions through a remote control of providing destructive military hardware for use against their own citizens.

Now, individual Muslims who sit around and do not even think about these matters that face their fellow Muslims cannot be said to anticipate the appearance of the twelfth Imam. These people do not have the necessary preparation to institute Islamic world government, even if they repeat a hundred times: allahumma 'ajjil farajahu-shsharif, meaning, "O God, hasten the deliverance through this noble [Imam]!"

This is what I have understood from the traditions that speak about the merits of anticipating the appearance of the twelfth Imam (peace be upon him). The entire philosophy of intizar ('awaiting,' 'anticipation') is summed up by Imam Sadiq who said:

Prepare yourselves for the revolution of our Qa'im, even if it means to gather an arrow [for ghting God's enemies.[338]

Abd al-Hamid Wasiti mentioned to Imam Baqir: 'In anticipation of the occurrence [of the Qa'im's revolution] we have even withdrawn from engaging in trade!' The Imam said:

O 'Abd al-Hamid, do you think that the one who has given up his life in the way of God, God does not make deliverance guaranteed for him? By God, God will certainly deliver him. May God have mercy on the one who keeps our mission alive.

Abd al-Hamid asked: "What happens if I die before the deliverance comes?" The Imam replied:

Any of those who say: 'If I meet the Qa'im I will help him,' then

---

[338] Ibid., p. 366

such a person will share the status of the one who will have fought near the Imam [defending him]. Indeed, he will share the status of the one who will have been killed [defending him].[339]

According to Abu Basir, one of most prominent companions of the sixth Imam, one day Imam Sadiq told his companions: "Should I inform you about a deed without which God does not accept people's achievements?" Abu Basir told the Imam to do so. The Imam said:

To bear witness about God's unity and Muhammad's prophethood; to acknowledge God's commands and prohibitions; to love us and disassociate from our enemies; to accept the authority of the Imams, and to act with piety and seriousness; to adopt gentleness and to await the deliverance through the appearance of the Qa'im.

He, then, went on to say:

We will have the authority, which God will establish at the proper time. Whoever wishes to be a companion and close associate of our Qa'im should await deliverance through him. Moreover, such a person should adopt piety and virtuous life and continue to anticipate our Qa'im in that state. If they live like that and if they die before the advent of the Qa'im, then they will reap the reward of someone who has actually been with the Qa'im. O my followers, be serious and work hard while awaiting the Qa'im's emergence. O you who are blessed with God's mercy, may you taste the sweetness of the nal victory.[340]

---

[339] Kamal al-din, Vol. 2, p. 644

[340] Nu'mani, Kitab al-ghayba, p. 211

Investigation into the Traditions against the Rise (qiyam)

Engineer Madani: Mr. Hoshyar! From your discussions on the subject of awaiting the appearance of the Mahdi, it would seem that during the occultation of the twelfth Imam the Shi'is are required to adopt an active posture and work to establish an Islamic government, to endeavor to execute an Islamic political and social system, and to engage in the jihad to achieve all that. By doing so, as you have pointed out, they would be actually preparing the way for the emergence of the Imam to launch his global revolution.

I suspect that your interpretation might not be in agreement with the subject of some other traditions. As you know there are a number of traditions which forbid any involvement of the Shi'is in the revolutionary movements before the rise of the Mahdi. It would be highly benecial to discuss some of those traditions.

Mr. Hoshyar: I am grateful to you for reminding me of a different perspective on the philosophy of awaiting. It is relevant to investigate these traditions in order to evaluate their authenticity. Thus, rst we should examine their chain of transmission to determine their reliability. Second, we should examine their content to determine the validity of the view that is derived from them. However, let me preface our investigation into these two areas by a general remark on the following two topics:

1. The question of governance in religion
2. The investigation of the hadith-reports

Governance Within Religion

On the basis of the teachings of Islam one can say that Islam is not a religion conned to belief and worship. It is a complete system of belief, worship, ethics, politics and society. Islamic principles and teachings can be generally classied into two parts:

1. Individual injunctions that are required of each believing man and woman, such as the ve daily prayers, fasting of Ramadan, ritual purication, annual pilgrimage, and so on. A person does not need a government or social organization in order to carry these out. He is capable of performing them on his own, because these injunctions deal with the God-human relationship.
2. Collective injunctions that are required of a group of believers, such as engaging in just war (jihad), commanding the good and forbidding the evil; administering justice, resolving conicts, instituting legal punishments, and so on. These injunctions are social and political, dealing with the individual's relationship to other humans. As a member of a society, each person needs to learn to respect the rights of others and to protect his own. God has provided principles of inter-personal human relationships

which are fundamentally based on justice and equity.

Hence, the Islamic system has taken care to regulate this relationship with due consideration to cover all spheres of humans' involvement with each other. In other words, Islam provides a comprehensive legal and religious system that caters to the needs of the society without making any distinction between temporal and spiritual realms of human existence. For instance, jihad in God's way is an obligation to defend oneself and others living in the society. Islamic law furnishes all the necessary regulations to cover every aspect of the Muslim community's obligation to defend and ght for its rights. Thus, the Qur'an in requiring the obligation of jihad says:

"Fight them, till there is no persecution and the religion is God's." (The Holy Qur'an, Surah al-Baqara 2:193)

"But if they (i.e., the unbelievers) break their oaths after their covenant and thrust at your religion, then ght the leaders of unbelief; they have no sacred oaths; haply they will give over." (The Holy Qur'an, Surah at-Tawba 9:12)

There are numerous such verses that indicate that Muslims have an obligation to spread Islam and ght the forces of unbelief and persecution. It, moreover, calls upon Muslims to mobilize themselves and stand rm against the enemy:

"Make ready for them whatever force and strings of horses you can, to terrify thereby the enemy of God and your enemy, and others besides them that you know not; God knows them." (The Holy Qur'an, Surah Anfal 8:60)

Consequently, it is correct to surmise that establishing and instituting social and political structures to further the cause of the Muslim community is part of Islamic religious teaching. Muslims have the obligation to do everything within their means to further these interests and to inspire the enemy with a fear and awe of Islam so that they will not try to intervene and interfere with their affairs.

The Obligation to Command the Good and Forbid the Evil

This obligation is one of the most important teachings of Islam for achieving Islamic justice. It actually forms the basis for the existence of government in Islam. It is the duty of every Muslim to stand rm against any act of injustice and corrupt sinful behavior. The spread of true religion is impossible without moral purication – which provides the justication for this social duty. There are numerous verses in the Qur'an that require Muslims to undertake the responsibility to command the good and forbid the evil as part of their moral responsibility as believers in One God. Thus, the Qur'an says:

> "Let there be one nation of you, calling to good, and bidding to honor, and forbidding dishonor; those are prosperers." (The Holy Qur'an, Surah al-'Imran, 3:104)

> "You are the best nation ever brought forth to men, bidding honor, and forbidding dishonor, and believing in God." (The Holy Qur'an, Surah al-'Imran 3:110)

Concluding Remarks

All the above discussion instills in us a condence that Islam as a religion demands the creation of a worldwide society which acknowledges, on the one hand, an individual's personal relationship with God by requiring him or her to carry out the injunctions imposed on them by God; and, on the other, an individual's responsibility as a member of a society in which interpersonal relationships are regulated by the principles of justice and equity as dened by God's revelation.

Consequently, the establishment of government to manage the affairs of humanity was part and parcel of the Islamic creed. Just as God provided the laws to direct human affairs, God also provided directives pertaining to the exercise of authority in Muslim society. How can one imagine a duty to ght without any guidance in the matter of who can command the Muslim army, or make critical decisions about the war strategies, and so on? In other words, Muslims needed both the law and the executor of the divine will on earth. Hence, it is accurate to say that governance is an integral part of Islamic faith and tradition.

The Prophet as the Leader of the Muslims

The Prophet (peace be upon him and his progeny) was in actuality the head of the Muslim community during his lifetime. As God's representative he managed the affairs of the community. He had been given a wide range of authority in matters related to the everyday existence of his community and the rst Muslim polity. He, according to the Qur'an, had discretionary control over his followers' affairs.[341] In another place the Qur'an says:

> "So judge between them according to what God has sent down, and do not follow their caprices." (The Holy Qur'an, Surah al-Ma'ida 5:48)

Accordingly, the Prophet of God held two positions: on the one hand, by means of revelation he was connected to God, from Whom he received the injunctions which he conveyed to the people; on

---

[341] Nu'mani, Kitab al-ghayba, p. 211

the other, he was in charge as the head of the community, which he organized politically and socially by promulgating the laws of Islam.

A study of the Prophet's biography reveals that he was practically in charge of the affairs of the community and ruled over them. He used to appoint governors and commanders, judges and administrators; he used to declare war, dispatch armies for defense and oversee every aspect of community life in the Muslim polity.[342]

The position that he held in the community was divinely ordained. In accordance with his appointment he was to legislate in the areas of the social and political life of the people as members of the Islamic umma, and see to the law's execution. Whereas Muslims were required to participate in the warfare, the Prophet was to prepare them for it and to call upon them when it was the proper jihad. For instance, the Qur'an commands the Prophet to encourage people to participate in warfare in the way of God:

> *"O Prophet, urge on the believers to ght." (The Holy Qur'an, Surah al-Anfal 8:65)*

> *"O Prophet, struggle (jihad) with the unbelievers and hypocrites, and be thou harsh with them." (The Holy Qur'an, Surah at-Tawba 9:73)*

> *"Surely We have sent down to thee the Book with the truth, so that thou mayest judge between people by that which God has shown thee. So be not an advocate for the traitors." (The Holy Qur'an, Surah an-Nisa' 4:105)*

---

[342] For details see: Shaykh 'Abd al-Haqq, Kitab al-taratib al-idariyya and Hafiz Abu 'Ubayd, Kitab al-amwal

Besides being the Prophet, which meant that he received the message from God and delivered it to the people, he was the head of the Muslims, invested with power to make decisions and give judgements, administer justice and institute penalties. In other words, to perform all those functions that strictly speaking belong to the head of a state. In this regard, the Qur'an required Muslims to obey the commands of God that were relayed to them through the Prophet. Thus the Qur'an says:

> *"O believers, obey God, and obey the Messenger and those in authority among you." (The Holy Qur'an, Surah an-Nisa' 4:59)*

> *"And obey God, and His Messenger, and do not quarrel together, and so lose heart, and your power depart." (The Holy Qur'an, Surah al-Anfal 8:46)*

> *"We sent not ever any Messenger, but that he should be obeyed, by the leave of God." (The Holy Qur'an, Surah an-Nisa' 4:64)*

In all these verses obedience to the Prophet is prefaced by obedience to God. Muslims are commanded to obey God and the Prophet. Obedience to God is materialized by accepting the ordinances sent through the Prophet. In addition, Muslims are specially required to obey the Prophet's commands, which include all that he, as the head of the community, requires Muslims to carry out. It is evident that obedience to the Prophet is derived from an obedience to God, and it is in this sense that it has become obligatory. It is accurate to maintain that governance was, from the very inception of Islam as a religion, an integral part of the Prophet's function as the leader of the community and its social-political structure.

Islamic Governance after the Prophet

Following his death, the prophethood and the revelation were terminated. But the ordinances and laws of religion, including the Islamic social-political programs, remained with Muslims as the directives of Islam. Here one should raise an important question: Did the end of the Prophethood mean that the governance of the community also was to be terminated? Did the Prophet himself conceive of the future of his community? Did he not leave any directives to ensure that his legacy would continue after him? Or, did he simply leave the entire issue of the leadership to the community to do as it pleased?

The Shi'a believe that the Prophet of Islam was also the statesman and ruler over the affairs of the community. He effected the programs that were revealed to him. He understood fully the critical importance of leadership for the umma. In order for Muslims to continue as a community they needed governance under a qualied leader who would implement the Islamic goals for humanity.

The Prophet himself was aware that his community could not survive without a just government to carry on his mission. It was for this reason that from the beginning of his mission, as the opportunity presented itself, and in accordance with the instructions received from God, the Prophet introduced 'Ali b. Abi Talib as his caliph and the Imam of the community after him. The books written by both the Sunni and the Shi'i scholars have recorded several occasions when 'Ali b. Abi Talib was introduced as the vicegerent of the Prophet. Among these occasions is the monumental speech of the Prophet during the Farewell Pilgrimage, in the Ghadir Khumm, when he stood in the midst of his community, including the major gures of early Islam, and said:

'O people who is more worthy ('awla) [in the eyes of] the believers than their ownselves?' They said: 'God and His Messenger know better.' He said: 'God is my Master and I am the Master of the Believers and I am worthier in their eyes than their ownselves. Whoever has me for his Master has 'Ali for his Master.' He said it thrice, and according to Ahmad, the Imam of the Hanbalis, four times.[343]

The above proclamation at the Ghadir Khumm regarding the leadership of Imam 'Ali b. Abi Talib occurred in the last year of the Prophet's life (10 AH/632 CE). Following the proclamation 'Umar b. al-Khattab met 'Ali and congratulated him saying: "O son of Abu Talib, congratulations for attaining the new position. From now on you are my master and the master of all believing men and women."

There are far too many such reports in the sources to mention. However, they all establish the fact that the Prophet made sure that his position as the ruler of the community would continue in 'Ali b. Abi Talib. He prepared him for this day on many occasions by giving him the necessary information about the responsibility he had. Moreover, he knew that 'Ali was endowed with infallibility and it was with the designation from God that he had acquired the position

---

[343] Yanabi' al-mawadda, p. 3

of the Imam after him.

'Ali too was aware of the great responsibility that was placed upon his shoulders. He was the protector of the Islamic ordinances and their executor. As such, the event at Ghadir Khumm was the culmination of a process that had begun in the early days of the Prophet's mission. In fact, 'Umar's statement while congratulating 'Ali indicates that he understood the meaning of the word mawla in its proper signication of a 'master.' Other Muslims also understood the Prophet's statement: 'Whoever has me for his Master has 'Ali for his Master,' as a statement of designation and, therefore, they paid their allegiance and remained loyal to him. Had the statement had any other than a political meaning, there would have been no need to pay allegiance.

'Ali b. Abi Talib, the Designated Caliph of the Prophet of God

Although the Prophet had ensured that his right to governance would continue through 'Ali b. Abi Talib's designation to the Imamate, after his death a number of his close companions decided to acquire the caliphate for themselves. Taking advantage of the ignorance and weakness of the people they usurped the legitimate right of 'Ali to rule. This marked the deviation of Islamic governance from its true path. His refusal to pay allegiance to those who came to power and his several orations in which he critically evaluated the situation after the death of the Prophet, indicate that 'Ali b. Abi Talib clearly saw the rupture between the ideal Islamic governance and the one that was pursued by the companions.

Moreover, these orations show the importance that was attached to the question of the comprehensive governance of the community, and not simply its religious and spiritual dimensions. The caliphs had not usurped the religious and spiritual authority of 'Ali, to whom they referred all their problems in those areas; rather, they had usurped his political power, the power to effect the laws of Islam.

When, nally, he assumed the caliphate in 35 AH/656 CE, he

shouldered the comprehensive power which included everything that the Prophet had done as the ruler. When Talha and Zubayr opposed his caliphate, they opposed this comprehensive aspect of his governance. They never opposed his religious and spiritual authority per se. Mu'awiya had disputed Imam 'Ali not in the matter of interpretation of an ordinance; rather he disputed him on his right of governance and his position as a comprehensive leader of the community.

From all this discussion it is possible to conclude that Islamic governance did not come to an end with the death of the Prophet. On the contrary, by appointing 'Ali, the Prophet ensured its perpetuity for posterity. It also demonstrates that the lawgiver of Islam never conceived of a system for the people which could do without governing the community's social-political structure. In other words, Islamic governance should be a permanent part of Muslim life in general throughout history.

Imam 'Ali b. Abi Talib designated his son Hasan to follow him in his position as the Imam of the Muslims. In turn, Imam Hasan appointed his brother Husayn to succeed him in the Imamate. From Imam Husayn the Imamate went to his son Zayn al-'Abidin and in this way it continued until the line reached the last Imam, Hujjat b. al-Hasan (peace be upon him).

All these twelve Imams, besides being endowed with divine protection in the form of infallibility and profound knowledge of Islamic revelation, were also granted the wisdom to govern and rule in accordance with the divine laws and scales of justice. Hence, the Imamate of the community and the governance of the infallible leader are indispensable aspects of the ideal Muslim public order. And yet, apart from the short time of the governance by 'Ali b. Abi Talib, no other had been given the opportunity to rule in accordance with the laws of God and to restore a true direction to and generate condence in Islamic public order.

Islamic Governance during the Period of Occultation

Now the question arises about the status of Islamic social-political programs during the occultation. What should the Muslims do when they do not have access to the Imam, the rightful ruler? Who should take charge of leading the community to its divinely ordained goal? Should the faithful simply abandon the idea of following the tradition of the Prophet in matters of governance? Were the directives given by the Prophet relevant only during his own short period of earthly life, and will they again be implemented only when the Mahdi appears?

Must the majority of God's ordinances dealing with social-political-legal matters remain in abeyance during this period of the invisible presence of the twelfth Imam? In other words, are we to read these verses of the Qur'an and discuss them in the light of the hadith-reports in order to enlighten ourselves without trying to effect them in our contemporary social and political existence?

Doubtless a Muslim ought not regard these Islamic ideals and directives as in abeyance until a qualied leader like the Imam himself assumes the governance. In particular, no scholar would ever concede that these ideals were given to the Prophet so that later generations should merely discuss them, dispute about them and ultimately write them down for the future generations. If this is so, then one has no choice but to agree that neither the Prophet nor the Imams left all these directives for an Islamic governance only in the future age of the Mahdi. Under no circumstance can one say that Islam came to provide the community with ordinances and social-political legislation without providing it the means for executing these ideals through the executor of the divine will, the leader, the Imam.

The Obligations of Muslims during the Occultation

It is true that the Prophet and the infallible Imam were appointed by God to undertake the governance of the community affairs as their rulers, and that the Prophet and the Imam should exert themselves to execute the divine will in this regard. Nevertheless, the essential obligation lies on the shoulders of the people who should provide the critical support needed by the Prophet and the Imam to attain the power and use it for advancing the purposes of God.

As long as the people do not show their loyalty and obedience to these divinely designated leaders, it is simply unthinkable to see the ideal governance being effected. By the same token, during the absence of the Imam, as in our own times, Muslims have the responsibility to seriously work for the establishment of the Islamic form of government. Islam, even under present conditions, has not suspended the duty of Muslims to implement and to follow its directives. In fact, many Islamic rulings are directed towards the generality of the Muslim community:

"Go forth, light and heavy! Struggle in God's way with your possessions and your selves; that is better for you, did you know." (The Holy Qur'an, Surah at-Tawba 9:41)

"Struggle in the way of God with your possessions and your selves." (The Holy Qur'an, Surah as-Saff 61:11)

"And ght in the way of God with those who ght with you, but aggress not." (The Holy Qur'an, Surah al-Baqara 2:190)

"As to the thief, male and female, cut off the hands of both, as a recompense for what they have earned, and a punishment exemplary from God; God is All-mighty, All-wise." (The Holy Qur'an, Surah al-Ma'ida 5:38)

"The fornicatress and the fornicator – scourge each one of them a hundred stripes, and in the matter of God's religion let no tenderness for them seize you . . ." (The Holy Qur'an, Surah an-Nur 24:2)

"O believers, be you securers of justice, witnesses for God, even though it be against yourselves, or your parents and kinsmen, whether the man be rich or poor." (The Holy Qur'an, Surah an-Nisa' 4:135)

All these verses are addressed to the generality of the Muslims and demand from them that they respond to their social obligations that are related to the betterment of Islamic public order. It is evident that carrying out these social injunctions cannot be possible without an authority who can ensure its fair execution. The nature of injunctions dealing with public order inevitably requires a governing body invested with executive powers to effectuate Islamic ordinances.

In other words, the comprehensive realization of an Islamic public order with all its spiritual, moral and legal dimensions is impossible without a government invested with executive powers. To practice Islam in all its dimensions necessarily requires the existence of a government that is committed to do its bidding. Thus the Qur'an says:

> *"He has laid down for you as religion that He charged Noah with, and that We have revealed to thee, and that We charged Abraham with, Moses and Jesus: 'Perform religion, and scatter not regarding it.'" (The Holy Qur'an, Surah ash-Shura 42:13)*

It is possible to conclude from these general addresses of the Qur'an to all believing Muslims and the provisions made by the Prophet for giving permanence to the governance of Islamic public order through Islam's social-political-legal-moral teachings that during the occultation of the twelfth Imam Muslims have the obligation to work seriously towards the implementation of Islamic ideals in their everyday personal and social lives. As long as we believe that Islam came to provide happiness in this and the next world and, therefore, it legislated laws to cover every aspect of God-human and human interpersonal relationships, then we must maintain the necessity of managing our affairs in accordance with these laws.

This conclusion becomes even more pertinent if we remind ourselves that we also believe that these laws were not given for the short period of the Prophet's life only; they will be with us until God resurrects us for the Final Judgement. Hence, our endeavors to effect these norms today assume some urgency.

Muslims must resolve to prepare themselves to be worthy of supporting the nal revolution of the Mahdi by constantly evaluating their shortcomings and reforming themselves to undertake the great responsibility of making the Islamic public order the only viable order that can guarantee peace with justice and harmony on the earth.

Two Evidences

1) The need to establish a government and to endeavor to make it stable is a rational need upon which all reasonable persons agree. Islam has not only not rejected this rational deduction, it has actually sanctioned it. During the Battle of Uhud in the early days of Islam, when the false news about the Prophet having been killed was spread among the Muslims, the consequence of such a story was the demoralization of Muslim soldiers who immediately abandoned their positions and were scattered. That moment has been captured in the following verse of the Qur'an:

> *"Muhammad is naught but a Messenger; Messengers have passed away before him. Why, if he should die or is slain, will you turn about on your heels?" (The Holy Qur'an, Surah al-'Imran, 3:144)*

Does it mean that after the Prophet dies Muslims should revert to their old habits? In other words, Islam is a reality that will remain even after the Prophet dies. Consequently, Muslims should assess their loyalty to the teachings of Islam and should work for its implementation without interruption. No explicit duty imposed by the Qur'an becomes invalidated by the death of the Prophet or the occultation of the Imam.

2) The second evidence is provided by the Muslims during the early history in the aftermath of the Prophet's death. The companions had gathered in the Thaqifa of Banu Sa'ida, all in agreement that the governance of the Muslim polity had to continue through a new leader, the caliph. The disagreement touched upon the question of who that leader would be, not upon the need for the leadership itself. The Ansar maintained that the leader had to be one of their group; the Muhajirun disputed them and contended that the leadership actually belonged to the Meccans. The compromise that was proposed suggested a caliph from one and a commander from the other group. However, no one ever said that there was no need for a leader and that they could continue an umma (community) without anyone directing their social and political life.

More importantly, even 'Ali b. Abi Talib, who disagreed with the outcome of the Thaqifa deliberations and opposed their decision, knowing very well that he was being denied his right to lead the community at its most critical stage, did not even for a moment dispute the fundamental need for someone to continue to provide governance to the nascent Islamic polity. The caliphate, as it emerged after the Thaqifa was, in 'Ali b. Abi Talib's opinion, a deviation from its original goal, but it was still a necessary instrument for the continuation of the social-political life of the umma.

It was for this reason that he never attempted to undermine the caliphate.

On the contrary, realizing the danger that was posed by the political turmoil to Islam, he never refrained from offering the best advice for Islam's preservation. Moreover, he never prevented his most loyal supporters and family members from accepting ofcial assignments under the caliphs. He was fully committed to the principle of governance for the continuation of Islamic public order in the future. In his dispute with the Khawarij, who seceded from his army in rebellion, and who had misused the Qur'anic verse: 'The judgement is God's alone' to rebel against 'Ali's authority, he refuted their interpretation by pointing out:

The statement is in itself a truth, but they infer an erroneous conclusion out of it. Indeed, there can be no judgement except that it belongs to God. However, they are implying that there should be no governance except that exercised by God. People necessarily need a ruler, whether he be godly or unjust, so that under his government a believer may be able to continue doing what he does, and an unbeliever may continue enjoying [his life] in it, until God's decree reaches its nal decision in their regard.

[Moreover, the need to have the governance is underscored by the fact that] under his governance taxes can be collected and the enemy can be fought, and the highways kept secure and safe. [In addition,] the rights of the weak can be exacted from the strong, so that a godly person can live in peace and remain immune from the harm of a wicked person.[344]

Accordingly, one should not doubt the principle that establishment and continuation of the government is among the necessary things. Moreover, this responsibility has been laid on the shoulders of the people. When the Prophet or the Imam is accessible, the people should support and help him to manage the affairs of the nation; when the Imam is in occultation, the people should search for and elect a well qualied jurist (faqih), knowledgeable in the detail of the laws of Islam, fully experienced in the social and political realm, and endowed with political insight to administer the Muslim public

---

[344] Nahj al-balagha, Speech No. 39

order.

The justication for electing a qualied jurist to govern the Muslim polity is found in the hadith of the Imams who not only accepted the jurist's governance in the absence of the twelfth Imam, but even recommended that their followers seek such leaders among themselves. Such a person is capable of leading the Muslim umma and of executing the Islamic social and political program.

It is relevant to point out that the debate about Islamic government and its relation to the 'governance of the jurist' (wilayat-i faqih) is intricate and needs a detailed exposition which we cannot undertake at this point in our discussion about the twelfth Imam (peace be upon him). Nevertheless, we will briey treat the subject and conclude our discussion.

Our purpose in going through all these details about the necessity of Islamic governance during the occultation is to make you aware that when we consider traditions that object to any active involvement in social and political movements prior to the advent of the Mahdi, we should be aware that all those obligations are classied as part of the collective duties – such as warfare, defence, institution of penalties, administration of justice, and so on and therefore are among the required matters of Islamic juridical tradition.

Accordingly, one can not doubt about their execution in a Muslim public order. In order to do so effectively, there ought to be a Muslim authority invested with the power to execute the social and political agenda of Islam. Hence, we should examine the traditions that encourage political quietism within the context of the need to manage Muslim affairs. I hope to take up this issue next time we meet and to elaborate on it in some detail so that we can arrive at our conclusion more objectively. It is running late, and we should adjourn now.

Dr. Jalali: Let me extend to you the invitation to meet once again here in my house for our next session.

Dr. Jalali: I would request Mr. Hoshyar to continue our previous discussion on the traditions about the merits of awaiting deliverance (faraj) through the advent of the Mahdi.

Mr. Hoshyar: Let us get into our main topic of investigation in the traditions dealing with opposition to political and social activism during the occultation.

As we have pointed out a major part of Islamic teachings which deal with ordinances which relate the Muslim public order to the religiously required deeds. These include participation in the defense of one's family, home, property, and so on; warfare with those who oppress the people; commanding the good and forbidding evil; and all other duties that constitute a necessary prerequisite for a Muslim as a member of society, of a public order. However, it is possible that some people might escape from the burden of these societal obligations and cite a hadith or two to justify their complacency and satisfaction with merely performing some rituals that please them. It is for this reason that I think the traditions that they employ to justify such behavior must be carefully examined to determine their source and validity.[345]

---

[345] These hadith can be studied in several important collections, such as Wasa'il al-shi'a, Vol. 11, pp. 35-41; Bihar al-anwar, Vol. 52

First Group of Traditions

There are traditions that advise the Shi'is not to accept the invitation to join a person who rises in armed revolt without first carefully examining his credentials and goals. These traditions, furthermore, require the Shi'is to reject the claims of leadership and the lofty goals of such individuals, even if they happen to be among the descendants of 'Ali b. Abi Talib.

First hadith: It is narrated from Muhammad b. Ya'qub, from 'Ali b. Ibrahim, from his father, from Safwan b. Yahya, from 'Isa b. al-Qasim, who said: I heard Imam Sadiq say:

Do not leave taqwa (fear of) God, the One and without any partners, and watch over yourselves constantly. I solemnly declare that if someone has chosen a shepherd to care for his sheep, but afterward finds someone else who is more wise than the first one for the task, he will leave the first one and employ the services of the wiser one. By God, if you had two life-times, and you experimented with the first one, and were left with the second lifetime, then there would be no difficulty in utilizing the experience of the first lifetime. But the reality is other than this. Every person has no more than one self, for which, if it falls into peril, there is no possibility for repentance or return.

Therefore, it is necessary for you to carefully evaluate and select the best way for your selves.

Hence, if one among us came to you and called upon you to revolt, think carefully and nd out for what purpose he has revolted. Do not simply say [to justify his revolt by saying something like:] "Well, Zayd b. 'Ali also had arisen before!" The reason is that Zayd was a learned and truthful person and had not called upon you to acknowledge his own leadership; rather, he was calling towards a person who would be acceptable and endorsed by the ahl al-bayt. Had he succeeded, he would have acted upon his promise and would have handed over the power to its owner.

Zayd revolted against the government so that he could overthrow it. But what is the one who has emerged today calling you? Is he calling you towards a person who is acceptable and endorsed by the ahl al-bayt? No, absolutely not. I am calling you to bear witness that we are not pleased with this person's revolt. This man has not even reached power and he has already started opposing us. And when he does seize power and raises his ag, he would certainly not submit to us in obedience.

Hence, accept the call of the one about whom all the descendants of Fatima are in agreement. That person is your Imam and your leader. When the month of Rajab dawns, come to the help of God. There is no problem if you wish to delay it until the month of Sha'ban. And, it is even better for you, if you wished to keep the fast of Ramadan with your family. If you need any signs, it is sufcient to remind yourselves about the rise of Sufyani.[346]

The hadith is regarded as authentic because the entire chain of

---

[346] Wasa'il, Vol. 11, p. 35; Bihar al-anwar, Vol. 52, p. 301. The tenth hadith in this section is also from the same narrator and, as such, should not be seen as a different tradition

transmission has been accredited by scholars.

Meaning and Implications of the hadith

The warning given by Imam Sadiq deals with the problem of individuals from the ahl al-bayt rising against the tyrannical power of the caliphs and claiming for themselves the leadership. The Imam provides the criteria of accepting such claims: if the individual is truly qualied or if he is honest about his goals and about the leader for whom he is revolting, then his Shi'a should have no problem in responding positively to his call.

This was the situation during the times of practically all the Imams before the twelfth Imam went into occultation. The hadith apparently addresses the revolt of Muhammad b. 'Abd Allah b. Hasan b. 'Ali b. Abi Talib, which the Imam compares with an earlier revolt of Zayd b. 'Ali b. Husayn b. 'Ali b. Abi Talib. The Imam warns people not to conate the two upheavals, and thereby justify their positive response to the later revolt. For Zayd's revolt was launched in order to restore the true Imamate to the rightful Imam; whereas there was no such noble goal in Muhammad's revolt.

Moreover, there was a difference in the leadership of the two movements. Zayd's personality was far more credible than Muhammad's. Imam Sadiq's observation that the latter would not obey him clearly explains his misgivings about the goal of the recent revolt.

Abu Faraj Isfahani, writing about Muhammad b. 'Abd Allah, says that the ahl al-bayt used to call Muhammad the Mahdi, and believed that he was the promised Mahdi of the traditions. The belief was so widespread that a group of people belonging to the Hashimites, descendants of Abi Talib, and the 'Abbasids paid allegiance to him. To add to this atmosphere of expectation and revolution, according to Abu Faraj, Muhammad b. 'Abd Allah used to publicly conrm his own candidacy to Mahdiism.[347]

In any case Muhammad b. 'Abd Allah arose as the Mahdi during Imam Sadiq's period and called upon people to join him. It was in this context that the above cited hadith was related as a warning to the Shi'a not to be taken in by such messianic claims. In other words, the purpose of the Imam was not to issue a blanket prohibition against any kind of activist response to social and political turmoil. Rather, his efforts were directed towards educating his followers to distinguish between the well-intended revolt of Zayd and the ill-intended rise of Muhammad, both members of the ahl al-bayt. In fact, on the basis of the above narrative, it appears that Imam Sadiq gave his approval to the former, including people's participation in that, while condemning the latter.

It is important to understand the goals of the revolution of Zayd, which received positive commendation from Imam Sadiq. Of course, in the limited space that we have in this study, we can only treat them in brief:

1) Zayd was a pious, knowledgeable, and truthful person. He had the necessary qualications for becoming a leader of the movement. Imam Sadiq's own evaluation of his uncle's character provides the main evidence for his endorsement of his revolution. He says: "My

---

[347] Maqatil al-talibiyyin, p. 233-240

uncle Zayd was benecial to us in this and the next world. Indeed, he attained martyrdom in God's way. He is like those who were killed and attained martyrdom ghting with the Prophet, 'Ali b. Abi Talib, Hasan and Husyan."[348]

In a tradition reported by Abu Faraj Isfahani, the Prophet told Imam Husayn: "Among your descendants will be born a son whose name will be Zayd. He and his supporters will be resurrected with a brilliant and beautiful face on the Day of Judgement, and will enter Paradise."[349]

2) Zayd's goal in his revolt was sound. He was not claiming to be an Imam. His main aim was to overthrow the unjust government and to restore the authority to the rightful Imam among the ahl al-bayt. If he had succeeded he would have kept his promise. Again, Imam Sadiq used to say: "May God have mercy on my uncle Zayd! Had he succeeded in his mission he would have fullled his promise. He used to call people to acknowledge a person among the ahl al-bayt who was acceptable to and endorsed by them."[350]

In some sources there are statements to the effect that Zayd claimed to be the Imam. His son Yahya, however, denied that ascription to him and regarded Imam Sadiq as the Imam. Among his followers and his soldiers also Imam Sadiq was acknowledged as the most learned of the Hashimites and the rightful Imam. 'Ammar Sabati relates the occasion when a man asked Sulayman b. Khalid, one of the soldiers in Zayd's army, who had revolted: "What is your opinion of Zayd? Who is more excellent, Zayd or Ja'far b. Muhammad [Sadiq]?" Sulayman replied: "By God, one day of Ja'far b. Muhammad's life is more valuable than the entire life of Zayd." When Zayd was told

---

[348] 'Uyun al-akhbar, p. 252

[349] Maqatilal-talibiyyin, p. 140-41

[350] Bihar al-anwar, Vol. 46, p. 199

about this he too acknowledged that excellence by saying: "Ja'far b. Muhammad is our Imam in all the questions that deal with the lawful and unlawful."[351]

3) Zayd's revolution was a calculated measure; it did not occur as an emotional outburst and without any preparation. The underlying intent was to command the good and forbid the evil, and to combat the forces of tyranny and wickedness. Zayd wanted to overthrow the unjust government by use of force and to replace it with a qualied member of the ahl al-bayt, who had the support of every one. It was mainly for this reason that a large number of Muslims had rallied to his cause. In Kufa alone, 15,000 thousand people had pledged their support for him. His army was made up of peoples from different regions of Iraq and Khurasan.[352]

The importance and legitimacy of Zayd's revolt was underscored by the fact that a great number of Sunni scholars had also responded to his call and joined his revolution. Some, like Abu Hanifa, the Imam of the Sunnis, had endorsed and sent him monetary help for his movement.[353]

Zayd had discussed his intention to rise against the unjust authority with Imam Sadiq, beforehand, to which the Imam replied: "Uncle, if you are willing to be killed and your body hanged in the trash of Kufa, then do what you think is right." Zayd was so determined to go ahead with his plan that in spite of what the Imam had predicted he was willing to die for his cause. He fought in God's path until he was killed. Imam Rida said the following about him:

Zayd was the learned one among the descendants of Muhammad. He was angered for God's sake and fought against God's enemies

---

[351] Bihar al-anwar, Vol. 46, p. 135ff

[352] Maqatil al-talibiyyin, p. 146-47

[353] Ibid., p. 99

until he became a martyr in God's path.[354]

Let us once again come back to our main inquiry about the tradition. It is evident that one cannot use the tradition reported by 'Isa b. Qasim as being against an activist response to the political turmoil in the Muslim public order. On the contrary, it is among those reports that support a legitimate movement against injustices. The purport of the Imam's warnings is to make sure that his followers do not blindly follow this or that person and movement and put themselves in an unnecessarily dangerous condition.

As long as the necessary criteria, as discussed above, were fullled, there was no prohibition against joining the leader and his movement. Accordingly, one cannot regard the tradition as among those opposed to any action on the part of the Shi'a during the occultation of the twelfth Imam.

Second hadith: It is reported from Ahmad b. Yahya al-Maktab, from Muhammad b. Yahya al-Suli, from Muhammad b. Zayd al-Nahwi, from Ibn Abi 'Abdun, from his father, from Imam Rida (peace be upon him), who told Ma'mun, the 'Abbasid caliph:

Do not compare my brother Zayd with Zayd b. 'Ali b. Husayn. Zayd b. 'Ali was among the learned authorities of Muhammad's descendants, who was angered for God's sake and fought against God's enemies until he was killed in God's way and attained martyrdom. My father, Musa b. Ja'far said that he heard from his father, Ja'far b. Muhammad, who said: "May God have mercy on my uncle Zayd. He called people towards a person acceptable to and endorsed by the ahl al-bayt. Had he succeeded he would have denitely fullled his promise." He also used to say: "Zayd consulted me about his mission and I told him, if you are willing to be killed and your body hanged in the trash of Kufa, then do what you think is right."

---

[354] Bihar al-anwar, Vol. 46, p. 174

Imam Rida then said:

Zayd was not claiming something that was not his right. He was so godfearing that he could never claim something that did not belong to him. On the contrary, he used to tell the people: "I am calling you to acknowledge a person who will be acceptable to the family of the Prophet."[355]

The hadith is not sound, as far as the chain of transmission (sanad) is concerned. The narrators have been described by scholars of biographical dictionaries as "lacking credibility." As for its content, it cannot be regarded as being opposed to an activist stance during the occultation. After all, it is describing positively Zayd's movement and personality. However, another Zayd, that is, Zayd b. Musa, Imam Rida's brother has been criticized. This Zayd had emerged in Basra and had called people to acknowledge him as their leader. He destroyed the people's homes and plundered them. He was nally defeated and arrested by the caliphal authority. Ma'mun forgave him and sent him to see Imam Rida. Imam Rida ordered him released but asked his brother not to speak to him ever again.[356]

Evidently, even this hadith is not evidence against an activist response to the injustices in the Muslim polity during the absence of the twelfth Imam (peace be upon him).

---

[355] Wasa'il al-shi'a, Vol 11, p. 39

[356] Bihar al-anwar, Vol. 48, p. 315

Second Group of Traditions

These are the traditions that indicate that any revolution before the nal widespread revolution of the Mahdi will end up in defeat.

First hadith: It is reported from 'Ali b. Ibrahim, from his father, from Hammad b. 'Isa, from Rab'i, reaching back to 'Ali b. Husayn (peace be upon him), who said:

By God, none among us will rise before the revolution of the Qa'im, except the one resembling a chick that leaves its nest before it can y. Such will fall in the hands of children who will play with it.[357]

This tradition is regarded as weak in transmission because it is incomplete. As such it is not regarded as reliable.

Second hadith: It is reported from Jabir, from Imam Baqir, who said:

The mode of our Qa'im's revolution will resemble the Prophet's emergence. The mode of revolution of any one among us, the ahl al-bayt, before the emergence of the Qa'im, will resemble a chick that leaves its nest [before being ready to y], and becomes a plaything

---

[357] Mustadrak al-wasa'il, Vol. 2, p. 248

for children.[358]

Third hadith: It is reported from Abu al-Jarud, who heard Imam Baqir say:

None among us, the ahl al-bayt, rises in order to stand against injustices and ght for the truth, except he becomes entangled in difculties and faces defeat. Until that time, when those who were present in the Battle of Badr, and who went swiftly to help those who were ghting, and did not have any one killed in need of burial nor any one injured in need of treatment, rise.

The reporter asked: 'Who does the Imam mean by that?' Abu Jarud replied: 'Angels.'[359]

Fourth hadith: It is reported from Abu al-Jarud, from Imam Baqir. He asked the Imam to recommend to him something for his benet. In response the Imam said:

I recommend to you that you be godfearing, and remain in your home. And live with these common people. Avoid the people among us who rise up, because they do not have any goals. . . Be aware that there is no group that rises in order to combat injustice and restore the glory of Islam except that they are struck on the ground by calamities until that time when a group that was present in the Battle of Badr arises . . .[360]

The rest of the hadith resembles the previous tradition. These last three traditions, again, on account of a weak chain of transmission are regarded as unreliable. Moreover, one of the narrators is Abu Jarud who followed the Zaydi faction and was the founder of the Jarudiyya sect. He has been regarded as a weak transmitter by scholars of biographical dictionaries.

---

[358] Ibid

[359] Wasa'il al-shi'a, Vol. 11, p. 36; Bihar al-anwar, Vol. 52, p. 302

[360] Mustadrak al-wasa'il, Vol. 2, p. 248

Investigation into the Meanings and Implications of these hadith-Reports

The traditions show Imam Baqir encountering those among his followers who want to know the reason he has not arisen. They relate the external truth about the situation encountered by individuals belonging to the ahl al-bayt who emerged and who initiated a movement against the unjust forces, but met with resistance and destruction. It also recounts the faith in the future revolution of the Mahdi who will receive divine help from the angels, just as those who fought that monumental battle of Badr in the early days of Islam received such miraculous help. In other words, the traditions are engaged in explaining the reason why the Imams could not arise against the unjust authority without adequate preparation and without divine aid.

There is also another aspect to these traditions: as reminders for those who insisted on radical responses at inopportune times for the success of such actions. These are grim reminders about those 'Alawids who had been killed at different times because they had taken off "before they could y out of the safety of their nest." In other words, success was not guaranteed to any uprising before the revolution of the Mahdi. Nevertheless, the traditions do not convey that the legally and morally imposed obligation of jihad in God's way, defence of Islam and the Muslims, commanding the good and forbidding the evil, confronting injustices and wickedness, were all in abeyance since the Imams had no discretionary authority to effect these duties.

If one is informed of the adverse outcome of a struggle, it does not mean that he is unable, then, to make a decision to put up the struggle. Here Imam Husayn serves as a good example. He knew the outcome that would ensue because of his stance against the injustices of the Umayyads, and still he decided to fulll his legal and moral obligation of defending Islam and the Qur'an. There is absolutely no doubt that today Islam has survived because of the sacrices that were made by Imam Husayn, his family and his companions. Hence, it is accurate to maintain that none of the above hadith-reports imply that the obligations to defend and protect the Muslim public order specied by the Shari'a are in suspension until the twelfth Imam returns.

Third Group of Traditions

These are the traditions that require the Shi'a to refrain from joining any movement before the nal appearance of the twelfth Imam. First hadith: It is related from several narrators, from Ahmad b.

Muhammad b. 'Uthman b. 'Isa, from Bakr b. Muhammad, from Sudyar, who said that Imam Sadiq said:

Stay in your homes. As long as day and night are motionless, you too remain calm. When you hear that Sufyani has arisen, then commute towards us, even if it be on foot.[361]

The transmission of the hadith is problematic, because the persons cited in the chain include a waqi, that is, one of those who stopped believing in the Imamate's continuation after the seventh, Imam Musa Kazim. 'Uthman b. Sa'id was Imam Kazim's agent while the Imam was alive. After his death he became a waqi, and refrained from sending the Imam's share of khums to Imam Rida. The latter had shown his severe disapproval of him for that. He repented later on and returned all the goods belonging to the Imam. Equally

---

[361] Wasa'il al-shi'a, Vol. 11, p. 36

problematic is the reliability of Sudayr b. Hakim Sayra.

Second hadith: It is related from Ahmad b. 'Ali b. al-Hakam, from Abi Ayyub al-Khazzaz, from 'Umar b. Hanzala. He said he heard from Imam Sadiq, who said:

"There are ve signs that will occur before the rise of the Qa'im: (1) The cry [from the sky]; (2) the [rise of] Sufyani; (3) the sinking [of the earth in some parts]; (4) the killing of Nafs Zakiyya; and, (5) the emergence of a Yamani." The narrator asked: "O son of the Prophet, what if one of the members of the ahl al-bayt rises before these signs occur? Should we follow him?" The Imam said: "No."[362]

The chain of transmission in this hadith is also problematic because of the inclusion of 'Umar b. Hanzala, who has not been accredited.

Third hadith: It is reported from Muhammad b. al-Hasan b. al-Fadl b. Shadhan, from al-Hasan b. Mahbub, from 'Amr b. Abi al-Miqdam, from Jabir, from Imam Baqir. He said:

Remain still on earth; do not move your hands and feet, until the signs of which I inform you occur. [These are:], dispute among the family of so and so; and the call of a caller from the sky; and the sound that will come from the direction of Damascus.[363]

This tradition also lacks reliability because of its chain of transmission, which includes an unknown narrator by the name of 'Umar b. Abi al-Miqdam. Shaykh Tusi has narrated the tradition from two sources which both happen to be unreliable.

Fourth hadith: It is related from al-Hasan b. Muhammad al-Tusi, from his father, from al-Mud, from Ahmad b. Muhammad al-'Alawi, from Haydar b. Muhammad b. Nu'aym, from Muhammad b. 'Isa, from al-Hasan b. Khalid, who said: "I told Abu al-Hasan al-Rida that 'Abd Allah b. Bukayr has related a tradition which I would like to

---

[362] Ibid., p. 37

[363] Ibid., p. 41

tell you." He said, "Go ahead and tell me what is this hadith?" I said: "Ibn Bukayr has related from 'Ubayd b. Zurara who said: 'When Muhammad b. 'Abd Allah b. Hasan revolted I was with Imam Sadiq (peace be upon him). One of the companions came and said: May my life be a sacrice for you! Muhammad b. Hasan has revolted. What is your opinion about this matter?' The Imam said:

As long as the earth and the heavens are calm you too remain motionless. Hence, if this is the situation there will neither be a Qa'im nor a revolution.

Imam Rida said:

Imam Sadiq is right. But the meaning of what he said is not as Ibn Bukayr has inferred. Rather, the intention of the Imam was to convey that as long as the sky is silent from the nal cry and the earth from sinking the army [of God's enemy] you too remain undisturbed.[364]

This hadith is not sound in its transmission, because Ahmad b. Muhammad has not been identied by scholars of biographical dictionaries. Likewise, three other persons have not been authenticated in this chain, namely, Hasan b. Khalid, Abu al-'Ala' and Sayra.

Fifth hadith: It is related from Muhammad b. Humam, from Ja'far b. Malik al-Fazazi, from Muhammad b. Ahmad, from 'Ali b. Asbat, from some of his companions, from Imam Sadiq. He said:

Hold your tongues, and remain within the connes of your homes, because you will not get anything that the rest of the people do not get. Moreover, Zaydis will be your shield [against the atrocities that are being committed].[365]

This tradition too suffers from a weak chain of transmission and, hence, it is not that reliable. A number of transmitters are omitted and the tradition is taken from 'Ali b. Asbat without any information

---

[364] Ibid., p. 39

[365] Mustadrak al-wasa'il, Vol. 2, p. 248

about his sources. Moreover, Ja'far b. Muhammad b. Malik is regarded as a weak link.

Sixth hadith: It is narrated from 'Ali b. Ahmad, from 'Abd Allah b. Musa al-'Alawi, from Muhammad b. Sinan, from 'Ammar b. Marwan, from Minkhal b. Jamil, from Jabir b. Yazid, from Imam Baqir. He said:

As long as the sky is calm, you too remain calm and do not revolt against anyone. Indeed your situation is not obscure. The exception [to this calmness] is that there are stings from God, on which people have no power.[366]

The chain of transmission of this hadith also suffers in reliability because Minkhal b. Jamil has been identied as weak and harmful in his narration.

---

[366] Ibid., Vol. 2, p. 247

Investigation into the Meanings and Implications of these hadith-Reports

Before examining the implications of these reports, it is relevant to point out that the Shi'a and the companions of the Imams lived in anticipation of the awaited Mahdi's rising. This anticipation was founded upon the traditions that had been handed down from the time of the Prophet and the Imams (peace be upon them) in which it was promised that when the Mahdi appears he will ll the earth with justice and equity as it is lled with tyranny and wickedness.

They had also learnt from the traditions that when that person comes forth he will be triumphant and will enjoy God's special favor. It was for this reason that the subject of the rise and the nal victory of the Mahdi and so on was prevalent among the Shi'a. The followers of the Imams used to ask them the reason for their silence in the face of all sorts of atrocities and the inhumanity suffered by the generality of Muslims under the caliphs. At times, they used to ask a very specic question: "Why does not the Qa'im from the ahl al-bayt rise?"

At other times, they wanted to know the signs of the Imam's appearance. It was such conditions that some descendants of 'Ali b.

Abi Talib took advantage of appearing as the promised Mahdi of the family of Muhammad (peace be upon him and his progeny) and ght against the evil power of the caliphs.

However, within a short time they were defeated, arrested, and mercilessly killed.

This was the background of these hadith-reports that we have examined in this section. Hence, when the Imam advises his followers to adopt quietism in the face of the existing turmoil, he is actually informing them that the person who has revolted is not the promised Mahdi. They have to wait for his appearance which will be attended by some specic signs as well as a movement of resistance. These hadith, then, are meant to warn their followers not to fall into any trap before the real event has taken place. They do not, in any way, relieve them from assuming the tasks laid down by the law for their own and their religion's survival. There is no evidence, whatsoever, to ascribe such illegitimate views to the Imams whose sole purpose in uttering these traditions was to save them from being meaninglessly destroyed. Hence, these traditions cannot be regarded as opposing all activist responses which seek to preserve Islamic public order.

Fourth Group of Traditions

These are the traditions that recommend the Shi'a not to make haste in rising against an unjust government.

First hadith: It is reported from several companions of the Imam, from Ahmad b. Muhammad b. Khalid, from Muhammad b. 'Ali, from Hafs b. 'Asim, from Sayf al-Tammar, from Abi al-Marhaf, from Imam Baqir, who said:

The dirt gets into the eye of the one who stirs it up. Those who make haste destroy themselves. . . .

Surely, they (i.e., the government forces) intend to see people rising against them [so that they can get rid of them]. O Abu Marhaf, do you believe that those who persevere will not receive any release from God? Indeed, by God, they will certainly receive deliverance.[367]

The chain of transmission of this hadith is weak, because it includes Muhammad b. 'Ali, the Kufan narrator, who is regarded as weak by scholars of biographical dictionaries. Moreover, Abu al-Marhaf's identity is unknown.

The context of the hadith is the period in which a group of people

---

[367] Wasa'il al-shi'a, Vol. 11, p. 36

had revolted against the caliphal authority, and were defeated. It is for this reason the narrator appears to be anxious that Shi'is might also be targeted. Hence, the Imam consoles him and assures him that God will deliver those who remain steadfast. Accordingly, this tradition cannot be classied as one of those which opposes any active participation in movements led by legitimate individuals with well-dened goals.

Second hadith: It is related from al-Hasan b. Muhammad al-Tusi, from his father, from al-Mud, from Ibn Qawlawayh, from his father, from Ahmad b. Muhammad, from 'Ali b. Asbat, from his uncle Ya'qub b. Salim, from Abi al-Hasan al-'Abidi, from Imam Sadiq (peace be upon him). He said: "Anyone who for God's sake adopts perseverance, God will make him enter Paradise."[368]

This hadith is relatively well authenticated, since its reporters are all regarded as trustworthy.

The context of the hadith is not evident from the text. But it is clear that the Imam is recommending patience in general and the reward that accrues to the person who perseveres. It does not deal necessarily with circumstances of revolt or other social-political turmoil.

Third hadith: Imam 'Ali b. Abi Talib says:

Stay where you are, and when visited by calamities be patient. Do not move your hands and swords in the way of fullling the inclination of your tongues. Do not be in haste. Surely, any one of you dying on his bed while acknowledging the right of his Lord, and the right of his Prophet and his ahl al-bayt, dies a martyr. He deserves to receive the reward for the intention of his righteous deed. He will also reap the reward for the intention to ght with his sword [in defence of truth and justice]. Undoubtedly, there is a time and specic limit for

---

[368] Ibid. p. 39

everything.³⁶⁹

The hadith is also part of the Nahj al-balagha, and is regarded as authentic.

Fourth hadith: It is related from Muhammad b. Yahya, from Muhammad b. al-Hasan, from 'Abd al-Rahman b. Abu Hashim, from al-Fadl al-Katib. He said that he was in the presence of Imam Sadiq when he received the letter from Abu Muslim [Khurasani]. He told the messenger that there was no reply to carry back and that he should leave his presence immediately. And then he added:

God does not expedite a matter because His servants are in a hurry. To be sure, it is easier to dig a mountain from its place than to overthrow a government whose term has not been decreed to end.

The narrator asked for a sign of such an imminence that would be recognized by the Imam and his followers. The Imam said:

Do not move from where you are until the Sufyani has arisen. At that time run towards us. And, he repeated the sentence thrice: "The rise of Sufyani is bound to happen."³⁷⁰

The hadith is regarded as reliable on the basis of its chain of transmission.

Fifth hadith: It is reported from Muhammad b. 'Ali b. al-Hasan, from his sources, from Hammad b. 'Amr, from Anas b. Muhammad, from his father, from Imam Sadiq, from his forefathers. This was a recommendation from the Prophet to 'Ali b. Abi Talib. He said:

It is easier to dig huge mountains than to remove those in power whose time to vanish has not come yet.³⁷¹

This hadith has a problem when examined for its chain of transmission. It includes Hammad whose identity is unknown. In addition,

---

³⁶⁹ Ibid., p. 40
³⁷⁰ Ibid
³⁷¹ Ibid., p. 38

Anas b. Muhammad and his father are regarded as lacking credibility.

Sixth hadith: It is reported from Humayd b. Ziyad, from 'Ubayd Allah b. Ahmad al-Dihqan, from 'Ali b. al-Hasan al-Tatari, from Muhammad b. Ziyad, from Aban, from Sabah b. Siyaba, from al-Mu'alla b.

Khunays who said, 'I took letters from 'Abd al-Salam b. Nu'aym, Sudayr, and others to Imam Sadiq at the time when the black-clothed one had arisen. This was just before the 'Abbasids revolted. The letter said: "We have decided that the matter of leadership should be handed over to you. What is your opinion about it?" The Imam threw the letter on the ground and said: "Alas, alas, alas! I am not their (i.e., the insurrectionists') Imam. Do they not know that the awaited Mahdi will kill the Sufyani""'[372]

The hadith is not reliable as far the chain of transmission in concerned. The problem is that Sabah b. Siyaba is unidentied.

---

[372] Ibid., p. 37

Investigation into the Meanings and Implications of these hadith-Reports

It is important to bear in mind what we have said earlier: the followers of the Imams unfailingly anticipated emancipation from tyrannical conditions through the rise of the Qa'im from among the family of the Prophet, as predicted in the traditions from him and the Imams (peace be upon them). In addition, we must not forget that the Shi'a were living under most cruel circumstances in this period. They were under surveillance, in prisons, executed, burnt alive, and so on. Consequently, whenever a member of the ahl al-bayt promised to lead the movement to redress the wrongs committed against them, they did not hesitate to follow him. They even accepted their claim to be the promised Mahdi, and rallied around to lend them support for their revolution.

On the side of the government, the Umayyads, and then the 'Abbasids, were fully aware of the messianic traditions and the political activism it generated among the dispossessed people. They also knew that the Shi'a exerted lot of pressure on their Imams to ght injustices and to replace unjust rulers by assuming power themselves. It was for this reason that 'Abbasid spies constantly reported the whereabouts of the Shi'i Imams and their contacts with their Shi'a, expecting that they would eventually conspire against the government.

This general observation about the times in which the Imams lived and guided their followers explains many traditions cited in this chapter. The main point that the Imams wanted their followers to realize was that the time for the revolution of the promised Mahdi had not as yet arrived. There were specic signs that would precede that revolution under the leadership of the Qa'im of the family of the Prophet. More importantly, there was a realistic assessment of the power of the unjust authorities in such statements as "It is easier to dig huge mountains than to remove those in power whose time to vanish has not come yet."

Hence, the Shi'a were admonished to bear with patience their burdens and to remain alert without causing destruction to themselves at the hands of the wicked rulers. This does not teach submission and quietism, as others have interpreted. On the contrary, it requires the Shi'a to assess each instance of upheaval carefully in order to avoid being drawn into them without any advantage. In fact, all the traditions point towards using one's intellect to understand the realities and not to respond simply emotionally and in reaction.

In the nal analysis, the implication of these traditions is an explicit demand that the followers of the Imam, who happened to be in the minority and under the constant hostile watch of the rulers, deliberate and conceive better strategies to work for their self-preservation as well as for the preservation of an Islamic public order. To be sure, the purport of Imam 'Ali b. Abi Talib's statement: "Stay where you are, and when visited by calamities be patient. Do not move your hands and swords in the way of fullling the inclination of your tongues," is a warning not to submit to emotional outbursts, but to learn from experience the wisdom of caution when the power is unjust and wicked.

Fifth Group of Traditions

These are the traditions that regard the person who leads any revolution prior to the revolution of the Mahdi as an evildoer, taghüt.

First hadith: It is related from Muhammad b. Yahya, from Ahmad b. Muhammad, from 'Isa b. al-Husayn b. al-Mukhtar, from Abu Basir, from Imam Sadiq, who said:

The leader of every ag [in an uprising] that is raised before the rising of the Qa'im is an evildoer who is worshipped (taghüt) [by the people for his daringness] beside God.[373]

This hadith is authenticated on the basis of its narrators who are all regarded as reliable.

Second hadith: It is reported from Muhammad b. Ibrahim al-Nu'mani, from 'Abd al-Wahid b. 'Abd Allah, from Ahmad b. Muhammad b. Rayyah al-Zuhri, from Muhammad b. al-'Abbas, from 'Isa al-Husayni, from al-Hasan b. 'Ali b. Abi Hamza, from his father, from Malik b. A'yan al-Jihani, from Imam Baqir, who said:

The leader of any ag that is raised before the raising of the Mahdi's

---

[373] Ibid., p. 37

ag, is an evildoer.[374]

---

[374] Mustadrak al-wasa'il, Vol 2, p. 248

Investigation into the Meanings and Implications of these hadith-Reports

To be sure, "raising of the ag" is a metaphor for beginning a battle against a system in order to establish a new government, and a new system. The standard-bearer is the leader of the movement who is in the process of overthrowing the ruling regime and installing a new government. For this he calls upon the people to join him. Taghūt, as we have seen in other traditions, is a tyrant who has attacked God's creatures and has forced them to accept his rule without opposition. The credo of the leader is captured in the phrase: "the one who worships other than God." Accordingly, he is engaged in undermining God's authority among His people, so that he can pursue his personal ambitions. It is in this sense that the word taghūt is applied to the leader of such a movement.

The meaning of the tradition is that any ag that is raised before the revolution of the Qā'im, and of which the leader calls the people towards himself, that bearer of the ag is to be regarded as an evildoer.

Hence, the hadith implies that insurrection for purposes other than the correct religion is to be rejected outright. However, if the purpose of the revolt is to restore violated justice and to make people aware of their spiritual and moral responsibilities, then it is to be regarded as legitimate. The leader of this latter kind of revolt does not call people to himself; rather, he is inviting people towards God. As such, his ag is leading the people in the same direction as that of the Qa'im. It is not engaged in negating the achievements of the other Imams and the Prophet, who all at different times stood rm against injustices and atrocities committed against innocent peoples.

Conclusions of the Discussion

The majority of the traditions that we examined in this section were classied by the scholars of the science of hadith as weak. As such, they cannot be used as evidence for the argument that is being put forward in opposition to an activist response during the occultation of the twelfth Imam. The traditions, however, provide the guidelines for the Shi'a to consider in acknowledging valid and invalid religious movements led by one or another leader. They also serve as a reminder to them that the time for the appearance of the Mahdi had not arrived yet. Under the circumstances that existed for the Shi'a community living as a minority under those most unfavorable circumstances that were prevalent under the caliphate, it was expedient for them not to join the bandwagon of anyone who invited them to rise against tyranny. In fact, under those conditions patience is a virtue.

Furthermore, it was a duty to determine both the leadership's claim and intent, before making the decision to support or reject an uprising. Not every ag that is raised in the name of ghting injustice deserves unquestioning support from the Shi'a. The criteria for judging a just cause provided in the traditions function as a deterrent rather than as a total prohibition against taking up arms against tyrants. In other words, the traditions do not propose complete withdrawal for the followers of the ahl al-bayt from defending God's laws and the Muslim public order. It simply requires them to be alert at all times about their duty to God and to God's purposes for humanity as specied in the teachings of Islam on interpersonal justice.

* * *

To recapitulate our lengthy discussion, let us summarize our major propositions and then derive the nal overall conclusion.

1. Islam is not simply concerned with the spiritual aspects of human religiosity. It has legislated comprehensively on every aspect of human existence – as individuals related to God, and as members of the human community related to fellow humans. Thus, all the chapters of Islamic law, whether they deal with prayer or with fasting, with warfare or defence, reveal this bi-dimensional feature of Islam.
2. There is no doubt that Islam was revealed in order to be implemented as a vital aspect of meaningful human existence.
3. The implementation of Islam depends upon the establishment of a Muslim polity and government that is committed to executing the divine plan on earth by creating an ideal society.
4. The Prophet was not merely an envoy of God who had come to deliver the message. He was also the executor of the divine will on earth. An integral part of his prophetic obligation was to organize his people and lead them to establish divine scales of justice on earth.
5. This obligation of implementing the divine will on earth did

not end with the death of the Prophet. It continues as long as Islam remains the religion of humankind.

6. It is the duty of the people to support and assist the Prophet and his rightful infallible successors who also are invested with the power to create the ideal Muslim public order. This requirement is extended to the times when there is no infallible leader in power or when such a leader is in occultation. As long as there is a Muslim polity that needs support and maintenance through government, a military apparatus, and nancial structures, Muslims have the obligation to provide that support. During the occultation, when the twelfth Imam lives an invisible life, the people should choose a most qualied jurist to provide the necessary Islamic governance. This is the meaning of Islamic government. It is a government that is headed by a pious, well-versed jurist, not merely in matters of religion, but also in matters of governance and in administration of an Islamic polity.

In the second part of our discussion we examined all the traditions that are used as documentation for the opinion that opposes an active response from the people during the occultation. As we have demonstrated, it is impossible to take these traditions in that meaning and to regard the fundamental duties of a Muslim as a member of the community as being in abeyance until the twelfth Imam (peace be upon him) emerges as the Mahdi. In view of all the verses and the hadith-reports that require Muslims to take up jihad, to command the good and forbid evil, to defend the rights of the dispossessed and downtrodden, and other related public obligations, it is impossible to maintain, even hypothetically, that since the actual ruler of the Muslims is in invisible existence, we cannot undertake these duties that require the presence of an infallible leader like the twelfth Imam as a precondition.

More importantly, if the religion of Islam is faced with a danger, no Muslim can be excused for sitting around and doing nothing about it. Nor can they be forgiven if they do not resist any intervention or interference in Muslim affairs by external or internal enemies. None of the hadith can possibly be interpreted to dictate such irresponsible behavior from Muslims simply because the Imam is in occultation. All the above-cited verses and many more passages of the Qur'an form the most explicit response to those who want to escape that most critical obligation of being a Muslim, namely, to work towards the creation of an ethical public order which reects God's will.

When there is no ambiguity in such unequivocally required duties to maintain the Muslim public order, there can be no possibility of deducing a quietist attitude that would avoid facing these religious and moral obligations of the Shari'a. Regardless of the need for sacrices, Muslims at all times must, as a fundamental duty of being a believer in God and His Prophet, protect Islam and its public order.

The scholars of Islam, especially the jurists, have an even greater responsibility in this regard. As heirs to the Prophet's function and as protectors of the true religion, they are the refuge of the people. They cannot acquiesce in the face of a threat that is posed by the ungodly powers to the Muslims. Imam 'Ali b. Abi Talib has reminded these leaders saying:

I swear by God, Who has caused the seed to germinate and the human being to be created, if that crowd had not come to pay their allegiance to me, and through that act of theirs, the duty that I had to undertake had not been made clearer, I would have tossed away the reins of the camel of the caliphate and let it go anywhere it pleased. Moreover, had it not been that God has exacted a promise from the learned that they would not give their consent to the wrongdoer to ll his belly while the wronged person goes hungry, then [I would have never accepted the caliphate.[375]

Imam Husayn also made similar remarks when he had to confront the injustices of the Umayyads, by quoting the Prophet, who said:

Whoever sees a tyrant ruler making lawful what God made unlawful, breaking God's covenant with those who exercise authority, opposing the Prophet's tradition, and becoming the enemy of the people by committing acts of disobedience against God, and does not oppose him by action and opinion, then God will make him enter the same place [of hell-re] as the tyrant.[376]

Imam Husayn goes on to explain the reason for such a severe indictment of any who fails to oppose wrongdoing:

This is so, because the execution of the laws and administration of affairs is in the hands of those who are knowledgeable about God, entrusted with the preservation of God's legal order dealing with the lawful and unlawful. Hence, it is you who have lost this position. And, this status has not been snatched from you except that you separated yourselves from the truth and disputed in the matter of the tradition of the Prophet after a clear proof was afforded. Had you been patient with the hardships and borne your livelihood for the sake of God, then those matters related to God would have reverted to you, would have been issued by you, and would have been referred to you.

But you let the wrongdoers take your place and you handed over God's affairs to them, being fully aware of their following their ruse and their giving in to their lower appetites. It was your running away from death and your being attracted to life that made them dominate you. It was you who let the downtrodden people fall into their hands, so that they would make some of them their slaves and

---

[375] Nahj al-balagha, Second sermon

[376] Ibn Athir, al-Kamil fi al-ta'rikh, Vol. 4, p. 48

others their source of feed. All this allowed the tyrants to rule the way they wanted, and brought shame and humiliation to themselves and their subjects. In this behavior of theirs, they follow evil people, and they have become daring in their opposition to God.

There is no doubt that the learned in the community have great responsibilities. If they failed to execute them they would suffer severe sanctions on the Day of Judgment. The duty of the 'ulama' is not limited to teaching, discussing, commenting, leading congregational prayers and so on. Rather, their greater responsibility is to protect the religion of Islam and the Muslims, to ght against unbelievers and evildoers, who are engaged in destroying Islam, and to implement Islamic legal and moral precepts. If they fall short in this then they do not have any excuse in the presence of God. By referring to those weak and brief traditions, they will not be able to exonerate themselves from this extremely critical responsibility.

Can God, the Exalted, and the Prophet of Islam, allow us to remain indifferent to the heinous and dangerous conspiracies against Islam and the pitiful behavior of some of the Muslim countries; continue with our life of teaching, preaching, and leading the prayers as usual? No, never.

The session began promptly at 8 p.m. at Dr. Jalali's residence. He also opened the session by asking the rst question.

Dr. Jalali: Mr. Hoshyar, could you please tell us, how will the Master of the Command appear?

Mr. Hoshyar: On studying the hadith reported by the ahl al-bayt, it appears that when the world has become psychologically ready to accept the government of God and when general conditions have become favorable to the idea of the rulership of the truth, God will permit the Mahdi to launch his nal revolution. He will suddenly appear in Mecca and the caller of God will announce to the world that he has alighted. A few selected individuals, whose number has been fixed to 313 in some traditions, will be the first ones to respond to his call, and will be drawn to him like iron to a magnet in that first hour of his appearance.

Imam Sadiq relates: "When the Master of the Age appears, the young among his followers (shi'a), without any prior appointment, will rouse themselves and reach Mecca that very night."[377]

At that time the Mahdi will call upon the entire world to join his movement. Those who have suffered and lost all hope that their situation could improve will rally around him and will pay allegiance to him. In a short time a vast army made up of courageous, sacrificing, and reform-seeking peoples of the world will be prepared to be led by him. Imams Baqir and Sadiq (peace be upon them), have described the Qa'im's helpers thus:

They will occupy the east and the west of the world, will bring everything under his command. Each one of these soldiers will have the power of forty strong men. Their hearts will be harder than iron pieces so much so that in their march to the goal should they encounter mountains made of iron they will overcome them with their inner strength. They will continue their struggle until God's pleasure is acquired.[378]

At that time, the imperious, sinful rulers, lacking any conscience yet sensing the threat, would come out in defense, calling out the oppositional forces made up of their own followers. But the soldiers of justice and reform, having been disgusted with the injustice and persecution of those evil forces, will take the ultimate decision of attacking them in unison and with total effort. With God's help and sanction they will wipe them out. Awe and fear will descend upon the survivors who will finally surrender to the rightful, just government.

---

[377] Bihar al-anwar, Vol. 52, p. 370

[378] Ibid., p. 327

On seeing the fulllment of many of the signs promised in the traditions, a large number of unbelievers will turn towards Islam. Those who persist in their disbelief and wickedness shall be killed by the soldiers of the Mahdi. The only victorious government in the entire world will be that of Islam and people will devotedly endeavor to protect it. Islam will be the religion of everyone, and will enter all the nations of the world.

The Destiny of the Unbelievers

Dr. Jalali: What will happen to the unbelievers (kuffar) and those who associated partners with God (mushrikin)?

Mr. Hoshyar: From the readings in the Qur'an and the hadith literature it appears that during the Mahdi's rule the government and the power will be taken away from non-monotheistic and materialistic disbelievers, and will be vested in the hands of the Muslims and other worthy people of the world.[379] Let us, for example, look at certain verses from the Qur'an:

> *"It is He who has sent His Messenger with the guidance and the religion of truth, that he may uplift it above every religion, though the unbelievers be averse."* (The Holy Qur'an, Surah as-Saff 61:9)

God has promised those of you who believe and do righteous deeds

---

[379] The phrase kuffar-i ghayr-i kitabi refers to the disbelievers who are neither Christian nor Jewish nor Zoroastrian. These latter are regarded in the Shari'a as muwahhidun, i.e., monotheists. Tr

that He will surely make you successors in the land, even as He made those who were before them successors, and that He will surely establish their religion for them that He has approved for them, and will give them in exchange after their fear security:

They shall serve Me, not associating with Me anything."
(The Holy Qur'an, Surah an-Nur 24:54)

"Yet We desired to be gracious to those that were abased in the land, and to make them leaders, and to make them the inheritors, and to establish them in the land." (The Holy Qur'an, Surah al-Qasas 28:4)

These passages from the Qur'an give the glad tidings of that which will come when world power and government are in the hands of the qualied and worthy believers and Muslims, and the religion of Islam ("submission to the will of God") overshadows all other religions and actually eclipses them all.

The traditions speak about the period of the Mahdi's rule and assure the believers that the forces of disbelief and hypocrisy will be annihilated from the face of the earth. Everywhere there will be a true believer in God's unity. Thus, for example, the Prophet (peace be upon him and his progeny) said:

Even if there remains one day in the life of the earth, God will bring forth a man from among my progeny whose name and character will be like mine, and whose patronymic will be Abu 'Abd Allah. Through him God will revive His religion and bring it back to its early glory. God will also endow him with victory and there will remain on earth none other than the ones who will declare the Unity of God (tawhid).

The Prophet was asked as to which of his children's descendants he would be. The Prophet struck his hand on Husayn, and said: "From his [descendants]."[380]

Imam Baqir has related a hadith in which he says: "The Qa'im and his companions will ght so much that there will no longer be those unbelievers who associate partners to God."[381]

---

[380] Ithbat al-hudat, Vol. 7, p. 215, 247

[381] Bihar al-anwar, Vol. 52, p. 345

The Destiny of Jews and Christians

Dr. Jalali: Since Jews and Christians are the followers of the heavenly books that teach monotheism, what will happen to them when the Mahdi appears?

Mr. Hoshyar: The apparent sense of some of the verses of the Qur'an seems to suggest that they will be around until the Day of Judgement occurs. God says in the Sura Ma'ida, 14:

And with those who say 'We are Christians' We took compact; and they have forgotten a portion of that they were reminded of. So We have stirred up among them enmity and hatred, till the Day of Resurrection.

In the Sura Al 'Imran, 55, He says:

> *"When God said, Jesus, I will take thee to Me, and I will purify thee of those who believe not. I will set thy followers above the unbelievers till the Resurrection Day."*
> *(The Holy Qur'an, Surah al-Imran 3:55)*

Again, in Sura Ma'ida, 64, He says:

> *"The Jews have said: 'God's hand is fettered.' Fettered are their hands, and they are cursed for what they have said. Nay, but His hands are outspread; He expends how He will. And what has been sent down to thee from Thy Lord will surely increase many of them in insolence and unbelief; and We have cast between them enmity and hatred, till the Day of Resurrection." (The Holy Qur'an, Surah al-Ma'ida 5:64)*

As you can see, the literal reading of these verses suggests that the religions of the Jews and the Christians will be around until the Day of Judgement. Some of the hadith-reports corroborate this observation. Thus, for instance, Abu Basir asked Imam Sadiq: "What will the Master of the Command do to the 'protected peoples' (ahl al-dhimma)?" The Imam said: "Like the Prophet he will negotiate terms with them, and they will pay the jizya (poll tax), while accepting their inferior position [in the Muslim society]."[382]

In another tradition Imam Baqir says:

The Master of the Command was named as the Mahdi because he will dig out the Torah and other heavenly books from the cave in Antioch. He will judge among the people of the Torah according to the Torah; among the people of the Gospel according to the Gospel; among the people of the Psalms in accordance with the Psalms; among the people of the Qur'an in accordance with the Qur'an.[383]

There are traditions that speak just the opposite of what the Qur'an and above-cited hadith speak. These traditions relate that during the rule of the Mahdi there will no other communities except the Muslims. The Mahdi will offer the religion of Islam to the Jews and

---

[382] Bihar al-anwar, Vol 52, p. 376, 381

[383] Nu'mani, Kitab al-ghayba, p.237

the Christians; if they accept it they will be spared, otherwise they will be killed. Thus, for example, the following tradition in which Ibn Bukayr asks Imam Rida the interpretation of the verse: "To Him submits everything that is in the heavens and the earth, in obedience and in aversion." The Imam relates:

The particular verse is revealed in reference to the Qa'im. When he appears he will offer the religion of Islam to the Jews, Christians, Sabians, and the disbelievers in the east and the west. Any one who willingly accepts Islam will be asked to pray, give alms, and perform all the obligatory acts; and any one who refuses to do so will be killed. This will continue until there remains none but a believer in and worshipper of One God everywhere on the earth.

Ibn Bukayr said to the Imam that in that case there would be far too many people who would be killed. The Imam said: "Whenever God desires something to increase or decrease He can do so."[384]

In another tradition, Imam Baqir related that God will open the east and the west for the twelfth Imam. He will put up the ght until there is no other religion than the religion of Muhammad.[385] In his commentary on the verse that says: "He (God) will manifest it (Islam), even if the disbelievers are averse to it," The Imam said: "He will do it in such a way that there will be no one left except that he will have accepted the religion of Muhammad."

Hence, there are two kinds of hadith: one in favor and the other objecting. However, it must be pointed out that those traditions that agree with the Qur'an have preponderance over those that do not, and therefore the latter must be of necessity rejected as unreliable. Accordingly, the Jews and the Christians will remain under the government of the twelfth Imam, but they will have abandoned

---

[384] Bihar al-anwar, Vol 52, p. 340

[385] Bihar al-anwar, Vol. 52, p. 390

their belief in the trinity and all forms of disbelief connected with associating partners to God, and become worshippers of One God.

They will continue to live under the protection of the Islamic government. At the same time, the corrupt and tyrannical governments will come to an end, and power will be exercised by the well qualied Muslims. Islam will be the world's religion, gaining precedence over all other religions and the call of the Unity of God (tawhid) will be heard all across the world. In this connection Imam Sadiq has said: "When our Qa'im rises there is no place on earth where one will not hear the testimony: I bear witness that there is no deity except God, and Muhammad is the Messenger of God."[386]

According to Imam Baqir: "When the Qa'im takes the command all the godless governments will become permanently extinct." Furthermore, in explaining the verse "when they will be consolidated they will establish worship and give alms," the Imam said: "This verse was revealed to describe the Imams, the Mahdi and his loyal followers. God will make them the commanders of the east and the west, and through them God will fortify the religion and eliminate innovation and false [interpretations in it]. Indeed the ignorant people have ruined the truth. All this will be accomplished in such a way that there shall remain no trace of injustice. He will execute the duty of commanding the good and forbidding the evil."[387]

In another report Abu Basir says that he asked Imam Sadiq: "Who is the Qa'im of the ahl al-bayt?" He said:

O Abu Basir, he will be the fth descendant of my son Musa, the son of the best among the slave girls. His occultation will be prolonged so much so that a group will fall into doubt. Afterwards God will cause him to appear and will make him conquer the entire world.

---

[386] Ibid., p. 340

[387] Ibid., Vol. 51, p. 47

Jesus, the son of Mary, will descend [from heaven] and will perform his prayer standing behind him. In that afternoon the earth will brighten up with the Light of God and all spots on earth where other than God was worshipped will become a prayer house dedicated to God. Religion will be entirely God's, even though the disbelievers may be averse to it.[388]

Engineer Madani: I recall another related topic but, since the time is running short, I will raise it when we meet next time.

The session was concluded for that evening and it was decided that the group would meet in a week's time at Dr. Jalali's residence.

The meeting started promptly at Dr. Jalali's place. It was indeed gratifying to know the number of issues related to the subject of the twelfth Imam (peace be upon him) that were raised, discussed and critically analyzed in the sessions that had met so far. The next important issue was the destiny of other peoples under the government of the Mahdi.

---

[388] Ibid., Vol. 52, p. 378

Will the Majority of the Peoples on the Earth Be Killed?

Engineer Madani: As you all are aware Muslims today are a minority in the world. The sizeable majority inhabiting the planet is non-Muslim. The Shi'a are also a minority in comparison to other schools of thought among Muslims. Among the Shi'a, it must be pointed out in all honesty, there are many evildoers and corrupt people.

On the basis of the way things move in a society, in addition to some analogical deduction, this religious scene of the world is unlikely to change drastically. It is possible to speculate that at the time when the Mahdi appears the Shi'a will still be a minority. My question is this: Is it logical and credible to maintain that the majority of the world's population will simply submit and will not resist as they are being eliminated by the soldiers of the Imam of the Age? Moreover, if the majority of the inhabitants of the world are going to be killed, then this earth will look like a huge cemetery. Does it mean then that the Shi'a will rule over this large cemetery? Surely this action cannot be identied as an act of reform and such a government as the universal authority!

Mr. Hoshyar: Actually we do not have sufcient information about the future world. We cannot speculate about the future on the basis of the past. The Muslim assessment of the situation about the human condition is that humanity is already in a state of perfection in terms of capability and mentality. With the Mahdi's revolution they will be even more prepared to accept the truth.

We often hear that many intellectuals in the east and the west have become aware that their own traditions and religions do not have the ability to satisfy their conscience. At the same time, the natural thirst to worship God and to search for a religion has not been entirely quenched and does not leave them in peace.

As such, they are in search of a religion that is free from all sorts of superstitions and corrupt beliefs, and whose spiritual power can provide them with satisfying nourishment. It is in keeping with this human search for the path that can satisfy their spiritual quest that one can speculate about the future human society's movement towards discovering the truth about Islamic knowledge and the permanence of its ordinances. At that point, it will become evident to them that the only creed which can respond positively to the inner needs and guarantee physical and mental happiness is Islam.

Unfortunately, we are not well equipped, both in terms of courage and means, to inform the peoples of the world about the Islamic truth and its pure teachings. Nevertheless, the people's search for truth, on the one hand, and the well stipulated ordinances of Islam, on the other, will ultimately allow the problem to resolve by itself. At such an opportune time, peoples of the world will convert to the Islamic faith in the thousands, making them a majority.

In addition, on the basis of general prevailing conditions at the time of the appearance, one can speculate that when the promised Mahdi emerges and presents Islamic truths to the world, informing humanity about Islam's revolutionary and reformative aspects, large numbers of people will accept Islam. Hence, they will save themselves from being killed.

For, on the one hand, they will have perfected their ability to perceive religious truth and, on the other, they will have witnessed the miracles performed by the Imam of the Age. Moreover, they will nd the social conditions extraordinary and inexplicable, and the call of the leader of the revolution will reach their ears. These circumstances will lead thousands and thousands of people to convert to Islam at the hands of the Mahdi, thereby saving themselves from destruction.

As for those who persist in their disbelief after all these signs, the Peoples of the Book, that is, the Jews and the Christians, will continue to receive the protection of the Islamic government. Other sinful and corrupt disbelievers will be killed by the universal upholder of justice, the Mahdi. The number of the latter group will, consequently, be insignicant.

The Teachings of Islam Will Be Proclaimed to the World from Qumm

From the hadith-reports related by the ahl al-bayt it appears that in the near future the Shi'i religious establishment, having grasped better than ever before the teachings of the ahl al-bayt in matters of faith and practice, will come out from its state of disorder, regalvanize itself with modern communications technology, and begin to reach out to the people all over the world with correct information about the teachings of the Qur'an and Islam. They will reintroduce those Islamic teachings that guarantee human happiness and will emphasize the factors that underscore the eminence and advancement of Islam. In this way they will prepare the way for the appearance of the twelfth Imam (peace be upon him). May those days come soon!

In one of the hadith Imam Sadiq says:

Very soon Kufa will be empty of the believers. [Religious] knowledge will disappear from that region the way a snake disappears from its abode into a hole in the earth, [without leaving any trace]. Then it will reappear in the city known as Qumm. That city will become the treasure of religious knowledge and excellence. From there it will spread throughout the world, thoroughly eliminating ignorance in matters of religion among the destitute, including women [who will participate in this process of learning anew about Islam].

This will happen close to the appearance of our Qa'im. In this way, God will make Qumm and its inhabitants a substitute for His proof. If it does not happen so, the earth will sink, engulng its inhabitants, and there will remain no proof. Religious knowledge will spread across nations from Qumm and God's proof will have been provided to all people in such a way that there will not be a single person on earth who will not have heard about the religion and its wisdom. It will be following this event that our Qa'im will appear. God's punishment and tribulation will be ready for execution, because God exacts His revenge only when the people have rejected His proof.[389]

In another place the Imam says:

God made the city of Kufa and its inhabitants to serve as a proof over all other places. He will make Qumm also a proof to serve over other places, and through its inhabitants He will make an argument against all those, including humans and jinns, who reject the proof of His existence. God will not disgrace and humiliate Qumm and its peoples; on the contrary they will always enjoy God's grace and support.

He then went on to say:

The religion and the religious in Qumm, being decient, will not draw the attention of the people. Had it not been that they were going

---

[389] Safinat al-bihar, hadith related under 'Qumm.

to serve as God's proof both the city and its inhabitants would have perished, and there would have remained no divine proof for the rest of the world. In addition, the heavens would not have remained secure and no warning would have been given to the people. Qumm and its inhabitants will remain immune from all the calamities. There will come a time when Qumm and its residents will become a proof for God's existence for the entire world.

This will happen during the occultation of our Qa'im until he appears. If this does not happen, then the earth will engulf its inhabitants. God's angels will remove all afictions and calamities from the people of Qumm. Any oppressor who commits aggression against Qumm will be destroyed by those who ght against these oppressors. Furthermore, they will be met with distressful calamity or will encounter a powerful enemy who will keep them occupied. Just as these oppressors would have forgotten remembrance of God, God will make them forget Qumm and its inhabitants.[390]

Imam 'Ali b. Abi Talib predicted the following about Qumm:

There will be a man from Qumm who will call people towards truth. Some will respond to his call and will rally around him like pieces of iron [that are drawn towards a magnet]. Strong winds will not be able to move them from their place. They will not be tired of warfare and will be fearless. They trust in none but God. At the end the victory is for those who are godfearing.[391]

Dr. Jalali: You have predicted that Muslims will be in the majority in the future. This speculation is contradicted by some hadith-reports. Thus, for instance, the Prophet is reported to have said:

There will dawn a time when there will remain nothing but a trace from the Qur'an. And from Islam there will survive only a name.

---

[390] Ibid

[391] Bihar al-anwar, Vol. 60, p. 216

There will be people called Muslims, but they will be the farthest of all other people from Islam. They will have well built mosques; but these will be devoid of guidance.[392]

Mr. Hoshyar: In such hadith-reports the Prophet has not predicted more than a particular detail that there will be a time that the true Islam will disappear and no more than an image of it will remain; and that, although there will be Muslims, they will be far from the true Islam. However, this prediction is also in accord with Muslims being in the majority, because it is possible that in spite of being Muslims they will be little affected by the truth and spirituality of Islam. Yet the heavy dust of inconsistency and antiquated traditionalism that will have descended upon Islam will be eradicated by the very existence of the twelfth Imam, who will lay the foundation for a renewal of the religious edice. In this regard it is worth recalling the Prophet's tradition in which he said:

I swear by the One in Whose hand is my life that Islam and Muslims will always be in increase, whereas disbelief and those who associate other beings with God will be in decrease. He then added:

I solemnly declare that wherever night reaches this religion will reach.[393]

It is sufcient to point out that, rst of all, it is predicted that before the twelfth Imam appears the Muslim community will attain a majority status. Second, when he appears many people will convert to Islam because the level of human perfection will have advanced to such heights that it will enable people to accept the truth of Islam, as many traditions have reported. In the following tradition Imam Baqir has declared:

When our Qa'im rises, God will stroke the heads of His creatures

---

[392] Ibid., Vol. 52, p. 190

[393] Ibn 'Asakir, Ta'rikh (Damascus edition, 1329), Vol. 1, p. 87

with mercy, thereby making their mind more awless, and able to realize their dreams by means of it.[394]

Imam 'Ali b. Abi Talib said:

In the Last Days and the days of calamity and ignorance of the people, God will appoint a person and will support him and protect his followers through angels. He will help him through miraculous signs and will give him victory over all the people of the world, so that whether they like it or not they will convert to the true religion. He will ll the earth with justice and equity, and brilliance and rationality. The distances between places will shrink for him in such a way that no unbeliever will remain except that [the appointed one] will bring [to him] faith, and no sinful person will remain except that he will become pious.[395]

"Your Enemies Will Destroy Each Other"

Another matter that helps to resolve the problem raised by Engineer Madani is that the general conditions of the world, the advancements in dangerous scientic discoveries and the arms race between the western and eastern nations, in addition to a general moral decline in humanity, allow us to anticipate that great powers, including the Jews and the Christians, would engage each other in hostile activities, and would destroy a majority of the world's population by means of destructive weapons.

Another large group will become the victims of precarious diseases that will surface as a result of human destruction of the natural immune system provided by God in human bodies and in the environment.

A companion of Imam Baqir by the name of 'Abd al-Malik A'yan relates that he once stood up in the Imam's presence and, leaning on

---

[394] Bihar al-anwar, Vol. 52, p. 328

[395] Bihar al-anwar, Vol. 52, p. 328

his two arms, wept and said: "I was hopeful that I would witness the period of the Qa'im while there was still some strength left in me." The Imam, consoling him, said:

Are you not pleased that your enemies are busy with each other [in conflict], while you are safe in your homes? When our Qa'im arises each one of you will gain the energy of forty men. Your heart will become like pieces of iron, which, if hurled against mountains, will break them through. You will be the leaders of the world and its keepers.[396]

In another report Imam Sadiq predicted the following:

Before the Qa'im's rise two deaths will occur: one death red and the other white. These will kill five out of every seven persons. The red death will occur by means of killing and the white through epidemics.[397]

Zurarah b. A'yan, Imam Sadiq's close associate, on one occasion asked the Imam: "Is the call from heaven, [as predicted in the traditions about the Qa'im's rise,] a true thing?" The Imam replied: "I declare with solemnity that indeed that will occur just as all the peoples [having heard it] will repeat that [call] on their tongues." He then added: "The Qa'im will not rise until nine out of every ten persons is annihilated."[398]

---

[396] Bihar al-anwar, Vol. 52, p. 335

[397] Ithbat al-hudat, Vol. 7, p. 401

[398] Bihar al-anwar, Vol. 52, p. 244

War Is Inevitable

Dr. Fahimi: Is not it possible that the preparations of the Mahdi's revolution might be done in such a way as to avoid war and bloodshed in establishing his government?

Mr. Hoshyar: As things normally proceed in such events, it seems unlikely that this catastrophe can be avoided even when the level of people's thinking changes to the extent that the number of good people increases, the oppressors and egotistic persons will still be there in the midst of human society. This group will indisputably be opposed to justice and will never give up their stubborn antagonism against any power.

Such people will do anything against the promised Mahdi to protect their vested interests. Moreover, they will do anything within their power to demoralize and combat those who support the Imam. To crush the negative inuence of this group there is no other solution except warfare and bloodshed. It is for this reason that the hadith-reports from the ahl al-bayt have regarded warfare and bloodshed inevitable.

In one of the traditions Bashir, another companion of Imam Sadiq, asked the Imam about what the people were saying about the rise of the Mahdi: 'When he rises not even an amount of blood as small as that which is usually allowed to flow during the cupping procedure will be shed.' The Imam retorted that such a thing was impossible:

"Had such a thing been possible then it would have been done for the Prophet (peace be upon him and his progeny). Actually, in the battle against the enemy, the Prophet's blood flowed as his teeth and his forehead were injured. By God, the revolution of the one who will command the affairs [of the Muslim community] will not be accomplished until we sweat on the battlefield and blood is shed." He then wiped his hand on his forehead.[399]

* * *

---

[399] Ibid., p. 358

The Mahdi's Defense

Dr. Jalali: I have heard that the Imam of the Age will rise with a sword. This is something that does not seem to be right. The reason is that so far humankind has created and discovered various kinds of weapons to be used on the battleelds. Nuclear proliferation and weapons of mass destruction are recent additions to the array of weaponry in human arsenals. With the use of chemical and biological weapons, including remote detonation devices for binary weapons, thousands upon thousands of people can be destroyed in one blow. The question arises that with all these weapons existing now, how can one imagine that the Mahdi and his soldiers will be triumphant ghting with swords?

Mr. Hoshyar: Yes, indeed the subject of the Mahdi's rise with the sword is mentioned in the traditions. Let me cite some examples. Imam Baqir relates:

The Mahdi resembles his forefather, the Prophet, in that he too will rise with a sword to wipe out tyrants and those who mislead people, the enemy of God and the Prophet. He will attain victory by sword and scare, and none of his troops (lit. ags) will return [with a defeat].[400]

However, the rise with the "sword" is a metaphor for warfare. It indicates that war and bloodshed are part of the ofcial task of the Mahdi. He is commanded by God to make Islam a universal faith and to confront injustice and tyranny, even by force and by means of a sword. His circumstance is contrary to his forefathers' careers, which did not require them to face the situation in that forceful manner, as their charge was limited to admonition and counsel. Consequently, "to rise with a sword" does not mean that his weapons of defense are limited to a sword, and that he is to restrain himself from using any other kind of weapons. To be sure, he too might employ the weapons of the day or even create new weapons to overpower all the known weaponry of his time.

The truth is that our knowledge about the future events of the world is limited; nor do we know in any detailed manner about the future destiny of humankind and the course of its technological enterprise. As such, we do not have the right to judge the future on the basis of the past without any evidence. We do not know which country or nation will have a technological and civilizational advantage and superiority over others. It is possible that the weak and divided nations of the Islamic world will wake up and put aside their minor differences to create the universal brotherhood under the mighty banner of tawhid, the Unity of God, and adopt and implement the Qur'anic guidance as the constitution of the universal Muslim nation.

The united Islamic peoples could then utilize their natural resources to their advantage and come out of a self-cultivated laziness and self-imposed isolation to take up the challenge of becoming leaders of human civilization in sciences, industry, and ethics. They

---

[400] Ibid., Vol. 51, p. 218

can bring under their control the unleashed and boundless energies of the east and the west in order to channel them into preparing for the nal launching of the Mahdi's revolution.

At that time the Mahdi can appear and destroy the unjust and tyrannical powers with the help of the mighty forces at his disposal. Furthermore, with divine assistance and promises of victory, in addition to the extraordinary energy that emanates from the position of the wilayat (the exercise of divinely-ordained sovereignty under the Imamate) he can lay the foundation of a just and equitable government of God on the earth.

At that moment the scientists and scholars whose research made possible the discovery of all the tools and technology will feel sadness and remorse because their discoveries had not been used for the betterment of human life but were instead employed to colonize and to suppress the peoples of the world. Hence, in order to give recompense for the abuse of their scientic contributions, they will see no other way but to respond to the call of the Mahdi to ght for justice and work for the good of the peoples of the world.

We cannot foretell how people in the future will abandon their arrogance and stubbornness, come out from their ignorance and work towards the eradication of weapons of mass destruction and the decisive implementation of the nuclear non-proliferation treaty. But all the wealth that is now being used to produce such weapons could then be diverted for the elimination of poverty, the advancement of education and the well being of humankind.

* * *

The World under the Mahdi

*E*ngineer Madani: Could you give some indications about the conditions that would prevail under the rule of the Mahdi?

Mr. Hoshyar: It is possible to reconstruct the following picture of the future from the traditions related by the ahl al-bayt:

When the promised Mahdi, the twelfth Imam (peace be upon him), appears, following his victory over the evil forces of the world, he will administer the entire world under one Islamic government. He will appoint well-qualied individuals as the governors of different regions of the world with clear instructions and programs for the peaceful and just administration of the region under their governance.[401] The entire earth will ourish under their administration. The Mahdi will distantly oversee the whole earth himself, with its widespread regions and extensive affairs accessible to him like the palm of his hand. His disciples and helpers also will observe and talk to him from remote distances. The entire earth will be lled with justice and equity.

People will have become kind and will treat each other with

---

[401] Ibid., Vol. 51, p. 218

honesty and sincerity. There will be security everywhere as no one will wish to cause harm to another. The economic condition of the people will improve enormously. There will be plenty of rain to cause the earth to become lush with greenery and there will be all kinds of grains and fruits in abundance. Necessary improvements will be introduced in agricultural methods. People will pay more attention to God's presence than to sins. Islam will become the ofcial religion of the world, with the call of the Unity of God arising from all corners of the earth.

In the matter of building the roads, interesting programs will be introduced. Main roads will be sixty yards wide. In building the roads there will be so much diligence that the mosques standing in the middle will be demolished. Footpaths will adorn the streets. Pedestrians will be asked to cross the roads at the proper pedestrian's crossing; whereas the drivers will be asked to move into the middle. All the windows of the homes that open to the street will be closed. There will be prohibitions against constructing open drains and sewage on the streets. Imposing structures will be demolished. The highly decorative and elevated mosques as well as minarets and the grills separating the leader of the congregational prayers from the worshippers will be destroyed.

During the age of the Mahdi human reason will have reached perfection. General information among people will have advanced to such a degree that women will be able to formulate judicial decisions while at home. Imam Sadiq says:

Knowledge is divided into twenty-seven parts. No more than two parts has been acquired by human beings so far. When our Qa'im arises he will expose the rest of the twenty ve parts and distribute it among the people.[402]

---

[402] Bihar al-anwar, Vol 52, p. 336

People's faith will have attained excellence and their hearts free of malevolence and resentment. Finally, let me remind you that all this elaboration has been extracted from pertinent hadith-reports, and most of these traditions are rare and reported by a single narrator. Anyone desiring more details can refer to volumes 51 and 52 of Bihar al-anwar, volumes 6 and 7 of Ithbat al-hudat, and Nu'mani's Kitab al- ghayba.

* * *

The Victory of the Prophets

Dr. Jalali: From all the descriptions and excellences that have been related about the Mahdi, the twelfth Imam (peace be upon him) in the traditions, it would seem that he is more excellent than all the Prophets, including the Prophet of Islam (peace be upon him and his progeny). After all, none of them succeeded in reforming human society, establishing a world government founded upon the Unity of God, implementing the divine ordinances in their entirety, executing the divine scales of justice perfectly, and eliminating injustice and tyranny absolutely. The only person able to accomplish all these tasks is the Mahdi, and none other!

Mr. Hoshyar: In reality, the reform of human society, and the execution of divine laws has been the aspiration of all the Prophets. Each one of these divinely appointed reformers endeavored to accomplish their goal in accord with the possibilities and capacity that were available to them in their particular age and thereby drew the people closer to God. If they had not struggled and made the necessary sacrices, then government based on God's unity would have never taken off. In this sense, all these Prophets are participants and have a share in this nal success.

The accomplishment of the Mahdi should be regarded as the success of all God-worshipping peoples in the line of the Prophets and religious leaders. The Imam's victory is not his own personal victory; rather, with the amazing energy of this Imam this will be the victory of truth over falsehood, of piety over disbelief. It will be the fulllment of the past Prophets' promise to their followers, and the realization of their ideal for human society.

The accomplishment of the promised Mahdi, in truth, is the accomplishment of Adam, Seth, Noah, Abraham, Moses, Jesus, Muhammad, and all other Prophets (peace be upon them). They were the ones who, through their sacrices and perseverance, prepared this highway and, to some extent, the people's intellect to accept this call. The program was conceived and the struggle begun by the past Prophets.

Each one of them provided an example through their own conduct and pushed the level of the people's comprehension of God's purposes until the line reached the Prophet of Islam. He outlined the complete program and provided the comprehensive blueprint for the transformation of the world. At the time of his death he handed that over to his rightful successors, the Imams.

The Prophet and the Imams, then, endeavored on this path to execute the divine plan for humanity and in so doing encountered severe opposition and made great sacrices. Many more years should go by, and many more crises and revolutions must be faced by humanity in order for it to mature and become worthy of the government based on tawhid. It will only be then that the last barrier of disbelief and irreligiosity will be surmounted by the astounding energy of the Mahdi (peace be upon him), only then will the dream of humanity materialize.

Hence, the promised Mahdi is the executor of the Prophet's plans, including those of the past Prophets. His victory is the victory of the revealed religions. God promises victory to David in the Psalms, and in one of the passages of the Qur'an revealed to underscore the Mahdi's nal accomplishment, God reminds Muslims of that promise, saying:

"We have written in the Psalms that Our righteous servants shall inherit the earth." (The Holy Qur'an, Surah al-Anbiya', 21:105)

The Mahdi and the New Constitution

Dr. Jalali: I have heard that the twelfth Imam (peace be upon him) will bring a new religion, constitution, and laws for the people. The present laws of Islam will be abrogated by him. How reliable is this account?

Mr. Hoshyar: The source of this information are the traditions on this subject. Thus, to clarify the issue we must cite some of these hadith.

'Abd Allah b. 'Ata' asked Imam Sadiq about the character and conduct of the Mahdi. The Imam said:

He will carry out the same mission that the Prophet did. He will eradicate prevailing innovations, just as the Prophet destroyed the foundation of the jahiliyya (pre-Islamic Arab morals), and then rebuild Islam afresh.[403]

In another hadith Abu Khadija relates from Imam Sadiq, who said:

When the Qa'im rises he will come with a new commission, just as the Prophet in the beginning of Islam called the people to a new commission.[404]

In still another hadith Imam Sadiq says:

---

[403] Ibid., p. 352

[404] Ithbat al-hudat, Vol. 7, p. 110

When the Qa'im emerges he will come with a new commission, a new book, a new conduct and a new judgement, which will be strenuous for the Arabs. His work is nothing but to ght, and no one [among the disbelievers] will be spared. He will not be afraid of any blame in the execution of his duty.[405]

---

[405] Ithbat al-hudat, Vol. 7, p. 110

The Conduct of the Mahdi

However, these and other traditions point to an important factor in Mahdi's behavior – that his conduct will be based on that of his forefather, the Prophet. He will defend the religion and the Qur'an that were given to the Prophet. For instance, the Prophet is reported to have said: "One of my ahl al-bayt will rise and will act upon my tradition and my custom."[406] And, he said: "The Qa'im among my children, will have my name and my patronymic. He will possess my features and will follow my conduct. He will command the people to my obedience and to my law; and he will call them to the Book of my Lord."[407]

In another tradition he said:

My twelfth descendant will disappear in such a way that he will not be seen at all. There will come a time when there shall remain nothing but a name from Islam. And, there shall remain nothing but a trace from the Qur'an. At that time God will permit him to revolt

---

[406] Bihar al-anwar, Vol. 51, p. 82

[407] Ithbat al-hudat, Vol. 7, p. 52

and through him God will reinforce Islam and revive it.[408]

In still another hadith the Prophet said: "Mahdi is from my family and will ght for my tradition, just as I fought for the Qur'an."[409]

As one can observe, these traditions clearly indicate that the twelfth Imam's agenda and his plan of action are to propagate Islam and to revive the importance of the Qur'an. In order to execute the teachings of the Prophet he will strive with force. Hence, if there is any ambiguity in the earlier traditions cited in this section, the above traditions help clarify them. Over all, the traditions should be interpreted as follows:

During the occultation, innovations will appear in the religion, and the ordinances of the Qur'an and the teachings of Islam will be interpreted in accordance with people's likes and dislikes. As a result, many teachings and laws will be forgotten as if they were never even a part of Islam. When the Mahdi appears he will invalidate these innovations and will restore the ordinances of God as they were when they were commanded. He will institute the penal laws of Islam without any leniency. Evidently, such a program will be perceived by the people something new.

Imam Sadiq in another hadith has made the aforementioned role of the Mahdi explicit: "When the Qa'im rises he will emulate the conduct of the Prophet, except that he will elaborate the traditions of Muhammad (peace be upon him and his progeny)."[410]

Fadl b. Yasar heard Imam Baqir saying: "When our Qa'im rises he will face so much difculty from the people, that even the Prophet during the period of jahiliyya did not face." Fadl asked: "Why should that be so?" The Imam said:

---

[408] Muntakhab al-athar, p. 98

[409] Muntakhab al-athar, p. 98

[410] Bihar al-anwar, Vol. 52, p. 347

When the Prophet was appointed people worshipped stones and wood. However, when our Qa'im arises people will interpret the ordinances of God against his interpretation, and will argue with him and dispute by means of the Qur'an. By God, the justice of the Qa'im will enter inside their homes, just as the heat and the cold enter them.[411]

---

[411] Ithbat al-hudat, Vol. 7, p. 86

The Freshness of the Explanations Offered by the Mahdi

People, having abandoned the absolute principles and fundamental teachings of Islam, merely follow the outward forms of religion and regard those to be sufcient. These are the people who, besides the ve daily obligatory prayers, the fasting of Ramadan, and avoidance of external pollution (najasat), know nothing of Islam. Besides, some of them have limited religion to the mosque and, hence, its reality has very little impact upon their actions and behavior. In the life outside the mosque, that is in the market place or at work, there is no trace of their Islam.

They do not regard ethical behavior and moral precepts to be part of Islam. They give no importance eschewing to immoral conduct and make an excuse of not following moral guidelines since there is dispute about the obligatoriness and the prohibitions of certain requirements. They go as far as turning the prohibitions of the law, through trickery, into something permissible. They also shun their responsibility for paying the dues that are imposed by the law on them. In other words, they are engaged in interpreting the religion according to their desires.

When it comes to the Qur'an, they think it sufcient to pay attention to its formal recitation and to respect the conventions in that connection. Hence, when the twelfth Imam appears it is obvious that he will ask them as to why they have abandoned the essence of religion and have interpreted the Qur'an and the hadith to t their own preferred meanings. Why have they left the truth of Islam while being satised with mere outward adherence to it? Why have they not sought to conform their character and their actions with the true spirit of Islam?

Why have they twisted the meanings of the religion to accord with their own personal avarice? Since they pay so much attention to the proper recitation of the Qur'an, they should also put its directives into action. The twelfth Imam has the right to ask: "My grandfather, Imam Husayn, did not get killed for the sake of mourning. Why have you forsaken my grandfather's goal and destroyed it?"

The Imam will ask them to learn the Islamic social and moral teachings and apply them in their everyday lives. They should avoid the forbidden acts, and take care of their nancial obligations, without making imsy excuses. They should also keep in mind that remembering the merits of the ahl al-bayt and weeping for their suffering can never substitute for the zakat and khums and taking care of one's debts.

Nor can they substitute for such sinful behavior as taking interest and bribes, cheating others and treating them with dishonesty. They should recognize that weeping and sighing for Imam Husayn can never substitute for having ill-treated orphans and widows. More importantly, they should not limit piety to the mosque; rather, they should seek participation in the society and carry out the duty of commanding the good and forbidding the evil and ght the innovations that have crept into Islam.

Certainly, such a religion would seem new and difcult to these people, and they might not even consider it to be Islam, because they have imagined Islam to be something else. These people used to think that the progress and greatness of Islam lay in decorating the mosques and in constructing tall minarets. If the twelfth Imam says: "The greatness of Islam is righteous action, honesty, trustworthiness, keeping promises, avoiding forbidden acts," this would appear to them altogether new!

They used to assume that when the Imam appears he will make amends for all the actions of the Muslims and will retire with them in the corner of a mosque. But if they witness that blood is dripping from the Imam's sword and that he is calling people to jihad and to command the good and forbid the evil, and that he is killing the unjust worshippers and returning the goods they have stolen to their rightful owners, such actions of the Imam they will indeed nd new!

Imam Sadiq relates:

When our Qa'im arises he will call people anew to Islam, guiding them to the old thing from which people have turned away. He will be called Mahdi because he will guide people to the thing from which they have been separated. He will be called Qa'im because he will be commanded to establish the truth.[412]

In short, there is a total difference between the assumed Mahdi and his agenda, and the true Mahdi and his role. It is for this reason that since his actions will not be approved by the people, they will desert him in the beginning. However, since they will nd no one else who can deliver them they will submit to him. Imam Sadiq says:

I can witness the Qa'im wearing the particular garment and taking out the letter of the Prophet sealed with a golden seal, and after breaking the seal he reads aloud to the people. The people disperse from him as the sheep do from the shepherd. And no one besides

---

[412] Ithbat al-hudat, Vol. 7, p. 86

his vizier and eleven chiefs remain with him. Then people begin to search for a reformer everywhere. But, since they do not find anyone besides him who can help them, they rush towards him. By God, I know what the Qa'im is telling them which they refuse to acknowledge.[413]

---

[413] Bihar al-anwar, Vol. 52, p. 326

The Mahdi and Abrogation of the Ordinances

Dr. Fahimi: If I recall, you had said earlier that the Mahdi is not the lawgiver, and neither is he the abrogator of the law. This statement of yours does not agree with the substance of the following tradition:

Imam Sadiq said:

Two cases of bloodshed are permissible in Islam. But no one executes the divine ordinance in those two cases until God sends the Qa'im from the ahl al-bayt who can execute God's injunction in those cases without requiring any witnesses: one is the case of a married man committing adultery who will be stoned by him; and the other is the case of a person refusing to pay the zakat.[414]

In another tradition the Imam said: "When the Qa'im from the family of Muhammad appears he will judge among people without requiring witnesses in the manner of David and Solomon."[415]

These and other such traditions imply that Islamic ordinances

---

[414] Bihar al-anwar, Vol. 52, p. 326

[415] Ibid., p. 320

will be abrogated by the Imam who will substitute for them new ordinances. By holding such beliefs you are actually proving the prophethood of the Mahdi, even though you do not call him a prophet!

Mr. Hoshyar: First of all, allow me to point out that the source of such beliefs consists of rare traditions reported by a single narrator. Second, I do not see any problem with the proposition that God may reveal a law to the Prophet and inform him that the law will be applicable to him and his followers until the time when the Qa'im appears. When the twelfth among his descendants appears he should follow a second injunction. The Prophet also informs about this arrangement to his successor until the information reaches the last Imam. In such a case the ordinance is not abrogated, and the Imam does not introduce a new ruling that was revealed to him. Rather, the first injunction was already limited in time, and the Prophet was already informed about the second one.

Thus, for instance, social expediency required that the judge should confine his judgement to an objective proof, seeking witnesses, and an oath. The Prophet and the Imams were also required to follow the same procedure in their administration of justice. However, when the Mahdi appears and establishes the Islamic government, he is required to decide the case on the basis of his knowledge. Thus, this latter ordinance was already part of Islamic judisprudence, awaiting execution after the appearance of the Mahdi.

Is It Not Possible that the Mahdi Has Already Appeared?

Dr. Jalali: We recognize with you the fundamental belief about the Mahdi. Yet, how do we know that he has not appeared already? From the early days of Islamic history up until now there have been many individuals from different parts of the world, both belonging to the Quraysh and non-Quraysh, who have arisen with the claim to Mahdiism. Interestingly, they found supporters among the people and have even left their legacy in the sects that were named after them. In fact, some of them came to power and established dynasties that lasted for some time. Here we are awaiting the appearance of the Mahdi, and in all likelihood one of the pretenders to Mahdiism might have been a true Mahdi about which we have no information!

Mr. Hoshyar: As we have detailed in our previous discussions, we do not believe in an unidentiable Mahdi whose characteristics are unknown to us so that we might make an error in recognizing him. On the contrary, the Prophet and the Imams (peace be upon them), who informed people about this fundamental expectation and the existence of the Mahdi, provided all the detailed characteristics and qualications of the Mahdi to remove all doubts and ambiguities about his identity. The following hadith is the summary of such a description of the future Mahdi:

The Mahdi's name is Muhammad and his patronymic is Abu al-Qasim. His mother was a slave-girl by the name of Narjis, Sayqal and Sawsan. He will be a Hashimite, from the descendants of Imam Husayn, and a direct offspring of Imam Hasan 'Askari. He was born in the year 256/868 or 255/867 in the city of Samarra in Iraq. He has two forms of occultation: one short, the other long. The second occultation will be prolonged to such an extent that many people will doubt his very existence. His age will be very long.

The mission will begin in Mecca. He will launch his revolution with a sword and will annihilate all the oppressors and disbelievers. All the Peoples of the Book and Muslims will submit to his authority. He will establish a universal Islamic government on earth, will thoroughly uproot the forces of injustice and tyranny, and will replace these with justice and equity. Islam will become the universal faith and the Mahdi will expend his energy to spread it peacefully amongst all. Such are the traits and functions of the Mahdi for whom the Muslims are awaiting.

Sayyid 'Ali Muhammad Shirazi, "the Bab"

Mr. Hoshyar: Now, Dr. Jalali, let me ask you a question. Among all those who have claimed to be the Mahdi so far, have you come across anyone in whom all these characteristics that we have detailed above nds expression so that his claim could be ascertained as a possibility?

For example, a person who arose in one of the cities of Iran claiming Mahdiism was neither the son of Imam Hasan 'Askari nor had he gone into occultation for a long time or fought any battle against the unjust rulers or established a universal Islamic government to ll the earth with justice and equity. It is remarkable that he did not raise his hand even a little to stop people from doing wrong. Moreover, not only did he not spread Islam all over the world, he actually abrogated all its laws and established a new creed in its place. He did not possess any profound knowledge nor did he perform any astounding task. And, towards the end of his career, in spite of the fact that he repented and displayed remorse, he was executed.[416] Can any rational person endowed with intelligence assume that such an individual could be the promised Mahdi of the Muslims?

The story of this pseudo-Mahdi from the city of Shiraz is no different from one related in the Mathnavi of Jalaluddin Rumi about a man from Qazvin, who claimed to be strong but could not stand the pain that was caused by someone poking a needle on his arm to tattoo a lion that he had desired. The choice of a lion, as Rumi indicates, was intended to show off his toughness. However, at each stage of tattooing this pseudo-strong man from Qazvin was willing to omit drawing parts of the lion's image that would require the tattooer to poke his needle more frequently and deeper. These requests to omit major parts of the lion's body led the tattooer to poke fun at his client:

Who has seen a lion without a tail, a head, or a stomach? When did God ever create such a lion?

If you don't have the strength to bear the poking of the needle
Don't desire such a brave lion [as a symbol of your strength].

One of the interesting episodes connected with Sayyid 'Ali Muhammad Shirazi is that before the claim to being the Mahdi and Qa'im had got into his head he, had written a book entitled: Tafsir-i sura-yi kawthar (Commentary on the Sura Kawthar). In this book he reported traditions about the promised Mahdi which were not congruent with his own later claim of Mahdiism. Later on, this

---

[416] Nabil Zarandi, Talkhis-i ta'rikh, pp.135-138

issue became a source of aggravation and nuisance for him and his followers.

In this book he writes:

Musa b. Ja'far Baghdadi related that he heard from Imam Hasan 'Askari who said: 'I see you [in the future] disputing with each other in the matter of my successor. Nonetheless, be aware that whoever acknowledges all the Imams after the Prophet, and rejects my son, will resemble someone who will acknowledge all the Prophets but will deny the prophethood of Muhammad (peace be upon him and his progeny). And anyone who denies the Prophet of God will resemble someone who has denied all of the Prophets. The reason is that obedience to the last one among us is like obedience to the rst one among us; and denial of the last one among us is like the denial of the rst. Know that my son will have an occultation and all the people, except a few who will be protected by God, will fall into doubt.'[417]

Then he quotes another tradition as follows:

Imam Rida told Di'bil: "Imam following me is my son Muhammad; after Muhammad it will be his son 'Ali; after 'Ali it will be his son Hasan, and, following Hasan it will be his son Hujjat and Qa'im, who should be awaited during his occultation and obeyed when he appears. If there remains but a day in the age of the world, God will prolong it until the Qa'im arises and lls the earth with justice and equity just as it is lled with injustice and tyranny.

As to when he will appear this would be to inform about the time of his rise, whereas our forefathers have reported from 'Ali, who related it from the Prophet, who was asked: 'O Messenger of God, when will the Qa'im from your descendants arise?' He replied: 'His situation resembles that of the Day of Resurrection [about whose timing no one but God can reveal]. However, the matter is of grave

---

[417] Nabil Zarandi, Talkhis-i ta'rikh, pp.135-138

importance both in the heaven and on earth and accordingly will happen all of a sudden.'"[418]

It is evident that a number of things are resolved in these two traditions: first, Qa'im and Mahdi are the direct offspring of Imam Hasan 'Askari; second, he will have a lengthy period of occultation; third, when he appears he will fill the earth with justice and equity; and, fourth, no one can fix the time for his rise.

---

[418] Ibid

Sayyid 'Ali Muhammad's Acknowledgement of the Hidden Imam's Existence

In his book on the commentary of Sura Kawthar, Sayyid Muhammad 'Ali acknowledged the existence of the Hidden Imam and wrote about the signs and indications of that existence. Thus, for instance, he writes:

There is no doubt about the existence of the Hidden Imam. The reason is that if he did not exist no one else would have existed. As such, this matter is as clear as the sun in the sky. The problem is that the necessary corollary of doubt in his existence is doubt in God's power. Anyone who doubts the existence of God is a disbeliever. As for the Muslims and the believers among the followers of the Twelve Imams, the Imamiyya, the period of his birth is proven (may my spirit and the spirit of all those in the realm of the spiritual beings – malakut – be a sacrice for his excellency!).

Moreover, his short occultation and the miracles that took place in those days, as well as the signs that were given to his deputies, are also proven beyond any doubt. He (the twelfth Imam) is a righteous offspring. His patronymic is Abu al-Qasim. He is the one invested with God's command (al-qa'im bi-amr allah), the proof of God's existence for God's creatures, the remaining one (baqiyyat allah) among the servants of God, the Mahdi who will guide people to the mysterious matters. But I do not like to mention his name, except the way the Imam ['Askari] has mentioned it, that is, mim, ha, mim, da. There are texts in this regard, directly received from the [twelfth] Imam (peace be upon him). The Imam himself has written the note in which he says: "God's curse be upon the one who mentions me by my name in public."...

The Master of the Age (wali 'asr) will have two [forms of] occultation. During the lesser occultation, he had trustworthy and intimate deputies and agents. The period of the lesser occultation lasted for seventy four years and some days. The deputies of the respected master (may our spirits be a sacrice for him!) include: 'Uthman b. Sa'id 'Amri and his son, Muhammad b. 'Uthman, Husayn b. Ruh, and 'Ali b.

Muhammad Samarri.

In another place in the same book he writes about his own experience of having seen the twelfth Imam in Mecca:

One day I was busy praying in the holy mosque of Mecca, on the side of the Yamani pillar [of the Ka'ba]. I noticed a well built and good looking young man who was deeply involved in performing the circumambulation (tawaf). He had a white turban on his head and a woolen cloak on his shoulder. He was with the merchants' group from Fars. There was no more than a few steps of distance between us. All of a sudden a thought came to my mind that he could be the Master of the Command (sahib al-amr). But I was embarrassed to go closer to him. When I nished my prayers I did not nd him. Nevertheless, I am not so sure that he was the Master of the Command.

Sayyid 'Ali Muhammad and the Traditions about Fixing of the Time

The following hadith also appears in the commentary on Sura Kawthar:

Abu Basir reported that he asked Imam Sadiq: "May my life be a sacrice for you! When will the Qa'im arise?" He replied: "O Abu Muhammad, we, the ahl al-bayt cannot x the time of his appearance.

Moreover, the Prophet Muhammad (peace be upon him and his progeny) said: 'Those who x the time for the rising [of the Qa'im] are liars.'"[419]

This and other traditions of its kind make amply clear that the Imams themselves never xed the time of the appearance and they falsied anyone else who tried to do that. However, the followers of the afore-mentioned Sayyid from Shiraz have ignored these clear indications and, contrary to the textual proof to that effect provided by their leader, have searched and found a weak tradition attributed to Abu Labid Makhzumi and through a far-fetched and mysterious interpretation, extracted from it the year of the Sayyid's appearance in 1256 AH/1840 CE.

The books that have been written in refutation of the claims made by this particular faction based on the tradition reported by Abu Labid, are far too numerous to be mentioned here. Moreover, any further discussion about the subject would be a digression from our topic of discussion at this time. Sufce it to say that according to the hadith of Abu Basir, also relied upon by Sayyid 'Ali Muhammad in his commentary, any tradition that xes the exact time for the appearance of the Qa'im must be rejected as false. As such, its inclusion as evidence is not permissible, whether it is the hadith related by Abu Labid or by someone else. The following hadith also appears in the

---

[419] Ibid

commentary on Sura Kawthar:

Imam Sadiq has related in a lengthy tradition, saying: "The occultation of our Qa'im will be denied by the umma. Some will say, without any knowledge: The Imam was never born; others will say: he was born, but he died. Still others will become disbelievers and will say: The eleventh Imam had no offspring at all. Some will spread factionalism in the community by what they say, and will go beyond the twelve Imams and will count thirteen or more Imams. There will be those who will cause God's anger to engulf them by saying: The spirit of the Qa'im is speaking through another person."[420]

---

[420] Ibid

What Do the Sayyid's Followers Say?

In spite of all these clear afrmations in Sayyid 'Ali Muhammad's commentary on Sura Kawthar, of which we cited some examples, we do not know what his followers believe. If they regard him the promised Mahdi and the Qa'im, this belief not only does not conform with the teachings of the ahl al-bayt, it also goes against the Sayyid's own afrmations. The reason is that he himself regards the direct descendant of Imam Hasan 'Askari, whom he calls mim, ha, mim, da, as the Qa'im and the Mahdi. He also introduces his patronymic as Abu al-Qasim, regards his short and long forms of occultation necessary, and provides the names of his special deputies. Finally, he relates his encounter with the young man in the sacred mosque of Mecca whom he thought to be the Hidden Imam.

If the followers of the Sayyid believe that the spirit of the twelfth Imam has transmigrated into the Sayyid's body and that he is the manifestation of the Qa'im, then even this belief has no validity. First of all, it must be pointed out that such a tenet leads to the belief in the incarnation and transmigration of souls. Both these are proven to be false in Islam. Moreover, this belief is in direct contradiction with the hadith from Imam Sadiq which the Sayyid himself has cited. The

Imam in this hadith says: "There will be those who will cause God's anger to engulf them by saying: The spirit of the Qa'im is speaking through another person."

The Sayyid Repudiated Any Attribution of Prophethood and Babism

However, if his followers believe that he was a prophet or a bab ("gate," meaning mediator between the Hidden Imam and his community), then even this attribution has been declined by him. In the commentary on Sura Kawthar he writes:

Those who say that "Remember the name of Thy Lord" means that he himself (i.e., Sayyid 'Ali Muhammad) has actually claimed to have received revelation and the Qur'an, have indeed become disbelievers. Moreover those who say that the verse means that he has claimed to be the bab of the Remnant of God (the twelfth Imam), have also become disbelievers. O God, you are my witness that [I declare] any one who claims to be divine or to possess the wilayat or who has received the Qur'an and the revelation, or who has omitted or altered anything in Your religion, has become an unbeliever. I certainly seek to disassociate from such people. You are my witness that I have not claimed to be the bab.[421]

To be sure, when the Sayyid composed his commentary he had

---

[421] Ibid

no intention of putting forward any messianic claims. He simply considered himself a learned person and sensed pain when he saw himself conned to the house and found other learned authorities occupied with many tasks in the public life. In this connection he writes:

God has favored me by enlightening my heart. I would like to publicize the religion of God the way it was revealed in the Qur'an and demonstrated in the teachings of the ahl al-bayt.

He was troubled by the false messianic claims ascribed to him and took pains to decline them. Later on he realized that the absurdity of the people was beyond imagination. Not only did they accept whatever he said, they also added to it something more. It was at that point in his career that his proclivity towards the messianic role of the twelfth Imam became rm in his mind and he proclaimed himself to be the Qa'im.

The Bayan and Messianic Claim

In chapter seven, the second unit of his Bayan, the Sayyid writes:

Since the appearance of the Qa'im of the family of Muhammad is precisely the same as the emergence of the Messenger of God, he will not appear until and unless he manifests the fruits of Islam as deduced from the Qur'anic verses that have been implanted in the hearts of the people. There is no way to deduce the fruits of Islam except by faith in him and conrmation of his status. Now that it has borne fruits, to the contrary he has been made manifest in the midst of Islam and everyone proclaims Islam in relation to him while they situate him groundlessly in Maku.

We have no intention of investigating this new creed in any detail so as to refute it and demonstrate its absurdities. Much has been written on this subject and our readers can refer to these works. Nor do we intend to examine each and every claim to Mahdiism that has been made throughout the history of Islam or to investigate their claims and analyze critically the proofs produced to support them. These discussions, interesting as they may be, go beyond the specic scope of these sessions.

Let me reiterate that the promised Mahdi has been sufciently introduced and described in the authenticated traditions, and possesses an intelligible and unique personality, understood in the minds of the Shi'a. If they come, across such a person who ts into all the characterizations found in the reliable hadith-reports, then they should submit to his authority. If, on the contrary, they discover that the person is a pseudo-Mahdi, then they must absolutely reject him. Those who have so far claimed this messianic position have fallen far short of sustaining such a title. In order to prove their messianic claim, it is obvious that they cannot resort to rare and doubtful traditions transmitted by single narrators and interpret them to their advantage. This method of establishing a messianic claim is insufcient simply because of the critical role of the Qa'im in restoring God's religion to its pure, unadulterated meaning. No single tradition can compete in reliability and authenticity with already accredited traditions.

False Claims and the Existence of a Followership

Engineer Madani: If the claims of these pseudo-Mahdis were meaningless and false, why would they attract such a staunch followership?

Mr. Hoshyar: To become a believer in and an adherent of a person does not prove that person's truthfulness, because in the world there have always existed false beliefs and religions and staunch believers in those religions. The perseverance and sacrice demonstrated by ill-informed and simple people cannot be taken as a proof of the religion's and the leader's truthfulness. Even a cursory glance at the history of religions will reveal this general observation.

For instance, at this time in history when human beings have made great strides in rational and scienti c development, there are millions of people in India who worship cows and believe that this animal has an elevated status in the heavens. They regard killing a cow and consuming its meat a prohibition, and consider disrespect to it as sinful. The Hindus in India are willing to defend the cow at a great price. One of the causes of con ict between Hindus and Muslims in India is the slaughtering of the cow for food, which is permitted in

Islam.

Such examples are plentiful in the history of world religions. Hence, it should come as little surprise to see human beings following all kinds of creeds and religions, false or true.

I believe we have covered the majority of the fundamental aspects related to the belief in the Mahdi in Islam in general and among the Shi'a in particular. Since there are no more issues to discuss we might consider bringing our sessions on this subject to a close.

Dr. Jalali: I agree that we do not have any other related questions about the subject.

Dr. Emami: I must say that these sessions were extremely benecial for my understanding of the Shi'i beliefs. I wish we could continue to learn some more. However, it is appropriate to bring the sessions connected with our subject on the Mahdi, the Universal Just Ruler of the World, to an end.

Let me take this opportunity to thank you all. May God hasten deliverance through the appearance of the Supreme Remnant of God, the twelfth Imam, and may He make us all the servants of Islam and the helpers of the Imam.

Wassalamu 'alaykum wa rahmatullahi wa barakatuh!

And peace be upon you, and God's mercy and His blessing!

www.ingramcontent.com/pod-product-compliance
Lightning Source LLC
LaVergne TN
LVHW091652070526
838199LV00050B/2160